THE
Laura Lea
BALANCED
COOKBOOK

120+ Everyday Recipes *for* *the* Healthy Home Cook

THE
Laura Lea
BALANCED
COOKBOOK

120+ Everyday Recipes *for* *the* Healthy Home Cook

LAURA LEA GOLDBERG
CERTIFIED HOLISTIC CHEF & CREATOR OF *LLBalanced.com*

Foreword *by* ALICE RANDALL

SPRING HOUSE PRESS

Publisher: Paul McGahren
Editorial Director: Matthew Teague
Editor: Kerri Grzybicki
Design: Lindsay Hess
Layout: Michael Douglas and Lindsay Hess
Photography: Laura Lea Goldberg, Danielle Atkins, and Kate Davis
Index: Jay Kreider
Proofreader: Li Agen

Spring House Press
3613 Brush Hill Court
Nashville, TN 37216
ISBN: 978-1-940611-56-3

Library of Congress Control Number: 2017930203
Printed in China
First Printing: May 2017

The pantry organization as shown below and in other photographs of LL's kitchen was provided by The Home Edit
(TheHomeEdit.com).

Note: The following list contains names used in *The Laura Lea Balanced Cookbook* that may be registered with the United
States Copyright Office: 5-Step Animal Welfare Rating; Alice Randall; All-Clad; Alyssa's Cookies (Healthy Vegan Bites);
Amazon; Annie's Homegrown, Inc.; Applegate Farms; Bananas Foster; Banner MD Anderson Cancer Center Clinic; Bundt;
Canyon Bakehouse; Caroline Randall Williams; Chosen Foods; Cuisinart; Dandy Blend; Dirty Dozen; Deland Bakery; Elvis;
Environmental Working Group; Fig Newton; Frontier Natural Products Co-op; Gatorade; Glasslock USA; Google; GreenPan;
Health Warrior; Honeycrisp; Honeyville; Ina Garten; Joyva; Kerrygold; Kirkland's; Las Paletas; Le Creuset; Lightlife;
LL Balanced; LunchBots; Magic Shell; Manchego; Melissa Clark; Mestemacher; Mr. Coffee; My New Roots; Nashville Sounds;
Natural Gourmet Institute; Orblue; Pearson Farm; Pinewood Social; Pink Lady; Ponderosa; Popsicle; Primal Kitchen;
Publix; Rugby; Sarah Britton; Seafood Watch; Selina Naturally; *Soul Food Love; Spaceballs;* Spectrum; Terrasoul Superfoods;
The Farm Midwifery Workshop Program; The Fresh Market; The Kitchn; The Nashville Food Project; *The New York Times;*
The Peach Truck; The Post East; Thermos (Foogo, FUNtainer); Thrive Market; Trader Joe's; University of British Columbia;
U.S. Fish and Wildlife Service; Vitacost; Vital Choice; Vitamix; Whole Foods; Wikapedia; Wüsthof; Yeti; Yukon Gold; Zeroll.

acknowledgements

For Max, my best friend, who envisioned this book on a crisp October night more than 3 years ago; who believed in me when I didn't always believe in myself. It's hard to remember life before you, and I couldn't be more grateful to have you as my partner in crime. Also, thank you for graciously eating leftovers of the same dishes for 9 months straight.

For Mom, whose stews, stir fries, and Bundt cakes spoiled me so I could never settle for less. Thank you for showing me that the table is a port at which our and any family can safely gather.

For Dad, who always, always shows up, and who finds a way to be interested in everything that I'm interested in. I am incredibly proud to be your mini-me.

For Mom and Dad, who have consistently given the three of us unconditional and unwavering love, and who do the hard and right things.

For Wiwie, who reminds me that the world, that people, are fundamentally good. Oh, and who keeps me in the best kind of stitches.

For Jack, who continually shows this introvert the power of connection and of forgiveness; who I've looked up to and admired from wobbles and pigtails to today.

For CC, MK, and Tara, who exceeded any expectations I could have had about sisterhood, and who brought much needed estrogen to our slowly expanding clan.

For Kate and Vivian, who have shown me a new kind of love, and who fill a room with the most magnetic and authentic joy; who I am honored to watch grow up.

For Ella, my angel on earth, who set the bar for selflessness, courage, and empathy. I take your lessons with me wherever I go.

For Alice, for whom "mentor" is not lovely or whole enough a word—who saw beyond my 12-year-old frame to the me I was and would be. Thank you for my first job in the culinary world and thank you for taking the time to write this foreword.

For my best friends over the years, who chose me and choose me over and over again. You keep me grounded, hugged, and understood.

For my new family, who embraced me from the beginning, and who my heart is now fully intertwined with.

For Jolene and Ironman, our furry children, who never fail to put life in perspective and draw out my softest side.

For the Natural Gourmet Institute, who gave me the knowledge and confidence to move forward into uncharted territory, and reminded me of parts of myself that had gotten buried—for the year that changed everything.

For the Spring House Press team, who shared my vision for this book and worked doggedly alongside me to make it happen.

CONTENTS

recipe directory

······················

foreword

· ·

We've all been at a place where our life is in the balance; a place where our future is undetermined and at risk. America is at that place with food. Many of us have managed to get into a precarious, unbalanced relationship with our plate, our table, and our kitchens. This cookbook will teach you how to find balance again—and, if necessary, again and again. Balance is not something you get stuck in—it must be restored, over and over, bite after bite, meal after meal. It's something you work to achieve. No one does it better than Laura Lea Goldberg.

Laura Lea cooks edible poems. Her recipes break with convention and established food culture. They express her vision of a lush life: a life both serene and exciting, a world full of surprises—all of them good. Simply put, that is the essence of the recipes in this book and the theme of Laura Lea's kitchen—the surprises will be good for and to you.

Laura Lea creates recipes that work, that tell you exactly how to create a delicious dish, but they will not be expected recipes— they will be Laura Lea innovations. You will treasure this cookbook. The woman is non-stop when it comes to recipe development.

Laura Lea and I began working together at the end of the 20th century. When still a teen, she was part of a workshop examining the impact improbable alliances and friendships had had on the shaping of Nashville.

Ours is one such friendship. I am a black woman who writes about putting health and history on a tasty soul food plate, and I am particularly concerned with great food on a budget. There are budget and splurge items in this cookbook, easy- and harder-to-get ingredients, but Laura Lea and I have a common cause: food that's good to you and good for you; food that sustains by delighting. I am proud to say, my daughter Caroline Randall Williams and I put one of Laura Lea's chia pudding recipes into our cookbook *Soul Food Love,* and cooked that pudding for food justice workers in Baltimore.

When I was appointed Faculty Head of Stambaugh House at Vanderbilt University, one of my first acts would be to hire Laura Lea to curate a syllabus of food for the house so that my students could learn more about the world they lived in—and about themselves—by eating. That year we welcomed students to campus with Laura Lea's delicious coconut chia pudding with granola and fresh peaches, and invited them to engage in hard conversations sustained by the pure deliciousness of no-bake five-ingredient truffles. Week after week, she surprised the house with balanced deliciousness, with nutrient-rich taste revelations—things the students had never tasted before, like sweet potato wontons with garlic tamari dipping sauce, and sun-dried tomato and basil hummus.

Laura Lea has embarked on the audacious creation of an original food culture that I think of as "Laura Lea's elegant hippy food." Every one of Laura Lea's innovative recipes takes you on an adventure. Some of my favorite Laura Lea recipes in this volume include: Sweet Chili Pumpkin Seed Clusters, the Blueberry Ginger Breakfast Smoothie, Lightened-Up Green Pea Guacamole, and the Corn, Kale & Goat Cheese Chickpea Cake. These are tastes of my new South.

Nashville, a city where Laura Lea has deep roots, is located in Middle Tennessee—an area that has long been associated with the creation of intentional communities seeking to create ideal worlds in which individuals thrive. In the 19th century, three of the most famous American utopias were in Middle Tennessee: Nashoba, Rugby, and Ruskin.

This area is also home to The Farm, where the modern art of midwifery was reborn in the 20th century. In the 21st century, Laura Lea is building on these traditions in the reality of food to connect us to the ideal of loving balance, abundance, and a willingness to engage in new creations.

Laura Lea creates recipes that are bites of love, containing her loving ambition to feed the world well, and to feed the world deliciously— with positive intentions for our bodies, for the health of this planet we call home, and for restoring joy through the pleasure of taste.

Every year, each of us embarks on a 365-day journey around the sun. This cookbook invites you to make part of your journey a spa for the soul. Cook through these pages, and you will discover that Laura Lea provides an easy way to feed your body, your family, your friends, your lover, and any and all beloved by you in a way that restores balance by adding more joy, beauty, flavors, textures, elegance, energy, and calm. This cookbook is more than a cookbook—it is a map to a balanced way of life that reflects the graceful wisdom of a serene young chef, wife, and friend.

—**Alice Randall**
Author, with Caroline Randall Williams,
of *Soul Food Love*
Nashville, Tennessee, 2017

introduction

Finding balance, or even knowing what balance means, is something most of us struggle with. I certainly did. I spent four years in New York City after college, pinballing between health extremes. I either obsessed about and restricted food, or I prioritized late-night pizza and cocktails. Both approaches left me anxious and unhealthy. With food, I was either being "good" or "bad": I labeled indulgences as "cheats," and praised myself for being "clean" when I dieted. I spent countless hours researching the "hot" nutrition trends: vegan, raw, paleo, pescatarian, juice cleansing. I tried them all, but nothing gave me the health and balance that I desperately wanted.

After four years of this I discovered the Natural Gourmet Institute in the Chelsea neighborhood of NYC. NGI is an accredited chef's training program that focuses on nutrient-dense, whole-foods cooking. NGI offers a variety of approaches to wellness, and it is not dogmatic about any "right" or "wrong" way. This was revelatory—the idea that there is no "one-size-fits-all" when it comes to how and what we should eat. My time at NGI helped me to realize why my previous food strategies hadn't worked. I had been trying to mold myself into guidelines that were created by people with completely different lives and bodies than mine.

The truth is that sometimes I eat "paleo." I enjoy meat and veggies and potatoes, and they make me feel great. Sometimes I eat "vegan." I enjoy grains and beans, and they make me feel great too. I can eat gluten in moderation without experiencing negative side effects. I love butter and occasionally include goat cheese or yogurt in my meals.

I don't count calories, but I pay attention to my body's hunger cues. I like fat, carbs, and protein, all in different proportions at different times. I can fit into all of the trendy food diets and none of them, at the same time.

And I am 100% okay with that.

I finally understood that I didn't need to follow anyone else's ideal diet, despite how much I admired them. Becoming a Certified Holistic Chef gave me the confidence to create my own food "way," and to share it with my beloved Nashville community. Which is exactly what I did in summer 2013 when I started posting recipes on LL Balanced. The positive response to my website was, and continues to be, humbling and deeply gratifying.

I think LL Balanced provides a breath of relief for those who find themselves overwhelmed by the nutrition noise, as I was. People who don't fall into any specific diet or program, who want a variety of dishes to feed the variety of preferences in their household. LL Balanced food doesn't reinvent the wheel with exotic, one-use ingredients. My recipes are nutritious, creative versions of classic, familiar dishes. Most are quick, easy, and meant to encourage home-cooking. The aim of my cookbook is to make you excited to create your own nutritious food by removing the pressure of a dogmatic approach and by setting you up for success in the kitchen.

I took control of my mental, physical, and emotional health by learning how to take control of my kitchen. Now, my kitchen is my sanctuary whenever I need to regain my sense of balance, and this cookbook will help you do the same.

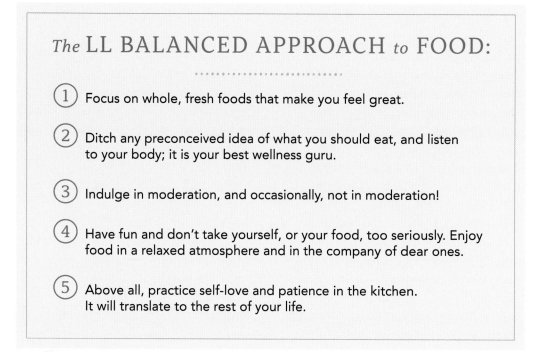

The LL BALANCED APPROACH *to* FOOD:

(1) Focus on whole, fresh foods that make you feel great.

(2) Ditch any preconceived idea of what you should eat, and listen to your body; it is your best wellness guru.

(3) Indulge in moderation, and occasionally, not in moderation!

(4) Have fun and don't take yourself, or your food, too seriously. Enjoy food in a relaxed atmosphere and in the company of dear ones.

(5) Above all, practice self-love and patience in the kitchen. It will translate to the rest of your life.

Special Recipe Symbols and Labels

Symbols are included throughout the book to make it easier to identify recipes that fit special diets and lifestyles. If a recipe fits into a diet as-is, without substitutions, it will have that diet's symbol on the left of the title bar. If substitutions are required, the symbol will appear on the right of the title bar, and the subs will also be designated with the symbol. Although there can be several interpretations for paleo, vegan, and vegetarian lifestyles, in this book, definitions should be taken to mean the following:

V VEGETARIAN

Free from: poultry, red meat, and fish/seafood. Note that in this book, recipes including eggs are classified as vegetarian. Note than any recipes including chicken stock can be made vegetarian by substituting vegetable stock.

Vg VEGAN

Free from: poultry, red meat, fish/seafood, eggs, dairy, and honey. Note that any recipes including the following can be made vegan by substituting.
- Mayonnaise can be swapped for vegan mayonnaise
- Dairy yogurt can be swapped for a non-dairy yogurt
- Honey can be swapped for maple syrup
- Chicken stock can be swapped for vegetable stock

DF DAIRY-FREE

Free from: dairy-based milk, cheese, yogurt, and butter. Note that most recipes with dairy in them can be made dairy-free through substitution of non-dairy counterparts.

GF GLUTEN-FREE

Free from: wheat, barley, rye, farro, or spelt. Note that any canned or packaged food should be certified gluten-free, such as (but not limited to): oats, canned tomatoes/paste, canned beans, soy sauce, mustard, ketchup, other sauces, flours, pastas, and crackers. All recipes in the cookbook are gluten-free unless otherwise noted, if certified gluten-free products are used.

Ⓟ PALEO

Free from: grains, gluten, legumes/beans, dairy (except butter), and refined sugar.

Note that any recipes including dairy yogurt can be made paleo by substituting a coconut or almond-based yogurt. Also be sure to use gluten-free prepared products as noted under Gluten-free. Some paleo diets do not include mayonnaise. If this describes your diet, replace any mayonnaise with paleo-approved mayonnaise.

ⓓ DAIRY-FREE NOT RECOMMENDED

These recipes are not recommended to be made dairy-free by making substitutions.

HANDS-ON AND TOTAL COOKING TIMES

Note that all total and hands-on times are approximate. Times don't include preheating the oven, boiling water, or making optional toppings or sauces. If marinating is required, the least amount of time required is included in the total time. For recipes with sauce or dressing, those instructions are included in the order in which the timing is most efficient for the entire recipe.

🕐 1 HOUR OR LESS

These recipes can be made completely within an hour.

💧 SOAKING REQUIRED

This label applies to recipes that include soaking an ingredient for 1 hour or more.

❄ CHILLING REQUIRED

These labels apply to recipes that require chilling for 30 minutes or more.

⊕ SECONDARY RECIPE

This label only applies if the secondary recipe isn't optional (e.g., teriyaki sauce for teriyaki meatballs). Even so, sometimes store-bought options can be subbed. This does not include salad dressings or optional toppings.

📻 SLOW COOKER

These recipes require the use of a slow cooker.

Important Tips & Tidbits

Understanding measurements. To avoid any wording confusion, let me clarify how dry measurements are described: If I say, "1 cup cucumber, sliced into ½-inch rounds," that means you are measuring a cup of ½-inch rounds, not a whole cucumber. Another example is: If I say "⅓ cup shallot, minced" you are measuring ⅓ cup minced shallot. A rounded cup means a few pieces of what you are measuring (often fruit) will stick up above the measuring line.

Basic recipes. Many cookbooks have a section on how to make healthy "basic" recipes, like properly cooking beans, making homemade nut milk, or making homemade stock. I do not have this, because the reality is: I don't make beans from scratch, I rarely make my own nut milk, and the few times I've made my own stock, it stunk up the kitchen for a whole day. Instead, I look for BPA-free organic canned beans and full-fat coconut milk, as well as low-sodium, free-range organic chicken broth. If you are interested in more of these DIY basics, there are ample book resources out there, if you do some noodling.

Preparing bananas for smoothies. My favorite smoothie foundation is the magical banana. A ripe frozen banana turns any smoothie into something creamy and decadent, even when it's packed with veggies. I always have a bunch of bananas ripening on the counter. When they are dotted with brown spots, I peel and slice them into 1-inch pieces. I then add them to a plastic food storage bag and lay the bag flat, horizontally in my freezer. They'll freeze in a layer that's easy to break apart.

Approximately 6 banana pieces equals 1 medium-sized banana.

Eggs. I always use large eggs, and eggs should be room temperature when used in baking recipes.

Canned coconut milk. If canned coconut milk feels a little heavy to you, try this: add 1 can coconut milk to a blender with 2 cups water. Blend until smooth and store to use as milk throughout the week. You can also use light

canned coconut milk or unsweetened almond milk. However, almond milk will create a product that is less rich and creamy, and I cannot vouch for the results.

Dates. In this book, I use medjool dates that come with the pit in. If you can only find pitted dates, you may need to soak them in hot water for 10 to 12 minutes, then drain thoroughly to make them juicy.

Nut/seed butters. Ideally, I try to use newer/runnier nut and seed butters, because they add moisture and are easier to blend. If that's not an option, then you can use this trick: Scoop out a few tablespoons less than the recipe calls for and add to a mixing bowl with the missing amount of tablespoons of very hot water. Stir to combine, then allow the mixture to sit 10 minutes. Then stir everything together thoroughly and measure out for the recipe. Also, assume nut butters are unsweetened and unsalted and peanut butter is organic.

Canned beans and butter. I always choose unsalted and unflavored options for these ingredients.

Extracts and caffeine. Technically, extracts like vanilla and maple are not considered strict paleo. Feel free to remove from recipes, noting that it will alter the flavor slightly. Or, you can order vanilla powder (look for Terrasoul brand online), which is pure ground vanilla beans. Sub ½ teaspoon vanilla powder for 1 teaspoon vanilla extract. Add powder with dry ingredients in baking. Technically, also caffeine is not considered paleo.

Oven rack position. I always use the middle rack. If I'm baking two things at once, I use the middle and bottom third rack, and switch the trays halfway through.

Cleaning salad greens. Though I don't specifically call for cleaning salad greens with a spinner in the recipes, you can assume that greens must be either cleaned or labeled as pre-rinsed before consuming.

Oat flour. To make oat flour, pulse rolled oats in a food processor or high-powered blender. It is important to pulse or blend until you have a very fine consistency. It should only be a little more granulated than all-purpose flour. It can be substituted 1:1 for all-purpose, whole-wheat, spelt, or gluten-free all-purpose flour.

Make ahead. All casseroles can be assembled the night before and baked the next day, but they will need another 5 to 10 minutes baking time because of the chill.

Leftovers. All estimated lengths of time for keeping leftovers with meat assume the meat was fresh when the item was prepared.

The LL BALANCED APPROACH to FOOD

....

Cooking isn't a rote set of steps to follow. It is a daily adventure; one that doesn't require airfare or jet lag. The temperature, time of day, age of your spices, seasonality of your ingredients — each time you cook, all of these factors and more come into play. And I do mean *play*. We live in an age of instant gratification, of science and technology and fact, and we've come to expect that in every aspect of our lives. But any true home cook will tell you that cooking often defies rules and logic, requiring instead intuition, risk, and experimentation. And that is the absolute real joy of the cooking experience. I have worked hard to create dishes that can be easily replicated, but embrace the concept that your versions will have their own nuances and characteristics.

....

> ## *The* THREE STEPS *to* ACHIEVING *the* LL BALANCED APPROACH TO FOOD:
>
> ① Fill your pantry and fridge with nutrient-dense, whole foods.
>
> ② Properly supply yourself with the basic kitchen equipment and ingredient staples.
>
> ③ Create a relaxed and happy eating environment.

① Fill your pantry and fridge with nutrient-dense, whole foods.

Eat Foods in Whole-Food Form Whenever Possible

I consider a whole food anything that comes directly from the earth that still contains all of its edible parts. A peeled orange is a whole food. A nut removed from its shell is a whole food. A deboned salmon fillet is a whole food. If you focus on filling your plate with whole foods whenever possible, you're automatically starting off on the right foot.

Protein, Fat & Fiber

Whenever I'm putting together a meal or snack, I focus on the trifecta of fat, fiber, and protein. High-quality fat will help keep you satisfied and provide lasting energy. Fiber,

in the form of vegetables and fruits, is where you'll usually find most of your nutrition. And protein is your powerhouse, building you from the ground up. Covering each of these categories helps ensure that you have a well-balanced dish. So what exactly does that well-balanced dish look like? Next you'll find a comprehensive breakdown of the major food categories and why they are so important.

note: What I've listed here are ideal food choices, but I understand that it is not always possible to have 100% grass-fed beef or organic everything. Check out my tips for eating healthy on a budget (page 36). The primary goal here is progress, not perfection. Do the best you can.

Whole foods, including fresh meats, vegetables, fruits, and nuts, are key to the LL Balanced approach to food.

This nutrition section has been reviewed and approved by the esteemed Dr. Santosh Rao, Medical Director for Integrative Medicine, Banner MD Anderson Cancer Center Clinic, Gilbert, Arizona.

HEALTHY PROTEINS

Proteins are the building blocks of our body, helping to properly form our skin, nails, hair, organs . . . you get the picture! Without enough high-quality protein, our bodies cannot grow and thrive. Healthy protein options include the following:

100% grass-fed, pasture-raised beef; pasture-raised pork; and pasture-raised lamb: "Grass-fed" refers to the actual diet of a cow, which should exclusively consist of grasses. Industrial farms often feed cows grain instead of grass, which is cheaper and fattens them more quickly. "Pasture-raised" refers to the environment and lifestyle of the animals. A pasture-raised cow, pig, or lamb is raised in a natural environment conducive to the health of the animal—that is, how they would ideally live if left to their own devices. When purchasing beef, look for grass-fed and pasture-raised. With pork and lamb, the best you can look for is pasture-raised. If you want to know what the animals have been eating, you can contact the company.

note: If you can find pastured-raised meat locally, that is the best option, because you'll be supporting sustainable practices in your own area, and the meat should be incredibly fresh.

Pasture-raised poultry: There are so many labels out there when it comes to poultry in general and chicken in particular. Here's a basic breakdown: "Free-range" simply means that the producers must demonstrate that chickens have outdoor access. However, this could mean (and often does) one tiny door leading to the outside in a crowded warehouse of chickens, so very few ever actually see the sunlight. "Organic" refers to the type of feed the animals are given, which can be completely unnatural, as long as it is certified organic. It doesn't speak to the care-taking practices, so it is our responsibility to inquire. I personally buy organic rotisserie chickens from Whole Foods, because they also meet the 5-Step Animal Welfare Rating criteria.

Eggs from pastured-raised poultry: Note, just because an egg is "local" doesn't mean that it comes from pasture-raised chickens. Again, do some digging on your own to understand the farm's practices. Egg yolks from pasture-raised chickens are one of the most healthful foods available. They contain a host of vitamins, including ample vitamin D, which is difficult to come by in food sources. They're full of minerals, such as magnesium, calcium, and iron, as well as antioxidants like beta-carotene. Generally, the darker and more golden/orange an egg yolk is, the more nutrient-dense it is.

Wild and sustainable shellfish and fish: Purchasing wild-caught, sustainable seafood ensures that you are getting the most nutrient-dense products, and you're not contributing to the extinction of any species. The omega-3 fatty acids found in wild, sustainable fish and shellfish are incredibly healing: they can help improve cholesterol levels, lower inflammation (see Healthy Fats, page 25, for definition), and boost mood, to name a few benefits. Depending on where you live, it can be easy to source affordable quality seafood. However, that is not the case for me in landlocked Tennessee. As a result, I order my seafood from Vital Choice (vitalchoice.com). It can be expensive, but if you order in bulk and use sparingly, it will last for months in the freezer.

To thrive, our bodies need healthy proteins like pasture-raised beef, wild-caught fish, eggs, tempeh, nuts, seeds, and legumes.

Tempeh: This is a fermented form of soybeans that usually shows up in a thin rectangular shape at the grocery store. Tempeh is a great protein alternative for vegans and vegetarians, as it has a pleasant, mild taste, mimics ground meat, and absorbs flavors easily. It's also quite affordable. The fermentation process in creating tempeh helps break down something called phytic acid, a natural plant defense mechanism that binds to nutrients, making them difficult to absorb. Tofu does not undergo this process and thus has a higher phytic acid content. I personally don't love the texture of tofu anyway, so I stick with tempeh. Whenever you consume soy (and I only recommend whole forms like tempeh, tofu, and edamame), choose non-GMO brands. I always look for organic tempeh, and

I particularly like Trader Joe's and Lightlife. Some brands use a combination of beans and grains other than soybeans, and I've found them to work equally well. However, soy is a controversial subject in the health and medical worlds. Consumption of soy has been implicated as problematic in relation to certain cancers, while other professionals believe it can be beneficial to cancer patients. Please see your health-care provider to learn more and determine how much soy is right for you. If you have the green light, I suggest trying some of my delicious tempeh recipes.

Nuts and seeds: I love everything in the nuts and seeds category—especially almonds, Brazil nuts, hazelnuts, macadamias, pecans, walnuts, and pistachios, as well as pumpkin, hemp, sesame, and chia seeds. This also includes nut and seed butters, such as almond or tahini (ground sesame paste). Peanuts are technically a legume, but they're generally enjoyed as a nut, so I include them here. I digest and tolerate nuts and seeds well, so you will see them throughout this book. However, nuts and seeds also contain phytic acid, and some people have a difficult time digesting them. If this is you, you can consider soaking your nuts and seeds, which makes them easier on your gut. I usually soak 2 cups of nuts or seeds in 4 cups of filtered water with 1 tablespoon sea salt. Soak, uncovered, at room temperature overnight. Drain and rinse thoroughly, and then place them in an even layer on a baking sheet on the counter until they dry out for a few hours.

note: My recipes do not call for soaked nuts or seeds, so your outcome might be different if you take this step before cooking.

Beans and legumes: I keep things simple when it comes to beans and legumes, which are a quick and easy source of plant-based protein and fiber. I purchase bulk amounts of organic BPA-free canned black beans, chickpeas, and lentils, and I use them for hummus, soups, and even my famous black bean brownies (page 341). BPA refers to bisphenol A, a harmful chemical found in many packaged products. I know that canned food in general isn't ideal, but this is where balance comes into practice: I am so careful about the quality of my meat, vegetables, home and beauty care products, etc., so if canned beans help me skip a step when I'm cooking in a hurry, I'm not going to worry about their imperfections. That said, you can absolutely cook your own beans

and legumes. The Kitchn (thekitchn.com) has a great article on scratch-cooking beans that I trust. You will see a few recipes in this book that use dry red lentils, which cook quickly and are extremely versatile.

note: Beans and legumes also contain phytic acid, which can cause digestive distress in some. If this is you, and you still want to use canned beans, just be sure to drain and rinse them extra-thoroughly.

Eliminate or minimize as much as possible:

- **Industrial, factory-farmed meat and poultry.** These proteins can contain all manner of chemicals and harmful fatty acids, and they do not contain the beneficial nutrient profile of their properly fed, pasture-raised counterparts. Factory-farmed eggs are one of the top allergens as well. Perhaps most importantly, most of these operations do not prioritize animal welfare, and I do not want to support the continuation and growth of any such practices.

- **Larger fish and endangered species.** In the seafood arena, enjoy larger fish, such as tuna and swordfish, in moderation. These larger fish tend to contain more toxins because they are higher on the food chain. Also, steer clear of endangered species (check fws.gov/endangered). As with meat and poultry, farmed seafood is likely fed an unnatural diet, which means you're not receiving the nutrition you deserve. For more information sourcing sustainable seafood in your area, I recommend visiting seafoodwatch.org.

HEALTHY FATS

Fat is essential for the function and maintenance of the nervous system and brain. We also need fats in order to absorb and synthesize crucial nutrients. Many people are lacking in the critical omega-3 fats and have an excess of omega-6 fats. This skewed ratio causes inflammation, which can eventually lead to chronic disease. Infla-what? You're probably familiar with the inflammation you see when you cut your finger—the skin around the cut gets red and inflamed. This acute inflammation is a good thing; it's a natural response to cellular damage and a signal that your body is trying to heal itself. However, inflammation can occur inside our bodies because of refined carbohydrate intake (aka white sugar and bread), polyunsaturated vegetable oils, antibiotics, pesticides, genetically modified organisms (GMOs), factory-farmed animal products, and more. Over time, consumption of these foods can cause chronic inflammation around your organs, which has been shown to contribute to the risk of cancer, autoimmune diseases, obesity, heart disease, and Alzheimer's.* Certain fats, particularly omega-3 from fish, are anti-inflammatory soldiers, helping to cool that silent fire that rages in many of us.

As my publisher once suggested, what if we referred to fat as "energy," instead of, well, *fat*? Dietary fat, the fat found naturally in food, has become synonymous with the fat on our bodies—the soft, buoyant flesh on our middle-sections and behind-sections. But here's the thing: they're *not* one and the same.

Eating high-quality, real-food sources of fat, such as avocado, coconut, or wild salmon, does not alone make you fat. These fats are a crucial element in a healthy diet. Not only can they promote and regulate brain health, reduce inflammation, and protect organs from trauma and injury, they are the most concentrated form of natural energy. Fats have twice the amount of calories found in proteins and carbohydrates—and this isn't a scary thing, it's a good thing! This means that a moderate amount of quality fat will give you sustained energy, and it won't leave you crashing and craving the way carbs alone can. Fats are the most satisfying macronutrient for your taste buds, making a dish taste rich and complex. Most low-fat packaged foods are higher in sugar than their whole-fat counterparts, because the sugar is required to make up for a lack of flavor.

Even more importantly, fats trigger the appropriate hormones for feeling content and satisfied, telling our bodies that it's time to stop eating. Because of this, you don't need to fear overeating healthy fats. Staying trim and losing body fat is so much more than the outdated concept of "calories in, calories out." All calories are not created equal, because they have varying impacts on our hormonal system. Our hormones are the real superstars behind our ability to burn fat, and depriving ourselves of healthy fat can wreak hormonal havoc.

This is not a low-calorie cookbook or a low-fat cookbook, and I wouldn't want it to be. I use whole sources of the highest quality fats,

---

*To read more about the effects of diet on inflammation, see the following studies:

Kiecolt-Glaser, Janice K., "Stress, Food, and Inflammation: Psychoneuroimmunology and Nutrition at the Cutting Edge." *Psychosomatic Medicine* May 2010; 72(4): 365–369. www.ncbi.nlm.nih.gov/pmc/articles/PMC2868080

Patterson, E., R. Wall, G. F. Fitzgerald, R. P. Ross, and C. Stanton, "Health Implications of High Dietary Omega-6 Polyunsaturated Fatty Acids." *Journal of Nutrition and Metabolism* volume 2012 (2012), article ID 539426. http://dx.doi.org/10.1155/2012/539426

and I use them in appropriate balance with everything else in any given dish. The LL Balanced way of eating will promote hormonal regulation and a healthy, energized body. Unless you have specific instructions from your doctor, I'd suggest you don't even look at calorie counts or grams of fat. Eat well, eat slowly, and eat without distractions, and your body will do the rest of the work.

Plant-sourced fats: Healthy sources of monounsaturated fats include avocados, nuts and seeds, olive oil, and toasted sesame oil. Another healthy plant-based fat is coconut oil. Coconut oil is a saturated fat (if a fat is solid at room temperature, it is saturated), and next I explain why that shouldn't scare you. However, coconut fat is unique in several ways. First, it contains a form of fat called *medium-chain-triglycerides,* or MCTs, which the body uses immediately for energy instead of being stored. Second, coconut also contains lauric acid, a fat that has potent antibacterial and antimicrobial properties. For these reasons, coconut oil is a great addition to a healthy diet. I purchase only extra-virgin organic coconut oil, which has a coconut-y taste, so I use it in recipes that fit this flavor profile.

Animal-sourced fats: Animal fats are saturated, and the term *saturated fat* can have negative connotations; but not all saturated fat is created equal. Moderate consumption of saturated fat from high-quality sources, such as pasture-raised animals, 100% grass-fed butter, and coconut, can be beneficial. These sources have anti-inflammatory omega-3 fatty acids and can improve nerve, brain, liver, heart, and lung health. You also don't need to be afraid that these saturated fats will have a negative impact on your cholesterol. In fact, our bodies require cholesterol to function properly. Our bodies actually make cholesterol on their own, but they can benefit from a moderate amount of additional cholesterol from high-quality saturated fats. Saturated fats are also incredibly stable, so they won't oxidize and become rancid in high-heat cooking the way vegetable oils do. True to form, I keep it simple and primarily use grass-fed butter as my choice animal fat. The brand Kerrygold is available at a fantastic price at Trader Joe's. Other fats, such as lard, tallow, schmalz, and ghee can be great options, again when sourced from pastured animals, so feel free to play around with these. Ghee is clarified butter, meaning that the milk solids have been separated and removed, so this can be a good option for people who do not tolerate dairy well.

Eliminate or minimize as much as possible:
- **Trans fats that come from hydrogenated, refined vegetable oils.** Some examples are safflower, corn, canola, cottonseed, and soybean oils. These unstable, easily rancid-ized fats are high in inflammatory omega-6. In addition, they tend to increase the "bad" LDL cholesterol and lower the "good" HDL cholesterol. If you stick to my guidelines for an LL Balanced way of eating, you should rarely come across trans, hydrogenated, or partially hydrogenated fats. They are typically found in packaged snack foods, fried foods, margarine, and frozen supermarket baked goods. "What about canola oil?" you might ask. Canola oil has been considered a healthy cooking fat for some time. However, it is chemically produced, often is genetically modified, and is partially hydrogenated. While it contains more monounsaturated fats than other vegetable oils, I don't see any place or need for it in a real-food diet.

FIBER

Grains: Certain grains can be a wonderful addition to a healthy diet. Grains are fiber-rich, contain high levels of B vitamins for proper metabolism and red blood cell formation, and they've been shown to improve cholesterol and blood pressure levels. I particularly love oats, which I use throughout the book as a gluten-free alternative to wheat flour (read more about gluten next). That said, some people experience irritable bowel syndrome (IBS) symptoms when they eat grains. Grains contain high levels of phytic acid, which we've seen can inhibit nutrient absorption. They also contain lectins, another plant self-defense, which can interfere with digestion and trigger an immune system response. If you eat grains and experience uncomfortable symptoms, or you see whole grains left in your stool after elimination, they might not be an ideal part of your diet. Besides oats, I only use a smattering of grains throughout the book in the form of white rice and quinoa. There are just so many other amazing foods available! Feel free to experiment with grains such as millet, barley, rye, amaranth, or buckwheat if you know that they agree with your digestive system.

Fresh vegetables: When it comes to the veggie kingdom, it's hard to go wrong. Barring any specific health conditions, I say go to town on plants, knowing that they're one of our best defenses against chronic inflammation. In addition, very few foods can rival the nutrient density of colorful vegetables, and their high-fiber content is great for feeling satisfied, aiding with digestion, and regulating blood sugar. The veggie recipes in this book are delicious and simple enough to convert even the strongest skeptic, so I hope you'll give them a try.

- **Cruciferous vegetables.** This family includes broccoli, Brussels sprouts, cauliflower, kale, radishes, collard greens, and cabbage, and they're some of my favorites when cooked properly. Cruciferous vegetables have particularly potent anti-inflammatory compounds.
- **Leafy green vegetables.** Kale has its own empire for good reason, but so should spinach, Swiss chard, bok choy, arugula, and collard greens. Leafy greens are packed with crucial antioxidants, which help quell damage from environmental toxins, chemicals in our body and beauty products, stress, over-exercise, processed foods, and medications. This class of vegetable is also rich in the alphabet of vitamins—A, B, C, D, E, K—and minerals, such as calcium, magnesium, and folate. And let's not forget about the lettuce family, such as Bibb, romaine, and butter lettuces, all of which contain many healing compounds.
- **Starchy vegetables.** My absolute favorites! Here we have jewel-toned beauties like sweet potatoes, yams, and beets, winter squashes like acorn and butternut, carrots, potatoes, and parsnips. These veggies have a higher sugar and starch content than others, making them ideal candidates for roasting and caramelizing. But they bring more to the table than just flavor—they contain a host of nutrients, insoluble fiber (which helps create bulk in your digestive system to push out waste), and soluble fiber (a natural stool softener . . . no other way to say it, guys).
- **Allium vegetables.** A.k.a., the smelly guys—garlic, onions, scallions, leeks, shallots, and chives all fit into this category. I say bring 'em on! The sulfides responsible for the pungent aroma in these bulbous vegetables

have been shown to improve cardiovascular and cholesterol health. While you may enjoy them raw (kudos), they're divine cooked up and softened in some good fat. A tip I learned from integrative oncologist Dr. Santosh Rao is to allow garlic to sit 10 minutes after mincing and before combining with something acidic, as this allows for the conversion of beneficial compounds. Also, when mincing garlic, first slice in half vertically to see if there's a green stem in the middle. If so, remove this garlic "germ"; it has a bitter flavor.

Non-starchy colorful vegetables. And this is the lovely category of everything in between! This includes bell peppers and other peppers, turnips, asparagus, artichokes, celery, eggplant, jicama, sugar snap peas, green beans, pumpkins, cucumbers, zucchini, summer squash, and tomatoes (which are technically a fruit but are generally viewed as a veg). All are gloriously nutritious and delectable in their own right, and I urge you to play around with different ways to enjoy them.

Gorgeous fruit: My husband and I usually prefer to eat fruit as a snack or with breakfast, and I enjoy several servings every day. Fruit is nature's candy, as scrumptious as it is beautiful to look at. Most fruits are fiber powerhouses, and each variety contains its own rainbow of vitamins and minerals. Some fruits are higher in sugar than others, so I've categorized them according to their sugar content. This is not a prescription for how much is too much—that's up to your body. However, it is worth understanding that fruit can have a significant impact on your blood sugar. When cutting dried fruit, rubbing a thin layer of oil on a knife before cutting makes it much easier and faster.

Cruciferous vegetables, like cabbage, kale, Brussels sprouts, and radishes, are a fantastic defense against chronic inflammation.

- **Low-sugar fruits.** Blackberries, cranberries, raspberries, avocado (indeed, it is a fruit!), lemons, limes, and rhubarb
- **Moderate-sugar fruits.** Strawberries, blueberries, watermelon, nectarines, peaches, papaya, apples, grapefruit, honeydew, cantaloupe, and apricots
- **High-sugar fruits.** Pineapple, banana, mango, plums, pears, oranges, kiwis, cherries, figs, and dried fruit

Allergy versus Intolerance versus Sensitivity

GLUTEN

I know your head is probably spinning from the gluten-free bug that's swept the nation in the past several years, but here's the deal with gluten. Gluten is a protein found in certain grains like wheat, barley, rye, and spelt. People who have celiac disease cannot tolerate even a speck of gluten because it will cause their bodies to start to attack its own tissue. Celiac disease affects only a small percentage of the population, but allergies, sensitivities, and intolerances to gluten are much more common. Allergy symptoms tend to show up immediately after ingesting a food, in the form of hives or rashes, difficulty breathing, nausea and vomiting, and irritation of the throat or mouth. A gluten allergy doesn't tend to cause the same amount of long-term damage to the intestines as celiac disease. Intolerances or sensitivities are more difficult to diagnose, because the symptoms can appear more slowly. Usually, these symptoms include mental and physical fatigue, digestive upset such as bloating or constipation, and headaches. If you experience any of these, I suggest working with a health-care professional to cut gluten out of your diet for

3 to 4 weeks, then reintroduce it slowly. Pay attention to how it makes you feel.

Personally, wheat and gluten don't bother me when I have them in moderation, so I do. However, you have to figure out what works for you. My recipes are mostly gluten-free, and I can guarantee you won't miss it.

DAIRY

I love me some dairy, but it doesn't agree with some people. Many people are allergic to dairy, in which case their bodies react negatively to the dairy protein casein. Dairy intolerance to the milk sugar lactose is also common. Dairy allergy and intolerance symptoms overlap and usually appear somewhat quickly in the form of stomach pain, bloating, gas, nausea, or diarrhea (or more severe in the case of allergy). Consult with your doctor to determine your condition if you think you and dairy aren't a good match. You won't be alone, and the good news is—the vast majority of my recipes are dairy-free, and almost all can be made dairy-free with appropriate substitutions!

On a different note, most factory-farmed dairy is the result of inhumane practices that I don't want to support, and the products themselves are poorer quality. Worse yet, many of the industrial dairy animals are injected with hormones, which compounds with the natural hormones found in cows already. Throw this on top of our own endocrine system, and we have a hormonal mess . . . which often shows up as acne and oily skin. In addition, "low-fat" yogurts and ice creams, as well as skim milk, are higher in sugar to make up for the lack of flavor, which isn't doing anyone any favors.

As with gluten, try eliminating and reintroducing dairy with the help of a professional to note any ill effects. If you are going to consume dairy, it should be full-fat, unsweetened, and from grass-fed, pasture-raised cows. My life would be a little sadder without grass-fed cheddar. I also find that people tend to digest goat's milk and cheese better than cow's, so that can be a good option if you have a trusty purveyor. If you can't find pastured and grass-fed, organic is the next best thing to look for. In the book, you will see a few recipes with cheese, and I certainly don't shy away from grass-fed butter. I use the best quality available in moderation, and I suggest the same for you.

CORN, PEANUTS & SOY

Be picky when it comes to corn, peanuts, and soy. These popular crops are mostly grown on large-scale industrial farms, where they are treated with pesticides and other chemicals, and often they are genetically modified. As a result, these foods are among the top allergens and food irritants, causing mild as well as severe immune system reactions and digestive upset. I enjoy all three of these foods, but I make sure to buy organic, non-GMO versions, and I eat them in moderation.

② Properly supply yourself with the basic kitchen equipment and ingredient staples.

Much of the stress that people feel around cooking comes from not having what they need to make a dish. This leads to multiple grocery runs, often last-minute, making the idea of a pleasant kitchen experience seem impossible. However, there's an easy fix for this major cooking roadblock: take the time and invest in pantry and kitchen staples. I have purposefully streamlined the tools and ingredients I use so that I know I have the building blocks of my dishes handy. The purpose of this guideline is to create the same ease for you.

Cooking Equipment Staples

FOOD PREP BASIC EQUIPMENT

- **Chef's knife:** This 8- to 10-inch knife with a wide blade and pointed tip is a home cook's best friend, and it is worth springing for a high-quality one if you can. I have several knife sets, and I rarely use any knife besides this and my paring knife. I like Orblue and Wüsthof.
- **Paring knife:** This is a mini chef's knife that comes in handy when you need to peel or chop more delicate and smaller fruits and vegetables, such as garlic or strawberries. I suggest the same brands as for the chef's knife.
- **Vegetable peeler**
- **Kitchen shears:** I use kitchen shears to trim fat off meat, snip herbs, and open plastic packaging.
- **Can opener**
- **Colander:** I suggest two large stainless-steel colanders, one with micro-perforations for smaller grains, and one with slightly larger holes for draining pasta or bigger vegetables.
- **Salad spinner:** This is almost an optional piece, but it makes life so much easier, so I highly recommend it. This dries delicate lettuce leaves without damaging them, ensuring you never have a soggy salad.
- **Mesh strainer:** I use this all the time for draining and rinsing beans and grains.
- **Pastry brush:** This is the best way to spread butter or oil evenly over ingredients for roasting and grilling, or for greasing a dish or baking sheet.
- **Stainless-steel whisk**
- **Wooden cutting board:** Use this for vegetables and fruit.
- **Plastic cutting board:** Use this for meat; bacteria can leach into wooden cutting boards. However, be sure to replace your plastic board if the cutting grooves become too deep and hard to clean.
- **Stainless-steel mixing bowl set**

A vegetable peeler and paring knife will make short work of prepping smaller vegetables.

- **Cheese grater**
- **Parchment paper:** I always use nonstick parchment paper, so assume that any parchment paper mentioned throughout the book is nonstick. Kirkland's brand is my favorite.

---

note: Not sure what these look like? Search online to see multiple options.

INVESTMENT PIECES

These items can be expensive, but I truly believe that they are worth the investment. I use them daily for smoothies, soups, sauces, salad dressings, and even making flour. The time you'll save hand-chopping, whisking, or mixing is invaluable, and they will earn their cost back quickly when you save money on take-out and dining out. Ask for them for birthdays, look into gently used options, or cut out a few indulgent habits every month. If you can only start with one of the two, I suggest investing in the high-powered blender. Food processors don't do well with liquid contents, whereas the blender can handle liquids and many solids as well—my Vitamix can make oat flour, pesto, and hummus. However, I do prefer to use my food processor for making veggie burgers, chopping nuts, grating vegetables, and making nut butters, when I do. Making nut butter is as simple as adding 1 to 2 cups nuts of choice to your food processor and blending until they form a creamy consistency. You can add a few tablespoons of coconut oil to get things moving if needed.

- **High-powered blender** (I have the Vitamix Standard original)
- **Food processor** (at least 8 cup; I prefer Cuisinart)

COOKING/BAKING
BASIC EQUIPMENT

- **Small sauté pan** (also called *fry pan*): 8- to 10-inch*
- **Large sauté pan** (with straight sides): 4 to 6 quarts*
- **Small sauce pot:** 2 quarts*
- **Medium sauce pot:** 4 quarts*
- **Large stock pot:** 8 to 12 quarts*
- **12½-inch cast-iron skillet**
- **Slow cooker**
- **13 x 9 x 2-inch baking dish**
- **8 x 8 x 2-inch baking dish**
- **Cupcake and loaf tins:** I suggest aluminized steel or green nonstick (see sidebar for more details).
- **1 to 2 large solid baking sheets:** This size has an inset of approximately 17 x 12 inches. I prefer to use aluminum or carbon steel.
- **1 to 2 perforated/slotted baking sheets:** I place these over a solid baking sheet to roast meat—this way the drippings don't make a mess.
- **Slotted and solid wooden spoons**
- **Indoor grill pan**
- **"Turner" spatula** (flat metal spatula for flipping pancakes and eggs)
- **2 to 3 rubber spatulas**
- **Stiff brush** (for cleaning stuck-on food)
- **Metal tongs**
- **Soup ladle**

COOKING/BAKING EQUIPMENT,
OPTIONAL BUT RECOMMENDED

- **Rice cooker**
- **Popsicle molds and sticks**
- **Enameled cast-iron braising pot** (Le Creuset has the best)
- **Meat thermometer**

---

*I recommend high-quality stainless-steel pots and pans, like All-Clad. They are nonreactive, cool down easily, and are very strong and corrosion-resistant. They don't distribute heat as evenly as aluminum or copper, but you don't need to worry about minerals leaching into your food. You can find copper lined with stainless-steel, which is a good option as well, but slightly more expensive.

UNDERSTAND YOUR SKILLETS AND PANS

Skillet versus sauté pan. A skillet or frying pan is shallow, with slanted sides that flare out. A sauté pan has taller, straight sides, with more surface area at the bottom. Throughout this cookbook, you will mainly "see" me using a stainless steel sauté pan, because it is cleaner (less sloshing over the side) and because I think it can do everything a skillet can do. However, if you already own a small and a large skillet, don't feel that you need to get sauté pans as well. Your skillets should work just fine.

Cast-iron skillets. A different animal altogether, these classic heavy pans are a great investment. They don't cost a lot and they get better with age, if properly taken care of. Cast-iron takes a little while to get hot, but it gets screaming hot and has excellent heat retention. I use my cast-iron skillet when I want to make sure that the dish is cooked evenly through, such as my Pesto Chicken & Spinach Frittata (page 137) or Summer Peach & Blueberry Crumble with Coconut Cashew Cream (page 323). I also use it for nonstick cooking, like with my Customizable Oat Johnnycakes with 20-Minute Chia Berry Jam (page 118). "Seasoning" your cast-iron skillet protects it from heat and makes it durable.

To season cast-iron: Preheat oven to 325° F. Wipe down skillet with a wet cloth and dry thoroughly. Apply a thin coat of any oil of choice to the skillet (I use olive oil). Place skillet upside down on center oven rack, and place a sheet of aluminum foil on bottom rack to catch dripping oil. Bake for an hour, turn off oven heat, and allow skillet to remain until completely cooled. You'll know you need to re-season your skillet when it is no longer smooth and shiny.

To clean your cast-iron skillet. Do not wash with soap or scrub with a metal brush or sponge; this will damage it. Wash under hot water with a textured sponge as soon as possible after cooking. If this doesn't clean it completely, add a few tablespoons of sea salt and scrub the salt into the skillet with a paper towel or dish rag. Rinse thoroughly.

Green nonstick pan. Traditional nonstick pans/skillets have been shown to release toxic gases at high temperatures, making them an unsafe option. However, some companies are now making "green" nonstick ceramic skillets that purport to eliminate health concerns. I have one grill pan from a company called GreenPan, and I've used it successfully. If you would prefer not to invest in a cast-iron skillet, you can look into "green" or "eco" pans to determine how you feel about them.

- **Immersion blender**
- **Ice cream maker**
- **Wire cooling rack** (can use a slotted baking sheet instead)

STORAGE EQUIPMENT

- **Variety of glass sealable containers** (I like Glasslock)
- **Food storage zip-top bags:** Perfect for frozen fruit and dry goods such as flours, nuts, and grains.
- **Insulated food and beverage containers:** I like Thermos brand. These are useful for food-to-go and in lunch boxes, for both hot and cold items. An optional item is a Yeti cup (or one from a similar, knock-off

brand), which keeps liquids hot or cold for a long time.

- **Mason jars:** Great for soups, salad dressings, smoothies, and salad dressings.

Pantry Food Staples

The following are MY staples and the staples for this book. If you buy and stock these, all you will have to do is purchase perishable items when you want to make a recipe: fruits, veggies, meat, eggs, dairy. Start here and feel free to experiment with ingredients as your comfort with cooking grows. Note I have tagged some ingredients with an *. These are ingredients that are a bit more exotic—I have included suggestions for using them starting on page 42.

Swapping healthy fats into your diet is as simple as using grass-fed butter, organic coconut oil, and olive oil, and leaving behind hydrogenated and trans fats.

FATS

- **Extra-virgin olive oil:** As classic as it gets; I probably use olive oil every single day in cooking. Its slightly savory umami flavor pairs with almost any protein or vegetable, and it is full of heart-healthy fats. When it comes to olive oil, make sure you are purchasing "extra-virgin first cold-pressed" oil, and look for a bottle that is dark/opaque (to protect it from destabilizing sunlight heat). This ensures you are getting the freshest, highest quality olive oil, which easily goes rancid.
- **Extra-virgin organic coconut oil***
- **Grass-fed butter:** What is left to be said about butter? It makes everything taste better, richer, more satisfying, and more complex. I use it in moderation, as I do all ingredients, but there are certain instances in which nothing beats butter— like slathered on a freshly baked muffin or tossed in pasta with a pinch of sea salt. I always have Kerrygold grass-fed butter in my fridge, and unless you have a dairy allergy or intolerance, I recommend the same for you.
- **Toasted sesame oil***

VINEGARS

- **White balsamic vinegar:** This is my go-to vinegar, and my husband actually introduced me to it. Made from white grapes and white wine vinegar, white balsamic has a lovely flavor and a clean aftertaste. It also has a hint of sweetness, and I think it is an ideal base for salad dressings. If you want a vinegar that is less intense than white vinegar, I highly recommend this.

note: When a recipe calls for this in the book, it is factoring in the natural sweetness of white balsamic. If you substitute a more acidic/less sweet vinegar, you should add more sweetener to taste.

- **Dark balsamic vinegar:** A classic and staple of our pantry. Good balsamic vinegar is made from simmering grapes for hours until they are syrupy and caramelized. Dark balsamic has a rich flavor that is ideal for adding complexity and acid to cooked dishes. To concentrate the flavor even more, you can purchase reduced balsamic vinegar or reduce it yourself: simply add it to a sauce pan and simmer until it reaches a syrupy consistency. This is a dream drizzled on fresh tomatoes in the summer.
- **Apple cider vinegar (ACV):** The most acidic of these three, apple cider vinegar is made from fermented apples. Used for centuries in home and health-care applications, apple cider vinegar has numerous purported health benefits, such as improving digestion, whitening teeth, and regulating blood sugar. Raw, unfiltered ACV contains "the mother," a cobweb-looking substance made from proteins, enzymes, and beneficial probiotic organisms. While I do not find apple cider vinegar to be the "cure all" that some have touted, I do find that it can help settle a stomach ache (I use 2 teaspoons in 1 cup of filtered water). Primarily, I use ACV for its astringent but neutral flavor when I want a nice hit of acid in a sauce or even a baked good recipe. I encourage you to do some ACV research on your own if you are interested in the health benefits.

HEALTY EATING ON A BUDGET

Follow the Dirty Dozen for organic selections.
I understand that organic food can get *real* expensive *real* quick. As a result, I follow the Environmental Working Group's list called the Dirty Dozen. This list includes fruits and vegetables that are highest in pesticide content. I try to buy organic versions of the Dirty Dozen items, such as berries, leafy greens, and apples. Visit EWG's website (EWG.org) for the updated list.

Buy seasonal and local produce. Produce is generally cheaper when it is in season, so look for items from local or regional farms. Buy in bulk. Chop fruits and vegetables into smaller pieces, place in zip-top storage bags, and freeze. Use as you would pre-packed frozen produce.

Check for sales and choose recipes accordingly.
Stay tuned-in to the sales going on at your grocery stores. Make a list of the whole-foods items on sale, then see which recipes in my book (or another book, *I guess*) use those items. Again, stock up and freeze anything that can be frozen (see page 53 for help with that).

Ditch bottled drinks for homemade options.
My husband and I get bored with plain water, and as much as we love seltzer and kombucha, the cost of bottled drinks adds up quickly. As an alternative, soak fruit in a pitcher of filtered water overnight to infuse the flavor. I also do this with cucumber and mint or basil. You can also try my Cleansing Raspberry Ginger Water (page 86) or Workout Water (page 89).

Eat eggs. Eggs are inexpensive and incredibly nutrient-dense. Always keep some in the fridge and enjoy them as your protein in any meal or snack. Stir a raw egg into some cooked grains over a little heat for a quick "fried rice." Make an easy egg salad with a few hard-boiled eggs, a dollop of mayo, a smaller dollop of Dijon mustard, and pinches of salt, pepper, and onion powder. Delicious!

Visit the frozen section. There is nothing wrong with frozen fruits and vegetables, so fill up your cart and freezer and feel good about it. I almost always use frozen organic kale and spinach in my green smoothies. Not only is it cost-effective and longer-lasting, but it makes for a creamier texture and better flavor. Most produce is frozen right when it's harvested, so it can have even more nutrition than some items that have traveled a long way to get to you.

Get slow cooker–friendly. Cheaper cuts of meat are generally tougher, but they can break down beautifully in a slow cooker. Add a few pounds of some of these tough cuts with enough water to cover halfway, throw in some seasonings, and let it cook for hours. Check out my Slow Cooker Indian Butter Chicken (page 238) for an example.

Condi-meat. Say what?! Think of meat as a condiment, not the centerpiece of each plate. Make sure you're offering plenty of vegetables with your entree and encourage family members to fill up on those first. If you can ditch the notion of meat as the main event, it will save you some serious bucks in overall quantity consumed.

continued on next page

continued from previous page

Meatless Monday. And while you're at it, have a meatless night or two every week, and try one of my absolutely delicious vegetarian dishes. Beans, grains, and tempeh are quite affordable, and I promise with the right cooking techniques and flavoring, you'll love them.

Make friends with leftovers. See my section on leftovers (page 54). This can save some major cash, it helps decrease waste, and it forces you to use your imagination (or your keypad and Google, whichever the case may be).

SPICES

I recommend replenishing your spices every 6 months. If you get rid of spices you don't use, and only stock the ones you do, this will be easy—you might even run out before then.

- **Ground cinnamon**
- **Ground paprika**
- **Ground sweet smoked paprika**
- **Turmeric powder***
- **Chili powder**
- **Garlic powder**
- **Onion powder**
- **Ground cumin**
- **Curry powder**
- **Ground ginger**
- **Ground cayenne pepper**
- **Sea salt**
- **Black pepper:** For adding to a dish that will be cooked (soups, casseroles, sautés), use pre-ground. For garnishing an already-prepared meal, use a pepper grinder.
- **Oregano**
- **Basil**
- **Tarragon**
- **Rosemary**
- **Red pepper flakes**

GRAINS (ORGANIC RECOMMENDED)

- **Quinoa:** Quinoa is technically a seed, not a grain. However, it has a similar nutrient profile and is prepared/eaten similarly to grains, so I'm designating it to this category. Quinoa is high in plant protein, and it is considered a "complete" protein. "Complete" proteins contain all nine essential amino acids that our body cannot produce and thus must obtain from food. There are very few plant-based "complete" proteins, and quinoa is one. Quinoa is also loaded with vitamins, minerals, and fiber, and it is gluten-free, making it a superstar in the health-food world. Before cooking quinoa, it is crucial to rinse the "grains" thoroughly, as they contain a bitter protective coating called saponin.

- **White rice:** My husband and I much prefer the flavor and texture of white rice to brown. Although brown rice, when properly prepared, contains more nutrients, we get so much nutrition from other foods that we don't worry about this. However, white rice can be a problem for those with diabetes or blood sugar issues. Quinoa, alone or mixed with brown rice, is a great alternative in those cases. Also, we always pair white rice with a fat or a protein, so it doesn't spike blood sugar the way it would if eaten alone. Absolutely feel free to use whatever grain you prefer.

note: When I mention white rice in recipes, I am referring to long-grain rice, not short-grain rice. Long-grain rice cooks up fluffy and separate, whereas short-grain rice tends to clump and stick.

Rolled oats: Oats—one of the inspirations of this book! You will see oats throughout this book in various applications, and that is for a few reasons. Oats are affordable, available at every grocery store, and they are extremely versatile with their mild, barely sweet flavor. Ground up, they can substitute 1:1 for wheat flour; they make a great binder, are a breakfast staple, and they can be used whole in bars, granola, or dessert toppings. On the health front, I much prefer homemade oat flour to wheat, as it is gluten-free and minimally processed. There are different types of oats. All oat variations start at oat groats, which are then processed to create three main oat categories. Steel-cut oats are simply groats that have been cut into chunky pieces, and they take quite some time to cook. Rolled oats are groats that have been steamed and flattened, which makes them more pliable and quicker-cooking. Instant oats have been further processed and flattened, and they lose texture/become mushy when cooked. Feel free to experiment with all three, but be sure to choose rolled oats for the recipes in this book.

note: Make sure your oats have "Certified GF/Gluten-Free" on the packaging if that is a concern.

Wild rice: Wild rice is actually the seed of a long-grain aquatic grass. It has a nutty, chewy flavor that pairs beautifully with nuts and fresh or dried fruit. It has significantly more fiber and protein than brown rice, as well as B vitamins and a host of minerals. Wild rice is gluten-free, making it a fun and unique alternative for those who might be sick of quinoa and oats.

what to do with

EXTRA WILD RICE

You can pop wild rice the same way you pop popcorn.

Fiber-rich grains can be a great addition to a healthy diet. In the recipes that follow, you'll find wild rice, quinoa, rice, and rolled oats.

DRIED/CANNED GOODS

- **Canned organic chickpeas**
- **Canned organic black beans**
- **Canned organic lentils**
- **Canned organic kidney beans**
- **Dry red lentils**
- **Canned organic cannellini or great northern beans**
- **Canned full-fat coconut milk**
- **Canned unsweetened pumpkin puree**
- **Nuts:** almonds, cashews, pecans, walnuts, hazelnuts
- **Nut and seed butters:** Almond butter, peanut butter (technically a legume, but we use it like a nut), and tahini paste*
- **Seeds:** Chia*, sunflower, pumpkin
- **Unsweetened coconut flakes:** Coconut flakes are different from shredded coconut. Shredded coconut is made of thicker, larger pieces than coconut flakes, so they're not a 1:1 substitution. If you use shredded, I cannot guarantee the exact same outcome, but it shouldn't impact a recipe dramatically.
- **Unsulphured dried apricots***
- **Medjool dates***
- **Nutritional yeast***
- **Pasta:** Brown rice, quinoa, spelt, black bean, or chickpea pasta
- **Wild-caught, boneless and skinless canned tuna and salmon**
- **Non-GMO popcorn** (as a snack)
- **Dandy Blend:** This is a caffeine-free coffee substitute made from ground chicory, beet, and dandelion root. Order it online at dandyblend.com.
- **Stock of choice** (low-sodium chicken or vegetable)
- **Canned artichoke hearts**
- **Figs**
- **Kalamata olives**
- **Tea bags**

- Salsa
- Unsweetened applesauce
- Organic crushed tomatoes
- Diced tomatoes
- Tomato paste
- Dill pickles
- Dried cranberries/dried cherries

REFRIGERATOR STAPLES

- **Tamari* or low-sodium soy sauce**
- **Sriracha:** The best condiment of all time, I'd wager! No, this is not a perfectly healthy product. It has added sugar and some preservatives, but this is the LL Balanced cookbook, and I'm not worried about a tablespoon of sriracha spread over multiple servings in a recipe. It has the perfect balance of sweet, savory, and spice, and I just adore it. You can sub 1 teaspoon honey + 1 teaspoon plain red hot sauce + 1 teaspoon water if needed.
- **Mayo:** As you will see in this book, I am not anti-mayo. I'm a Southern girl, after all! The problem with commercial mayonnaise is that it's usually made with hydrogenated vegetable oils, like soybean, and I've explained in my Healthy Fats section (page 26) why this is a NO. However; thoughtful companies like Spectrum, Chosen Foods, and my favorite, Primal Kitchen, have made mayonnaise with olive oil and avocado oil, both healthy choices that taste great. I buy my mayo on thrivemarket.com, or you can check out chosenfoods.com.
- **Dijon mustard:** A classic and staple! I adore Dijon mustard, and find that it adds a wonderful touch of acidity to countless recipes. A dear friend from college taught me to dip baby carrots into Dijon, and I still love this combo. My favorite Dijon ever is the Trader Joe's Moutarde de Dijon, but any basic variety will do.

• **Organic ketchup:** As with sriracha, ketchup is not a perfect food, but there are many brands now offering organic versions without high-fructose corn syrup. And sometimes, only ketchup will do. That is a culinary fact of life. I like Annie's Homegrown, which I buy on Thrive Market. It has a touch of cane sugar, but I don't spend a minute worrying about it.

• **Coconut water:** This is nature's Gatorade and something you will always see stocked in our refrigerator, because my husband drinks a glass every morning. Coconut water is packed with natural electrolytes, which keep you hydrated and help regulate the nervous system. I use coconut water as the base of smoothies, my Workout Water (page 89), and as a key component to any illness recovery. I just look for any brand that is 100% coconut water, without added sugars, flavors, or preservatives.

• **Tempeh**
• **Lemon/lime juice**
• **Cheese of choice**
• **Eggs**
• **Prepared horseradish**
• **Orange/grapefruit juice**
• **Yogurt**
• **Hummus**

Keeping staples in your refrigerator makes preparing healthy meals easy and stress-free.

FREEZER STAPLES

- **Wild-caught salmon, shrimp, halibut, cod, and scallops** (I order them from Vital Choice)
- **Bread:** I like Deland Bakery, Canyon Bakehouse (GF), Mestemacher rye, or a sourdough loaf.
- **Non-GMO corn tortillas**
- **Leftover pancakes and waffles** (separate with small pieces of parchment paper and stack)
- **Grass-fed ground beef; ground turkey**
- **Organic chicken breasts and thighs**
- **Frozen smoothie fruit** such as bananas, apples, pineapple, cherries, raspberries, blueberries, and strawberries
- **Frozen organic broccoli, spinach, edamame, peas, kale, or other green vegetables**
- **Frozen corn kernels**

FLOURS

A note on my flour choices: There are lots of healthy flours out there . . . countless, these days. But I keep things simple for myself, and I suggest the same for you. Certified gluten-free oats are cheap, accessible, and tolerated by most people. And when blitzed in a high-powered blender or food processor, they make a fantastic flour. I realize that not everyone can or will buy almond and coconut flour, though I make a strong case for them in the following description. As a result, I decided that oats/oat flour/oat bran could be the great equalizing flour in this book. It doesn't rise the same way as wheat flour, but it has a lovely mild taste that goes with almost everything. Feel free to sub wheat flour 1:1 with oat flour if you like.

- **Blanched almond flour***
- **Coconut flour***
- **Oat flour**
- **Oat bran**

Try natural sweeteners like honey, maple syrup, and coconut sugar.

SWEETENERS

- **Honey** (real honey, not from a teddy bear bottle!)
- **Coconut sugar***
- **Grade A maple syrup**
- **Medjool dates***
- **Molasses**
- **Organic liquid stevia:** Organic stevia can be a great sugar-free sweetening option, and it won't have an impact on your blood sugar the way other sweeteners will. However, it is incredibly strong and some don't like the flavor. I don't use it often, but I like to keep it around to add a drop to oatmeal, smoothies, or hot tea, where other flavors are more prominent. I do not recommend substituting stevia for sweeteners in baked goods/desserts, as it can throw off the liquid/dry ratio.

OTHER:

- **Baking powder**
- **Baking soda**
- **Vanilla extract**
- **Almond extract**
- **Maple extract**
- **Arrowroot starch* or non-GMO cornstarch**
- **Dark chocolate and/or semi-sweet chocolate chips**
- **Cacao nibs**
- **Cocoa powder:** There are three different chocolate powders out there. Raw cacao powder is made by cold-pressing raw cocoa beans. This is the most "natural" form, and it is extremely high in antioxidants. Natural cocoa powder is made by roasting cocoa beans at high temperatures, which decreases the nutritional content. Dutch process cocoa powder is natural cocoa powder that has been alkalized to become less acidic and astringent-tasting. The latter two still provide health benefits, however, and they are preferable for baking, as the baking process negates the point of having raw cacao. Cutting to the chase—I keep natural cocoa powder around, and I use it anywhere I'd need a chocolatey powder. If you want to amp up your nutrient game, however, feel free to also use raw cacao in smoothies or no-bake treats.

SOME FUNKY INGREDIENTS AND OTHER WAYS TO USE THEM

The vast majority of the ingredients in this book can be found in any grocery store and probably already sound familiar to you. This is how I cook—simply and from the same basic pantry—and it makes life so much easier. That said, there are a handful of ingredients you'll see scattered throughout that you might not recognize. If you choose not to buy a single one of these items, you

can still make most of my recipes. However, I recommend them. These are ingredients that have enhanced my cooking with their flavor and nutrition, and often take the place of less healthy foods. I believe they're worth the investment, and your body and tummy will thank you! Let me tell you a little bit about each, and why I think they're worthy of a spot in your pantry.

Extra-virgin organic coconut oil: Coconut oil has been a superstar on the health-food scene, touted for having countless miraculous and healing properties. While I don't think it's the panacea it has been blown up to be, unrefined organic coconut oil is an extremely nutrient-dense food. The monounsaturated fatty acids in coconut are anti-inflammatory, and they're used immediately by our body for energy instead of being stored first, as other fats are. One specific fatty acid called lauric acid has antiviral, antibacterial properties, which can benefit our immune system in helping fight pathogens. Plus, it's a great alternative to olive oil and butter in cooking, as it lends a lovely, mild coconut flavor to food.

Other uses: Topically, coconut oil can be a great body moisturizer for your skin—test a small amount to ensure there's no negative reaction.

Where to find: Most grocery stores, Whole Foods, The Fresh Market, Trader Joe's, Amazon, Vitacost, Thrive Market

Toasted sesame oil: Oh, how I love toasted sesame oil! It has the most wonderful nutty flavor. You only need a small amount to create that signature taste found in many Asian cuisines. There really is no good substitution for it, but know that one bottle lasts for a very long time. On the health front, sesame seeds and sesame oil are high in minerals such as zinc, which boosts collagen production for elastic, supple skin. Sesame is also a great source of specific anti-inflammatory compounds that promote heart health.

Other uses: Toasted sesame oil is amazing as a quick salad dressing—just drizzle it on greens with a splash of red wine vinegar, sprinkle on some sea salt and voila! Totally delicious. You can also use it as a finishing oil for any roasted meat, seafood, or vegetables.

Where to find: Most grocery stores (in the ethnic foods section), almost all health-food stores, most Asian stores, Whole Foods, Trader Joe's, Amazon, Vitacost, Thrive Market

Nutritional yeast: Okay, I know, not the best name for a food. But it makes up for it in versatility! Nutritional yeast is simply a dried mushroom/fungus, and it happens to have a delicious cheeselike flavor. Nutritional yeast adds a layer of umami, the elusive fifth taste found in meat and certain foods such as sun-dried tomatoes. Umami adds complexity to recipes and makes people ask "What's in here?" Nutritional yeast is also a fantastic source of B vitamins, which can be difficult to obtain in a vegan or vegetarian diet. If you are on the strictly plant-based train, nutritional yeast is likely a great addition to your cooking repertoire.

Other uses: Sprinkle it on popcorn, then drizzle with some olive oil and sea salt. Combine 1 cup nuts of choice with 2 to 3 tablespoons of nutritional yeast and ½ teaspoon sea salt, then pulse until it forms the consistency of a grainy flour. This makes a yummy alternative to parmesan cheese and can keep sealed tightly in your pantry for up to a month.

Where to find: Most health-food stores, Whole Foods, Amazon, Vitacost, Thrive Market

Tahini paste: You will see tahini paste scattered throughout this cookbook, and for good reason. Nutty, savory tahini paste is incredibly versatile, and it offers umami and depth to dairy-free dishes in particular. Tahini is simply ground sesame seeds, the seed version of an almond or peanut butter. Considered exotic only a few years ago, tahini can now be found in most grocery stores. I love tahini for its health benefits as well. It is a fantastic source of essential vitamins and minerals like copper, calcium, iron, vitamin E, and B vitamins. Tahini has been said to help with everything from lowering blood pressure to regulating hormones to improving skin health and nutrient absorption. Once you start playing around with this unique ingredient, you will always want it in your refrigerator.

Other uses: Besides the copious uses in my cookbook, tahini is fantastic as a simple spread. I love it on rye toast with a smear of raspberry jam. You can use it as a substitute for nut butters, but note that it will be less sweet.

Where to find: It is often near the other nut butters in grocery stores, but sometimes it is in the exotic ingredients section. You can also order it from Vitacost, Amazon, or Thrive Market. My favorite brand is Joyva.

Unsulphured apricots: When you think of dried apricots, your mind likely pictures something neon-orange. These apricots have been treated with preservatives, causing an unnatural color and mediocre flavor. Unsulphured apricots are in a league of their own. They have a wonderful rich flavor with caramel notes, as well as a softer texture. Dried apricots are fabulous for digestion with their high fiber content, and they also contain the antioxidant carotene. Don't fear their darker color—that's the good

stuff. I use them in my Apricot & Olive Oil Granola Clusters (page 150), and although you could absolutely substitute another dried fruit, I recommend trying these at least once. Note, when shopping, these might be called Turkish apricots instead of unsulphured; look for that tell-tale golden brown color.

Other uses: Use as a snack by the handful! One of my favorite nighttime treats is a few unsulphured apricots dipped in almond butter. An easy appetizer idea is crackers or crostini spread with goat cheese, sprinkled with sea salt, and topped with an apricot.

Where to find: Bulk bins at health-food stores, Whole Foods, Trader Joe's, Amazon, nuts.com. I like Terrasoul brand.

Medjool dates: Nature's candy! Medjool dates are the answer to refined sugar–free prayers around the world. These sweet, exotic delights can now be found in almost every grocery store, and they are so delicious. Although there are several kinds of dates, I think the medjool dates have the loveliest flavor. Their sticky nature makes them a wonderful binder for no-bake treats, or they can be soaked and pureed and used as a caramel sauce. In addition to their date-lightful taste (you see what I did there?), dates are high in fiber, antioxidants, potassium for electrolyte balance, vitamins A and K for healthy skin, nails, and hair, and trace minerals. You will see medjool dates sprinkled throughout this book.

Other uses: Similar to unsulphured apricots, I enjoy dates with a smear of almond or peanut butter and a sprinkle of cinnamon as a night-time snack. They also make for fantastic pre- or post-workout fuel. I use them almost daily to sweeten smoothies. Stuff them with goat cheese or marcona almonds, wrap each with a slice of bacon, and bake at 350° F

for 15 minutes or until bacon is crispy.

Where to find: Most grocery stores, health-food stores, Whole Foods, The Fresh Market, Amazon, Vitacost, Thrive Market

Coconut flour: Coconut flour is the first of two flours I'm going to politely ask you to invest in. There are only three flours used in this book—oat flour, which is cheap and easy, coconut flour, and almond flour. The latter two are not cheap, and they're not as easy to find, but they're worth it. One of the primary struggles I witness, with women in particular, is an uncontrollable sweet tooth: the once-you-start-you-can't-stop issue. This is exacerbated when one is eating foods made from highly refined flours, including many gluten-free flours out there like tapioca or potato. Coconut flour is made from the pulp of the coconut as a by-product of the coconut milk–making process. Coconut flour has a high fiber content and is low-carbohydrate, especially compared to grain-based flours. As a result, goodies made from coconut flour are very satisfying and filling, and I find they don't trigger the "more more more" desire that traditional treats do. Coconut flour cannot be substituted 1:1 for wheat flour, and it requires a lot of liquid, as it is highly absorbent. It also requires a lot of binder for the recipe to stick together, and eggs are really the best and only option. Instead of trying to convert a traditional recipe to a coconut flour recipe, I suggest starting from scratch with a recipe made specifically for coconut flour. After much experimenting with grain-free baking, I found that using almond flour and coconut flour produces a fabulous, tender, moist result that is even better than the baked goods I grew up with. I highly recommend investing in both of these flours if you are someone with a sweet

Nutritional yeast is a dried fungus packed with umami and a tasty cheeselike flavor. Try it on popcorn!

tooth who likes to bake. These will make you feel so much healthier and you'll enjoy the process more as a result.

Other uses: Add 1 tablespoon of coconut flour to smoothies for added thickness and fiber. You can also mix 3 tablespoons of coconut flour with 1 egg and a splash of milk, sweetener, and a pinch of cinnamon or sea salt in a small sauce pot. Heat to a simmer and cook, whisking and adding liquid as necessary, to reach a porridge-like consistency.

Where to find: Many grocery stores, health-food stores, Amazon, Vitacost, Thrive Market

Almond flour: Dovetailing on coconut flour, almond flour is the other grain-free flour I rely on in baking and cooking, and you will see it throughout the book. Almond flour is lower in fiber and lower in carbohydrates compared with coconut flour, but it is higher in fat and protein. As a result, it contributes to a very satiating baked good that you can have just one of and feel content. One important distinction to make is between almond flour and almond meal. Almond flour is much more finely ground than meal, and as a result, it creates a product more similar to wheat flour. Using almond meal will lead to a heavier, grainier, and soggier result. I use a company called Honeyville that sells large bags of blanched almond flour, which is the finest ground available. I order it online and store it in the fridge, and it lasts for a long time. Feel free to experiment with other brands, but I can't be sure how it will turn out. If you do not want to purchase almond flour, you can substitute it 1:1 for wheat-based flour. Note, however, that almond flour requires more binder, so it won't be a perfect substitution.

Other uses: Outside of baking, I use blanched almond flour instead of breadcrumbs in most of my ground-meat recipes because it provides moisture, richness, and a little extra protein. I also use almond flour to coat chicken tenders before baking, and it would be great as a coating for chicken parmesan or pan-seared shrimp as well.

Where to find: You can find brands of almond flour in most grocery stores, health-food stores, The Fresh Market, and Whole Foods. However, I recommend ordering Honeyville brand from honeyville.com, or from Amazon.

Arrowroot starch: Arrowroot starch is derived from a tropical South American tuber plant. I use it as a substitute for cornstarch as a thickener in my recipes. The process of extraction for arrowroot starch is gentler and more natural than cornstarch, and it is non-genetically modified, unlike many brands of cornstarch. To use arrowroot starch properly, you mix a tablespoon or two with an equal amount of water until it dissolves, and then add it into your hot soup or sauce. The result is magical, as you watch your recipe gain body and texture. If you do not want to invest in arrowroot starch, you can absolutely use cornstarch in its stead. However, please find a brand of cornstarch labeled "Non-GMO" or something similar.

Other uses: Use it as a coating before baking or pan-frying vegetables or protein to make them crunchy. Arrowroot can also substitute for eggs as a binder in baked goods—try 1 tablespoon starch plus 1 tablespoon water for each egg (you may need to adjust the liquid ratio). I also keep some arrowroot in a shaker and use it to make desserts look beautiful, without having to use refined powdered sugar.

Where to find: Most health-food stores, Whole Foods, The Fresh Market, Amazon, Thrive Market, Vitacost

Chia seeds: Chia seeds, tiny black and grey seeds that come from a plant in the mint family, are near and dear to my heart. My first post-corporate job was for Health Warrior, a company that sells 100-calorie chia seed bars. Although I now prefer to make my own bars, I still rely on chia seeds. The benefits of the little seeds fall into three main categories.

1. **Nutrition:** Chia seeds are high in fiber, protein, omega-3 fats, calcium, and magnesium, among other nutrients. That's some serious bang for your buck.

2. **Multi-purpose:** Chia seeds have an amazing capacity to absorb a great deal of liquid. As a result, soaking them in liquid for a few hours or overnight creates a creamy, pudding-like texture. In addition, chia seeds are a great substitute for eggs in some recipes, because they act as a binder (see Subsituting Eggs on page 51).

3. **Flavor:** Mild! These poppy seed lookalikes have a neutral flavor. This means you can pair them with almost any sweet or savory flavor. They form the base of my Chocolate Chia Avocado Pudding (page 124), and they serve as a binder in my BBQ Chickpea & Sweet Potato Veggie Loaf (page 274). You can also sprinkle them on salads or use them to thicken soups.

Chia seeds are a nutritious and versatile ingredient.

Other uses: Stir them into oatmeal or smoothies, or mix with water and a touch of honey for a homemade workout "energy gel."

Where to find: Most health-food stores, Whole Foods, The Fresh Market, Amazon, Thrive Market, Vitacost

Turmeric powder: Many spices have anti-inflammatory properties, which means they can help combat the common problem of low-grade, chronic inflammation. You're probably familiar with clove, ginger, rosemary, cinnamon, and cayenne pepper. But less known is turmeric, a tuber from the same plant family as ginger. Curcumin is the potent antioxidant found in turmeric, and it has been studied as a healing agent in autoimmune diseases, liver damage, cancer, diabetes, and more. Some stores sell turmeric whole, but I prefer the ease of using it ground. Turmeric has a mild, earthy flavor that blends well with many other spices, and its gorgeous golden color gives curry powder its signature yellow tint. As a result, you will see turmeric smattered throughout this cookbook, complementing other ingredients and offering its incredible health benefits. My Turmeric & Tahini Roasted Cauliflower (page 189) is a reader favorite, and turmeric also stars in my Green Immuni-Tea (page 106).

Other uses: Throw a pinch into smoothies, your coffee, scrambled eggs, oatmeal, or most soups, stir fries, or casseroles. It's incredibly versatile.

Where to find: Most health-food stores, Whole Foods, The Fresh Market, Amazon, Thrive Market, Vitacost

note: Check the expiration date to make sure your turmeric powder is fresh. It should have a vibrant, rich orange-yellow color.

Tamari: There is so much tamari action in this cookbook, and for good reason. Tamari is a wheat-free soy sauce, traditionally created as a byproduct of fermented miso paste. Not only is tamari a better option for those who are wheat- or gluten-free, it has a richer and less astringent flavor than your average soy sauce. Like nutritional yeast, tamari has wonderful umami, so I love to add it as the salty component in sauces and soups. Tamari isn't just great for taste; it has antioxidant and anti-inflammatory properties, contains B vitamins and minerals, and it can aid in the digestion of grains and vegetables. You can certainly substitute soy sauce where you see tamari in this book, but it might change the outcome slightly, so taste as you go. I buy and use low-sodium tamari because I find the regular version a little too strong for me.

Other uses: Splash tamari over any rice, grains, or cooked vegetables to jazz them up, or substitute for soy sauce when you order take-out sushi (or bring some with you!). Play with swapping tamari for sea salt in savory recipes and watch how it can transform other flavors. I even like it drizzled on my homemade Quinoa Lentil Pizzas (page 219).

Where to find: Most health-food stores, Whole Foods, The Fresh Market, Amazon, Thrive Market, Vitacost, most Asian markets

Tempeh: My favorite meat stand-in. Tempeh is made from fermented and compressed soybeans, and it usually shows up as a block or rectangle at the store. I know that has you salivating, right? Seriously though, tempeh is incredibly mild and pleasant-tasting, and it takes on whatever flavors you pair it with. I prefer tempeh over tofu, because the fermentation process makes it easier to digest and higher in easily assimilated nutrients. Tempeh is a fantastic source of minerals, vitamin B, fiber, and plant protein. It contains the entire amino acid profile found in meat, so you feel quite satiated after eating it. If you're looking for some plant-based meals that go beyond rice and beans, I urge you to try my Marinated Tempeh Sushi Burritos (page 289) and my Maple Balsamic–Glazed Tempeh & Mushroom Bake (page 290) to see how delicious tempeh can be. Look for non-GMO organic tempeh. You might see some made with other beans or grains besides soy. These will have a slightly different flavor but are usually mild and tasty.

Other uses: While tempeh can be safely consumed raw, it is much tastier pan-seared in some healthy fat or roasted in the oven. Cube it or cut it in strips to replace chicken in a dish, or crumble it as a substitute for any ground meat. You can also play with a tempeh burger, using chia seeds or eggs as the binder.

Where to find: Most health-food stores, Whole Foods, The Fresh Market, Amazon, Thrive Market, Vitacost

Coconut sugar: Coconut sugar is a natural sweetener derived from the sap of the coconut plant. Although coconut sugar has the same amount of calories and carbohydrates as refined sugar, it is a better choice for several reasons. Whereas refined sugar is devoid of nutrients, coconut sugar contains trace amounts of vitamins and minerals, such as vitamin C and magnesium. In addition, some studies have shown that coconut sugar has less of an offensive impact on blood sugar levels. At the end of the day, any form of sugar is detrimental to the body in excess and should be treated as an occasional indulgence, but why not choose something with added health benefits if you can? Lastly, I adore the flavor of coconut sugar, which is rich and caramel-like, and a great substitution for brown sugar.

Other uses: Use coconut sugar in recipes where you want the sweetener to add flavor, instead of disappear amidst the other ingredients. Try it on oatmeal, blended in a banana smoothie, stirred into coffee, in baking recipes that use warming spices like cinnamon, or wherever you'd normally use brown sugar.

Where to find: Most groceries stores, almost all health-food stores, Whole Foods, The Fresh Market, Amazon, Thrive Market, Vitacost

Cooking Notes and Tips

Part of properly stocking your pantry and kitchen is stocking your brain with the knowledge to make your cooking adventures go as smoothly as possible. With that in mind, here are some useful notes and tips to help you expand your cooking knowledge.

TECHNIQUES

- **Simmer versus boil.** When a liquid is simmering, you will see very small bubbles around the edges, but not in the middle. When a liquid is boiling, you will see large, rapidly forming bubbles all over the surface of the liquid.

- **Dice versus mince versus chop.** "Dice" refers to cutting food into specific cube sizes. A large dice is ¾-inch pieces, medium dice is ½-inch pieces, and small dice is ¼-inch pieces. A mince is even smaller than a small dice—smaller than ⅛th of an inch, and this is usually used for potent flavors like garlic, ginger, and jalapeño. "Chop" refers to a rougher, more casual style of cutting, usually where the ingredients will be pureed or blended.

- **Sauté.** To sauté food means to cook it in a little bit of fat over high heat, and it is how most vegetables are cooked at the start of the dish. Sautéing brings caramelization to the

Dicing is a basic food prep method. Depending on the recipe, you may want a large, medium, or small dice.

food without overcooking it. You will often see me use the word "sauté," but note I rarely request high heat. My high heat is really medium or medium high, and this is because I like to prevent the fats from smoking, which makes them rancid. So I will ask you to start with a sauté for color and flavor, then I'll often ask you to continue cooking a little longer at a lower temperature.

- **Deglaze.** When you sear meat or vegetables, it often leaves behind brown bits. These are gold. "Deglazing" refers to adding water or stock to a pan, then scraping with a spatula to loosen the brown bits. Unless they are actually burnt, keep this deglazed juice in the dish to add richness and flavor.

- **Getting the most out of your citrus.** To maximize the amount of juice you get out of your lemons and limes, roll them under the palm of your hand on the countertop, applying pressure. Do this for 10 to 15 seconds; the heat and pressure from your hand help loosen the insides, releasing more juice.

- **Properly pitting an avocado.** Carefully poke the avocado where it is widest with a sharp knife, until it hits the seed. Drag the tip of the knife down and turn the avocado with your hand, so that you are creating one long vertical cut all the way around. Release the knife and twist the two sides in opposite directions. You should have one side left with the pit. Hold that avocado half face-up in the palm of your non-dominant hand. With your dominant hand, hit the pit with the knife edge, just hard enough to stick. Twist the avocado and the knife in opposite directions. The pit should pop out. Hit the knife gently against a cutting board to get the pit off.

- **Keeping a clean kitchen.** A trick my mama taught me, which her mama taught her, is to keep a mixing bowl or two for trash and/or compost on the counter with you while you work. Having the bowls by your side makes it much easier and faster to clean up. At the end of the cooking session, you can dump them in the trash and/or compost.

- **Consolidating spices.** When cooking a recipe with more than one or two spices, I suggest mixing them together in a small bowl before beginning the recipe. That way, when it's time to add the spices, all you have to do is dump in your pre-mixed spices.

- **Substituting eggs.** Don't eat eggs, or want to veganize a baked goods recipe? Substitute a chia "egg." To make a chia "egg," which is equivalent to one large egg, whisk together 1 tablespoon chia seeds and 3 tablespoons water. Allow mixture to sit for 10 to 15 minutes, whisking every 2 to 3 minutes, until it has thickened to a gel-like consistency. At this point, you can add it to the recipe. Note: I have not tested all my baked goods recipes with chia "eggs" instead of regular eggs. Historically, I have had great success with this substitution, but please know that your outcome might be different than mine.

- **Shortcut for room temperature eggs.** When baking, it is important to use room temperature eggs instead of cold eggs. Cold eggs can affect the baking time, and they also can result in a denser product— something that is a hazard with grain-free baking anyway. I always forget to take my eggs out an hour before I'm going to bake, so I simply place them in slightly lukewarm (NOT warm) water for 5 minutes, and voila! They're perfect and ready for cracking.

- **Other uses for lemon rinds.** When you've squeezed the juice out of a lemon, you can rub the cut side over a wooden cutting board to help remove any garlic or other strong

Remove avocado flesh by slicing it into slabs in the shell, and then removing with a spoon.

smells. You can also put them down your garbage disposal to make it smell fresh and clean. Similarly, I like to keep one or two in my refrigerator, which helps eliminate funky odors.

- **Cooking with sea salt.** When I refer to salt throughout the book, I am referring to fine-ground non-iodized sea salt. This is the ideal all-purpose salt for cooking, baking, and seasoning, in my opinion. I prefer sea salt over traditional table salt. Sea salt retains beneficial trace minerals, as it is less processed, and table salt contains anticlumping preservatives. You cannot substitute one for the other, because table salt is much more finely ground and the same amount will yield a much saltier result. Table salt also often includes iodine, a crucial mineral, but one that we can get from eating wild saltwater fish and seafood. I prefer to control my intake of nutrients, and this is difficult to do if they're in the salt you use every day. My favorite brands are Selina Naturally and Frontier Natural Products Co-op. If you want to indulge in some lovely finishing salts, my favorites are sea salt flakes and pink Himalayan sea salt. Finishing salt is unrefined, natural salt, usually with a slightly larger grain, that is sprinkled on a dish before serving to enhance the flavor.

FREEZING LEFTOVERS

When you're trying to get healthy, whole-foods meals on the table every night, the freezer can become your best friend. That is, if you know what to do with it. Here are my tested tips and tricks for using your freezer to your advantage, as well as some ideas for how to get creative with leftovers.

- Always ensure that your freezer is set at 0° F.
- Freeze fruit, vegetables, and soups in zip-top storage bags in a thin layer and place horizontally in the freezer. This way, you can stack multiple bags, as well as easily break off pieces to use. I suggest double-layering the bags to prevent freezer burn if you plan to keep them in there longer than a week.
- You can also use silicone muffin trays or ice cube trays to freeze sauces. When frozen, pop out the chunks and store in a zip-top food storage bag.
- For quick meals, freeze individual portion sizes in plastic pint containers that you can order in bulk online.
- If you plan for an item to be in the freezer longer than a week, double-bag it or wrap it with plastic wrap before putting it in a container.
- LABEL all of your freezer bags and containers: what and when. You *need* to know how long something has been in there. Also make some sort of symbol that denotes if a food is about to go bad, and that's why you froze it. If you take it out to thaw, you'll know you need to eat it ASAP.
- Keep a notepad or whiteboard in your kitchen that lists everything you have in your freezer so you don't have to go rummaging around when deciding what to make for dinner.
- Invest in an insulated food and beverage container. They're an amazing tool for on-the-go lunches, keeping food either hot or cold. I like Thermos Foogo or FUNtainer food jars and LunchBots.

- Thaw food in the refrigerator, *NOT* at room temperature—this will increase the likelihood of harmful bacteria.
- When in doubt, BRINNER (aka breakfast for dinner)! Pancakes, waffles, muffins, and breads all freeze very well. I slide a piece of parchment paper between each so they don't stick. When I'm in a pinch for dinner, I'll pull a few out, scramble some eggs, and voila!
- Peanut or almond butter and jam sandwiches freeze well . . . seriously.
- Freeze pre-made smoothies in silicone muffin tins or large ice cube trays. Place in blender and add splashes of hot water as you blend to save time in the morning. Don't store longer than 1 week.

HOW LONG TO FREEZE FOODS*

Cooked
- Steak: 2 to 3 months
- Pancakes, quick bread, cookies, granola bars, and muffins: 3 months
- Bread, unfrosted cake or cupcakes, waffles: 1 month
- Casseroles, pasta-based dishes: 2 months
- Soups, stews, marinara sauce, stock, and broths: 2 to 3 months
- Chicken breasts, thighs, and wings: 4 months
- Burgers, meat patties, and meatballs: 1 to 2 months
- Taco or Bolognese meat: 1 to 2 months
- Vegetables: 8 to 12 months
- Grains: 3 months

Raw
- Chicken pieces: 9 months
- Shrimp and scallops: 3 to 4 months
- Raw lean fish (such as halibut): 6 months
- Raw fatty fish (such as salmon): 2 to 3 months
- Ground beef, turkey, or chicken: 3 to 4 months
- Steak: 4 to 6 months
- Whole chicken: 1 year
- Citrus fruit: 3 months
- Other fruits and popsicles: 6 months
- Vegetables: 8 to 12 months
- Nuts: 3 months

Don't freeze
- Water-rich foods: lemon, lime, tomato, and cucumber
- Dairy products: yogurt, cheese, sour cream, milk
- Fresh herbs (unless suspended in oil, such as the Arugula Walnut Pesto recipe on page 286)
- Onions, peppers, artichokes, radishes, sprouts, salad greens
- Uncooked rice
- Canned fish
- Hard-boiled eggs

*Assuming they are fresh going into the freezer

Freeze dairy-free sauces in ice cube trays or molds to create easy-to-thaw chunks.

• Make freezer wraps for an easy breakfast, lunch, or dinner. Start with brown rice or other gluten-free wraps and add cooked and cooled roasted veggies; cooked sliced chicken, ground meat, or scrambled eggs; and a thick spread of pesto. Roll into a burrito, then wrap tightly in aluminum foil. Freeze up to 1 month.

GET CREATIVE WITH LEFTOVERS

Use your taste buds and dishes/combinations you know you love to figure out what will taste good together.

• **Break the fast.** Any meat can be shredded and used in tacos or burritos with scrambled eggs, stirred into potato hash, or cooked into a frittata: use the proportions on my frittata recipes (pages 137, 143) as a guideline.

• **Southern-salad style.** Leftover chicken and seafood can be turned into a "salad" with some high-quality mayo, Dijon mustard, salt, pepper, and chopped pickles (or however you like it).

• **Comfort soup.** Leftover meat and veggies can be simmered in a chicken or beef broth with some extra salt and pepper to make soup. Stir in canned coconut milk or plain hummus to thicken if you like.

• **Not wimpy green salad.** Leftover meat, veggies, beans, and grains can all be thrown on a bed of fresh spinach, arugula, or baby kale to make an epic salad. Always have white balsamic and olive oil on hand for a quick dressing. Top with cheese, avocado, or nuts for added richness.

• **Make it a 'za.** Use my Quinoa Lentil Pizza Crust (page 219) and top with leftovers, sauces, and any ingredients you have laying around. Or, bake a brown rice tortilla in the oven at 400° F until firm. Add leftover meat and veggies, a sprinkle of grass-fed cheese, and bake again until crispy.

③ Create a relaxed and happy eating environment.

The environment and the mental and emotional space in which we eat matter enormously. Sometimes, they matter even more than the food itself. Proper digestion and assimilation of nutrients requires a low-stress eating experience. We've all either skipped meals or eaten mindlessly to excess because we were anxious, upset, distracted, or in a hurry. And we've all felt the ill effects of this choice—poor digestion (gas, bloating, cramps, etc.), a lack of feeling satiated or satisfied, or feeling overly stuffed. As Dr. Rao puts it, "The concept of mindful eating is important in so many ways and may take practice in our fast-paced world. It can improve digestion and make eating a time out from the stressful day to enjoy our food and socialize."

When we eat in our cars, in the middle of a business meeting, under a time deadline, or even in front of a screen, we rob ourselves and our bodies of the pleasure of eating. Just as the scent of muffins baking can make us hungry or make our mouths water, our bodies take cues from preparing a proper meal environment: setting a place with utensils on the table, turning off the TV, grabbing a glass of water, plating the food in an attractive way. These are not luxuries; they are necessities for

Take pleasure in preparing and plating healthy food to fuel yourself and your loved ones.

getting the most nutrition and pleasure out of your meal. I understand that this is not always a possibility, but I believe that most of us could make a few small changes in our eating routines that would have a positive impact on the way we experience food. Here are some of my tips for creating an ideal eating environment, even in the midst of life chaos.

Unplug. Wherever you are, turn off as many electronics as possible. Even if it's just for 10 minutes, turn off your cell phone and TV, and close your computer or put the screen in sleep mode if using a desktop.

Chew slowly. Or at least, chew! Most of us gulp our meals down, leaving little to no time to actually appreciate our food. Eating too quickly makes it difficult to know when we're full, so we may overeat as a result. Thoroughly chewing your meals will also help prevent digestive upset. Do you often find yourself bloated and gassy around 3 in the afternoon? It could be because your lunch disappeared in 10 minutes.

Look for company. We tend to eat more slowly and enjoy meals more in the company of friends. If you have a colleague or study-buddy nearby, see if you can align your lunch times. At home, do your best to accommodate your family's varying schedules so that you can all eat together.

Listen to relaxing tunes. Light, mellow, and preferably wordless music can help calm you down and set you up for a more pleasant eating experience. If you're at work and have to eat alone, you can fudge the no-electronics policy and put on some headphones.

Be an amateur food stylist. Taking care to arrange your food in a visually appealing way will make the act of eating seem more special—something to be savored, not hurried through. Wipe the edges of your plate free from sauce, add fresh herbs or a sprinkle of finishing salt . . . get creative. For meals on the go, invest in an attractive compartmentalized lunch box or bento box.

Set the table. If you're at home, take a few minutes to light some candles, use place mats, and set napkins with utensils. These details might seem silly, but they create a ritual of pausing and honoring your meal. Whenever I set a proper table, it makes me more mindful of and grateful for my food.

Check in with yourself. If you are stressed, anxious, upset, or angry, hold off on eating until you've had some time to cool down. You'll probably realize you're not even hungry anyway. Along those lines, make sure you're actually ready for your meals, instead of eating for the sake of eating. Most of us are fortunate enough to have an over-abundance of food, so we don't need to fear hunger. Wait for true hunger cues to kick in, and I guarantee this will make your eating experiences more enjoyable. Note: I'm not suggesting you become ravenous, just good, old-fashioned, grumbling-belly hungry!

Many of us constantly eat on the run—take the time to set the table and enjoy a meal with family.

recipes

2

SNACK-ITIZERS

· ·

*H*anger = hunger + anger. Hanger is a state that arises
when one has gone too long without eating, and the
body's alarm bell appears in the form of short-tempered, snappy
responses and a general distaste for anything that isn't food.
I tend to be susceptible to hanger. As a result, I am a snacking
queen! I always . . . *always* . . . have something edible in my
purse or car if I'm going to be away from home longer than an
hour. When I travel, I dedicate an entire backpack to healthy
snacks. If you've ever come to my house for dinner or taken one
of my classes, you know that there will be something to munch
on upon arrival.

My snack-itizer recipes will leave you feeling lightly satiated,
with room to spare for the main event. They range from casual
on-the-go favorites to more sophisticated options. Several are
fantastic for bringing to a game-day celebration or shower, when
you want something healthy but not obviously so. Although these
snack-itizers cover a wide range, they share the same basic traits:
wholesome, flavorful, easy to prepare, and "hanger"-busting.

· ·

rosemary roasted pecans

V **GF** **P**   HANDS-ON TIME: *5 min* | TOTAL TIME: *25 to 27 min* | YIELD: *6 to 8 servings* | OPTIONS: **Vg** **DF**

*I*n homage to my mother, who is a better chef than I'll ever be, this first recipe is an updated version of her holiday roasted pecans. Lavished in butter, the original recipe is too heavy for everyday consumption. I use just a kiss of butter and add some fresh rosemary for depth of flavor. These pecans may look simple, but they taste all kinds of rich and amazing! I often have a batch ready and waiting for my cooking class attendees, and I always have requests for the recipe afterward.

Preheat oven to 350° F. Line a baking sheet with parchment paper and add pecans and rosemary. Roast for 10 to 12 minutes, or until pecans are slightly darker in color with a nutty aroma.

Immediately upon taking nuts out of the oven, drizzle with butter and sprinkle with sea salt. Use a spatula to coat evenly. Allow to cool 10 minutes before enjoying.

2½ cups raw pecans

1 tablespoon minced fresh rosemary

2 tablespoons butter, melted
(**V** **DF** sub 1½ tablespoons olive oil)

1 teaspoon sea salt

---

ideas for

LEFTOVER ROSEMARY

Mince 1 tablespoon and toss with Turmeric & Tahini Roasted Cauliflower (page 189) before roasting.

Mince 1 tablespoon and toss with Crispy Garlic Smashed Potatoes (page 177).

Add 2 minced teaspoons to shallots when making Fig & Olive Tapenade (page 68).

pb&j no-bake energy squares
with peanut maple drizzle

Ⓥ Ⓥⓖ Ⓖⓕ Ⓓⓕ | **HANDS-ON TIME:** *15 min* | **TOTAL TIME:** *1 h, 15 min* | **YIELD:** *16 squares* ❄

*W*hat is there left to be said about the world's greatest flavor combination—peanut butter and jelly? You will know my deep and abiding love of peanut butter by the end of this cookbook, and I couldn't imagine my snacking routine without it. These PB&J No-Bake Energy Squares are everything you love about the classic sandwich, but with amped-up nutrition. Cashews are a wonderful source of heart-healthy monounsaturated fats and antioxidants, and rolled oats pack a serious fiber punch. Combined with protein-rich peanuts and the natural carbohydrates from dates, you have a perfectly energizing snack. I like to enjoy these squares as a pre- or post-workout snack.

If making Peanut Maple Drizzle, whisk all ingredients until smooth. Treat like Magic Shell—drizzle over bars and it will harden in the refrigerator.

Line an 8 x 8-inch baking dish with parchment paper, allowing a few inches to hang over the sides.

Place cashews and oats in a food processor and pulse until they form a flour consistency. Add remaining ingredients and process until incorporated into a sticky dough, and you can no longer see chunks of dates. You might need to stop and scrape down the sides to prevent dough from forming a ball.

With a small bowl of water nearby, scrape dough into the baking dish. Dampen fingers and pat dough into dish in an even layer. I usually have to rinse my fingers off once or twice to help prevent sticking.

If desired, top with Peanut Maple Drizzle and freeze-dried strawberries and refrigerate for 1 hour. Use overhanging parchment to lift bars out of the baking dish and slice into 16 squares. Keep bars refrigerated in a tightly sealed container for up to 1 week.

PEANUT MAPLE DRIZZLE (OPTIONAL):

2 tablespoons peanut butter

1 tablespoon maple syrup

1 tablespoon coconut oil

SQUARES:

1½ cups raw whole cashews

1 cup rolled oats

½ packed cup medjool dates, pitted (approximately 6 large; be sure they are soft and juicy)

⅓ cup all-fruit jam (I like strawberry and raspberry best)

¼ cup peanut butter (creamy or chunky, more liquid than solid, which is usually found with newly opened jars)

¼ teaspoon sea salt

Freeze-dried strawberries (optional for garnish)

kale & artichoke dip

GF HANDS-ON TIME: *25 min* | TOTAL TIME: *2 h, 25 or 40 min* | YIELD: *10 to 15 servings* | ♦ | OPTIONS: V Vg DF P

*T*his recipe holds a special place in my heart because it was one of the first dishes I cooked for my now-husband. He asked if I could make something healthy for football-game munching. I was nervous to serve this meat-and-potatoes guy a vegan dip, but he gobbled it right up and asked for another batch! Thus began our love affair through food, and I still get butterflies when I see how much he enjoys one of my recipes.

Add cashews to a high-powered blender or food processor with chicken stock. Blend until smooth.

Heat a large sauté pan to medium heat and add olive oil. When oil is slightly shimmering, add shallots. Cook, stirring, until softened and fragrant, approximately 3 to 4 minutes.

Add the minced garlic and cook for another minute, stirring.

Stir in the chopped artichokes, salt, pepper, onion powder, garlic powder, and nutritional yeast or cheese. Cook 1 minute, stirring. Add in the kale, lemon juice, and cashew puree and cook, stirring, until heated through. Serve immediately or follow the optional step next.

Optional: Preheat oven to 350° F. Place dip in a baking dish and sprinkle with extra nutritional yeast or parmesan cheese. Bake for 15 minutes before serving, or until cheese is melted (if using) and edges are golden brown. Dip will keep in a tightly sealed container in the refrigerator up to 4 days.

1 cup raw cashews, soaked 2 hours in lukewarm water and drained

¾ cup low-sodium chicken stock (V Vg sub vegetable stock)

1 tablespoon extra-virgin olive oil

½ cup shallots, minced (approximately 1 large or 2 small)

4 garlic cloves, minced

1 14-ounce can artichoke hearts, drained and roughly chopped

2½ teaspoons sea salt

½ teaspoon black pepper

1 teaspoon onion powder

½ teaspoon garlic powder

¼ cup nutritional yeast, plus more for optional topping (sub parmesan cheese)

1 10-ounce bag frozen kale, thawed and chopped into 1-inch pieces

1 tablespoon lemon juice

⅓ cup cheese of choice to sprinkle on top before baking (optional) (Vg DF P omit)

SERVING SUGGESTIONS

This dip is also amazing stuffed into mushrooms and roasted. After washing each mushroom and removing the stems, stuff with a tablespoon or so of dip. Bake by following the optional instructions at left and keeping an eye on them.

teriyaki slow cooker meatball skewers

GF DF | HANDS-ON TIME: *25 to 30 min* | TOTAL TIME: *5 h* | YIELD: *25 to 27 meatballs*

*I*t's hard to go wrong with meatballs and teriyaki sauce, but letting them tenderize in a slow cooker truly elevates them to another level. My homemade teriyaki sauce is much healthier than most packaged brands, and it tastes amazing on all sorts of protein and veggies (I also use it for my fish tacos, see page 265). However, if you're in a pinch and decide to use something store-bought, no judgment from me! These meatballs are melt-in-your-mouth goodness that will become the star of any tailgate or picnic.

In a food processor, combine chicken thighs, oats, egg, sea salt, and black pepper. Pulse until ingredients are combined into a textured paste. You might need to stop midway through pulsing to scrape down the sides with a spatula.

Empty chicken mixture into a large mixing bowl. Place a small bowl of water next to the slow cooker. Dampen fingers and roll chicken mixture into approximately 1½ inch balls, then place them side by side in a row at the bottom of the slow cooker. Stack meatballs gently in a second or third layer as necessary. It's okay if they stick together.

Combine arrowroot starch and 2 tablespoons water in a small bowl, stirring to dissolve starch. Set aside. Heat a small sauce pot to low heat and add tamari, 1 cup water, honey, garlic, and ginger. When the mixture is simmering, add starch mixture and stir until the liquid has thickened, approximately 30 to 45 seconds. Set sauce aside. The recipe makes approximately 1½ cups.

Pour teriyaki sauce over meatballs, turn to high heat, and cover with a lid. Cook meatballs for 4½ hours, or until golden and tender, stirring halfway through to cover the top layer with sauce.

Skewer meatballs and place on a serving tray, then garnish with sesame seeds and scallions if desired. Reserve extra sauce for dipping, drizzling, or another recipe. Meatballs will keep in a tightly sealed container in the fridge up to 4 days.

MEATBALLS:

2 pounds boneless skinless chicken thighs

½ cup rolled oats

1 egg

1 teaspoon sea salt

¼ teaspoon black pepper

Sesame seeds and thinly sliced scallions (optional garnish)

TERIYAKI SAUCE:

2 tablespoons arrowroot starch (sub non-GMO cornstarch)

¼ cup low-sodium tamari

1 cup plus 2 tablespoons water

¼ cup honey (sub maple syrup)

2 cloves garlic, minced

1 packed teaspoon freshly grated ginger (sub ½ teaspoon ground, but fresh is preferred)

SERVING SUGGESTIONS

Feel free to use this recipe as an entree. The meatballs are delicious served over Simple Spaghetti Squash (page 207) or Easiest Fluffy Quinoa (page 207) with my Pinewood Social Roasted Broccoli with Almond Dipping Sauce (page 190).

I also love to use my teriyaki sauce on stir-fried vegetables. I toss in a few toasted cashews at the end.

note

If saving extra teriyaki sauce, allow to cool 15 minutes before refrigerating. It will keep tightly sealed in the refrigerator up to 5 days.

fig & olive tapenade *with* whipped goat cheese crostini

V GF | HANDS-ON TIME: *15 to 20 min* | TOTAL TIME: *35 to 40 min* | YIELD: *1½ packed cups* | OPTIONS: Vg DF P

Whenever I make these crostini, I feel like I'm channeling Ina Garten, with her effortless sophistication and approachable but elegant dishes. My vegan Fig & Olive Tapenade is simply excellent, with a perfect balance of sweet and savory. When I combine this tapenade with the Whipped Goat Cheese Spread on a crunchy crostini . . . well, the result is "killer," as my mama would say. I cross my fingers that there will be leftovers when I make this tapenade, because I also love to spread it on toast with mashed avocado and a fried egg. It's even wonderful thinned with extra olive oil and used as a salad dressing.

If making the Whipped Goat Cheese Spread, combine all ingredients in a food processor and puree until smooth. Spread will keep tightly sealed in the refrigerator up to 5 days. The recipe makes approximately 1⅓ cups.

Preheat oven to 350° F and place walnuts on a baking sheet. Bake for 10 minutes, or until walnuts are fragrant. Set aside to cool.

While walnuts are roasting, place figs in a mixing bowl and cover with hot water for 10 minutes. Drain figs and set aside.

Heat a small sauté pan to medium heat and add 1 teaspoon olive oil. When oil is slightly shimmering, add shallots, oregano, and 1 teaspoon sea salt. Cook, stirring every minute or so, until shallots are translucent and fragrant (approximately 3 minutes). Add tiny splashes of water as necessary to prevent sticking. Turn off heat and set shallots on another burner to cool.

(continued on next page)

WHIPPED GOAT CHEESE SPREAD (OPTIONAL) (Vg DF P OMIT):

1 cup whole milk ricotta

½ cup goat cheese

½ teaspoon sea salt

Pinch black pepper

1 tablespoon olive oil

1 tablespoon lemon juice

FIG & OLIVE TAPENADE:

½ cup raw walnuts

¾ cup dried Mission figs, stems removed (sub purple raisins)

3 tablespoons plus 1 teaspoon extra-virgin olive oil

⅓ cup shallot, minced (approximately 1 small)

1 teaspoon dried oregano

1 teaspoon sea salt, plus more to taste

1 cup black Kalamata olives, pitted

2 tablespoons balsamic vinegar

1 teaspoon lemon zest (approximately 1 lemon)

1 tablespoon fresh lemon juice

ASSEMBLY:

Crostini of choice (I like sourdough, and there are also gluten-free varieties available)

Freshly minced parsley for garnish (optional)

fig & olive tapenade *with* whipped goat cheese crostini *(continued)*

Combine all remaining tapenade ingredients in a blender or food processor and pulse until it forms the texture of salsa, with small bits of olive, walnut, and fig still visible. Taste for salt and add accordingly. You can enjoy the tapenade immediately or refrigerate it, tightly sealed, up to 5 days.

To assemble, spread a thin layer of Whipped Goat Cheese Spread on each crostini and top with twice as much Fig & Olive Tapenade. Sprinkle with fresh parsley, if using.

GRAIN-FREE VERSION:

If you want to enjoy a grain-free version, you can sub out crostini for cucumber slices, cut approximately ½-inch thick.

---

ideas for

LEFTOVER FIGS

Figs make a delicious snack, especially dipped in almond or peanut butter.

I also love to make a Fig Tahini Smoothie: Blend ½ cup coconut milk, 1 frozen banana, ⅓ cup dried figs, 1 tablespoon tahini, pinch cinnamon, and ½ cup ice, adding water as necessary to reach desired consistency.

spicy golden deviled eggs

GF **DF** **P** | **HANDS-ON TIME:** *30 min* | **TOTAL TIME:** *30 min* | **YIELD:** *12 deviled eggs* | 🕐 | **OPTIONS:** **V**

*D*eviled eggs are a hallmark of classic Southern entertaining, and for good reason. They're two-bite, portable, napkin-friendly, and oh-so-delicious. My updated version has much less mayo than traditional recipes, and I kick it up several notches with spicy horseradish and antioxidant-packed turmeric. Protein-packed eggs are an ideal option for keeping "hanger" at bay, and I always choose local when I can. Look for bright yellow yolks, which signify a nutrient-dense and natural chicken diet—a win-win! Sometimes I chop up a few tablespoons of dill pickle and mix that into the filling for a fun variation.

In a medium-sized mixing bowl, whisk together mayonnaise, mustard, honey, turmeric, horseradish, sea salt, and pepper. Set aside.

For perfect hard-boiled eggs, place eggs in a small sauce pot and fill with water until eggs are covered 1 to 2 inches (in a 2-quart sauce pot, I use 2¼ cups water). Add vinegar, if using. Turn heat to medium-high and set a timer for 5 minutes. When water reaches a boil, start the 5-minute timer. When the timer goes off, remove pot from the heat, cover with a lid, and set timer for another 5 minutes. When timer goes off, place pot in the sink and run cold water over the eggs for 2 minutes. Allow to cool another 10 minutes before peeling.

Take a look at your hard-boiled eggs. Most will have a flat spot on the side that allows the egg to rest without rolling away. Using a sharp knife, mirror this spot on the opposite side by slicing off a thin layer of egg white. Eat or give the treat to your dog!

(continued on next page)

3 tablespoons mayonnaise

1½ teaspoons Dijon mustard

1 teaspoon honey

½ teaspoon ground turmeric

1 tablespoon plus 1 teaspoon prepared horseradish

¼ teaspoon sea salt, plus more to taste

⅛ teaspoon black pepper

6 large eggs

1 teaspoon white or apple cider vinegar (optional)

Cooked and crumbled bacon, chives, and scallions (optional garnish) (**V** omit bacon)

---

ideas for

LEFTOVER HORSERADISH

Make my Grilled Sweet Potato Avocado Toast (page 121).

Stir into plain hummus, mayonnaise, or ketchup (homemade cocktail sauce).

Use instead of wasabi with sushi.

Stir into scrambled eggs or my Sunday Tuna Salad (page 257).

spicy golden deviled eggs *(continued)*

Slice eggs vertically and gently scoop yolks into the mixing bowl that contains mayonnaise mixture. Place egg white halves face up on a plate. Use a fork to mash yolks into the mayo mixture, then whisk until smooth and incorporated. Taste for more sea salt, and add accordingly.

Wipe egg whites gently with a damp towel to remove any yolk stains. Now, you can either just scoop the yolk mixture evenly into each egg white, or you can make a "piping bag" by taking a small plastic food storage bag and snipping off approximately ¼ inch of plastic from one corner. Using a spatula, scoop yolk mixture into the bag. Push mixture into the corner of the bag that has the slit, removing as much air as possible.

To pipe, hold the open corner as close as possible to the inside of each egg white half, then squeeze gently. Fill each egg white approximately ½ inch above where the white ends. If you're feeling frisky, move your hand in a circular motion as you pipe to make a swirl.

Top each half with a sprinkle of garnish, if using. Eggs will keep tightly wrapped in the refrigerator up to 3 days.

green goddess avocado dip

(V) (GF) (DF)   **HANDS-ON TIME:** *10 min* | **TOTAL TIME:** *2 h, 10 min* | **YIELD:** *15 to 20 servings*   ❄   **OPTIONS:** (Vg)

*T*raditional green goddess dressing is fabulous, but it is heavily mayonnaise-based, and it includes anchovies. Try as I might, I don't enjoy anchovies enough to keep them in the pantry. So I took the parts I love about this classic dressing and turned it into a healthy dip, using my own favorite flavors. Avocado and white beans form a hearty base that stands up nicely to pungent fresh basil and touches of lemon juice and garlic. Although Wikipedia tells me that green goddess dressing was first made on the West Coast, it has come to represent spring and summer in the South, and that's exactly when I love it most!

Place all ingredients except olive oil in a food processor and puree until smooth, scraping down the sides as necessary with a spatula. When ingredients are pureed, slowly drizzle olive oil into the top open spout. Taste for more lemon juice and salt and add accordingly. Refrigerate 2 hours before serving. Dip will keep tightly sealed in the refrigerator up to 4 days. Stir before serving. To revive the color, stir in a little freshly squeezed lemon juice.

1 13½- to 15-ounce can white beans, drained and rinsed (cannellini or great northern)*

1 large ripe avocado, de-seeded and peeled (or 2 small avocados)

1 clove garlic, peeled and roughly chopped

1 tablespoon Dijon mustard

2 to 3 tablespoons fresh lemon juice (start with 2 and add to taste)

½ packed cup fresh basil leaves

2 teaspoons honey ((Vg) sub maple syrup)

1 to 1½ teaspoons sea salt (start with 1 teaspoon and add to taste)

Pinch black pepper

¼ cup extra-virgin olive oil

*I have used both 13 1/2- and 15-ounce cans of beans for this, and either work—just taste for more salt as you see fit.

SERVING SUGGESTIONS

This dip is also amazing as a pasta sauce. Cook noodles according to package directions and add sauce to taste. I like mixing in thawed green peas. Enjoy immediately or refrigerate for a cold pasta salad.

Serve the dip with freshly cut veggies, chips, or crackers, or spread on toast. This even works as a salad dressing, thinned with a little water.

anti-inflammatory root veggie hummus

V Vg GF DF | HANDS-ON TIME: *25 min* | TOTAL TIME: *3 h* | YIELD: *10 servings* ❄

I created this stunning, antioxidant-packed hummus for a lecture on the relationship between food and skin health. Whatever we ingest, we manifest outwardly, so truly radiant skin reflects a nutritious diet. The vibrant color in this dip represents free-radical–battling compounds, which can help repair your skin, nails, and hair. Anti-inflammatory garlic and turmeric are soothing from the inside out. Did I mention that this hummus is as scrumptious as it is beautiful and healthful? I've taught classes for professional male athletes who cannot stop devouring this bowl of hot pink goodness, and immediately requested the recipe.

Place sweet potatoes and beets in a small pot and fill with enough water to cover them by 1 to 2 inches. Bring to a boil and boil for 10 minutes, or until vegetables can be pierced with a knife. Drain in a colander and rinse with cold water for 30 seconds. Allow to cool for 10 minutes.

After vegetables have cooled, combine all ingredients except olive oil in a food processor and blend. While blending, slowly drizzle in olive oil. Scrape down with a spatula as necessary. Refrigerate 2 hours before serving. It will keep in the refrigerator tightly sealed for up to 5 days.

¾ cup sweet potatoes, peeled and cubed into 1-inch pieces (approximately ½ large sweet potato)

½ cup beets, peeled and cubed into 1-inch pieces (approximately 1 small beet)

1 15-ounce can chickpeas, drained and rinsed

1¾ teaspoons sea salt

2 cloves garlic, minced

¼ cup tahini paste

1 teaspoon ground turmeric (can omit, but recommended)

2 tablespoons nutritional yeast (sub parmesan cheese)

¼ cup extra-virgin olive oil

SERVING SUGGESTIONS

Enjoy with crackers, chips, or raw veggies, or spread on toast.

I love toasting a piece of my favorite bread, spreading it with this hummus, and adding a few slices of fresh avocado and a pinch of sea salt.

maple pecan pie balls

V Vg GF DF   HANDS-ON TIME: *20 min*   TOTAL TIME: *1 h*   YIELD: *15 balls*

I won't forget the time I first made these Maple Pecan Pie Balls. The idea sounded lovely in my head, but I wasn't prepared for just how mouthwateringly good these turned out to be! Since they first appeared on my website, they've been one of my most popular recipes, and I often make them as a gift during the holidays. Not only do they taste like gooey, caramel-y pecan pie in a healthy little package, they're a breeze to throw together. These are great as a quick breakfast or bedtime treat, as well as a snack.

1¼ cups raw pecans

1½ packed cups medjool dates, pitted

¼ cup rolled oats

½ teaspoon sea salt

1 teaspoon cinnamon

1 teaspoon maple extract

Line a baking sheet with parchment paper.

Place all ingredients in a food processor and blend until ingredients are the texture of wet sand—you should be able to pinch a small amount together and it will stick.

Carefully remove blade. Empty your "dough" into a bowl with a spatula.

Prepare a medium-sized bowl of room temperature–water by your side. Dampen fingers to prevent sticking, and roll dough into 1½-inch balls. Place balls on the baking sheet, side by side. If chilling, cover lightly with plastic wrap or aluminum foil and refrigerate 30 minutes before serving.

Store leftover balls in an airtight sealable container in the refrigerator for up to 1 week.

ideas for

LEFTOVER MAPLE EXTRACT

Replace vanilla extract with maple in LL's Daily Green Smoothie (page 90) or swap the almond for maple in my 10-Minute Whipped Banana Almond Porridge (page 127).

Add a drop or two to peanut or almond butter before spreading on toast or a banana with cinnamon.

Add a tiny splash to hot coffee or chai tea, then add to a blender with milk of choice for a quick latte.

note

You can enjoy the Maple Pecan Pie Balls immediately, but they will be very soft.

sweet chili pumpkin seed clusters

(V) (Vg) (GF) (DF) (P)   HANDS-ON TIME: *5 min* | TOTAL TIME: *1 h, 5 min* | YIELD: *1 cup*

I originally made these Sweet Chili Pumpkin Seed Clusters as a garnish for my Kale Caesar (page 299). As soon as I tasted them, however, I realized that they deserve a page of their own. Unlike other nuts and seeds, pumpkin seeds require a long time in the oven, but holy wow is it worth it! If you're anything like me or the clients I've made these for, you'll be scooping them by the handful throughout the day. Pumpkin seeds are loaded with fiber, zinc, copper, and plant protein, so you can feel great about these becoming your favorite new snack.

1 cup raw pumpkin seeds

2 teaspoons chili powder

2 teaspoons maple syrup

1 teaspoon sea salt

Preheat oven to 275° F. Line a large baking sheet with parchment paper. Combine all ingredients in a small mixing bowl and toss to coat evenly. Add pumpkin seeds to a baking sheet in an even layer, but try to keep as many touching as possible—this is what will allow them to form clusters.

Roast for 35 to 40 minutes, or until seeds are puffed and crunchy with a slightly darker green color. Allow to cool completely, at least 20 minutes, before gently breaking into small clusters.

sriracha garlic roasted edamame

V GF DF | HANDS-ON TIME: *10 min* | TOTAL TIME: *32 to 35 min* | YIELD: *8 servings* | OPTIONS: **Vg**

Organic, non-GMO edamame is a great staple to keep in your freezer. Almost everyone enjoys edamame, and the mild flavor makes it a perfect backdrop for whatever spices or sauces you have around—for example, the creamy sriracha-garlic sauce that I use in this recipe. When baked, it forms a tasty "crust" on the edamame that will transport you to your favorite Asian fusion restaurant. This recipe is my go-to when I need something truly last-minute that feels special. As I mentioned in Chapter 1, I am a fan of high-quality soy products in small amounts, so don't be afraid to add this to your snack-itizer rotation.

Preheat oven to 415° F and line a large baking sheet with parchment paper. In a large mixing bowl, whisk together all ingredients except edamame. Add edamame and toss to coat.

Spread edamame on your baking sheet in an even layer, including any excess sauce. Roast for 22 to 25 minutes, until the edamame has golden brown spots and edges. There will be some spots of burnt sauce, but that's okay. Use a spatula to toss the edamame in the sauce that has thickened on the parchment paper. Serve immediately, or refrigerate and serve chilled.

Tightly sealed edamame will keep in the refrigerator up to 3 days.

¼ cup mayonnaise
(**Vg** sub vegan mayonnaise)

1 tablespoon plus 1 teaspoon sriracha

1½ teaspoons maple syrup

3 tablespoons low-sodium tamari

¾ teaspoon onion powder

½ teaspoon garlic powder

½ teaspoon ground ginger

1 tablespoon nutritional yeast (optional)

10-ounce bag frozen organic edamame, thawed

ideas for
SNACKS

Dipping Jars: Add ⅓ cup of my Green Goddess Avocado Dip (page 75) or Anti-Inflammatory Root Veggie Hummus (page 76) to the bottom of a mason jar. Slice cucumbers, bell peppers, and carrots into vertical strips short enough to put the lid on and place in the jar.

Quick Spiced Olives: Add 1½ cups plain Kalamata olives to a bowl. In a small sauté pan, add 1 teaspoon olive oil and 1 clove garlic, minced. Cook on low, stirring, for approximately 30 seconds to a minute, until garlic is softened and fragrant. Stir in ½ teaspoon dried oregano, 2 teaspoons fresh orange zest, and ¼ teaspoon red pepper flakes. Cook another 30 seconds, stirring. Pour mixture over olives and serve.

recipes

3

BEVERAGES & SMOOTHIES

Oh smoothie, what can't you do? You're the ideal "gateway" for people who are striving for a healthier life but don't love eating or preparing veggies. You pack so much nutrient density into a creamy, drinkable, portable form. And you are a world of creative possibilities. Truly, smoothies and smoothie bowls are an absolute staple in my diet, for all of the above reasons and more. When I don't have the time or energy to whip up a "real" meal, I am always grateful for my Vitamix and my drawer of frozen produce. Over the years, I have experimented with countless variations, ingredients, and ratios, and this chapter offers you the fruits of my labor (see what I did there?).

I also offer several smoothie bowls, which are smoothies with less liquid, so they're the consistency of frozen yogurt. Also try some of my lovely non-smoothie beverages. My Workout Water (page 89) is a reader favorite in hot months, and my Green Immuni-Tea (page 106) will help keep you healthy when the temperature drops. Happy slurping!

cleansing raspberry ginger water

Ⓥ Ⓥⓖ Ⓖⓕ Ⓓⓕ Ⓟ | **HANDS-ON TIME:** *15 min* | **TOTAL TIME:** *2 h, 15 min* | **YIELD:** *4 to 5 servings* ❄

I really don't enjoy plain ole' water. There, I said it. And sometimes, a squeeze of fresh lemon juice isn't enough to get me into the water-drinking spirit. So I've played with various ways to "doctor" my H2O even more, and this Cleansing Raspberry Ginger version has to be my favorite. There is something so incredibly refreshing about this combination, and I always feel energized after a big glass. I also love to serve this when I have guests for lunch or if someone drops by in the afternoon—it looks special, which makes them feel special.

Add raspberries, ginger, and lemon or lime juice to a heat-proof pitcher.

Add water to a sauce pot and heat to medium. As soon as water starts to lightly simmer, pour water into pitcher. Use a spoon to mash raspberries and mix everything together.

Refrigerate at least 1 hour, then add stevia to taste, if using. Strain mixture using a fine mesh sieve. I strain mine into my Vitamix, rinse my pitcher, then pour it back into the clean pitcher.

Refrigerate until completely chilled before serving, approximately 2 hours. Water will last up to 4 days in the refrigerator.

¾ cup raspberries
(could use fresh or frozen)

1 tablespoon freshly grated ginger

Juice from 3 lemons or limes (doesn't need to be an exact amount)

Liquid stevia drops, to taste (optional)

6 cups water

---

ideas for

LEFTOVER STEVIA DROPS

For ideas on using stevia drops, please see Chapter 1, page 41.

SERVING SUGGESTIONS

I love to serve this over ice with fresh raspberries and sprigs of mint.

workout water

Ⓥ ⒼⒻ ⒹⒻ Ⓟ   HANDS-ON TIME: *15 min*   TOTAL TIME: *2 h, 15 min*   YIELD: *4 servings*   ❄   OPTIONS: **ⓋⒼ**

I developed this recipe when my husband was working long hours in the hot Tennessee sun, opening a restaurant in the Nashville Sounds' baseball stadium. I wanted him to stay hydrated, but no-way-no-how was he getting some pre-packaged beverage full of artificial ingredients and preservatives. This refreshing drink has natural electrolytes from coconut water and sea salt, vitamin C to help protect skin from harsh rays, and just enough sweetness for a gentle energy boost. This quickly became a summer staple in our family, and I think it will for you as well.

3 cups water

2 herbal tea bags*

2 to 3 tablespoons honey
(**ⓋⒼ** sub maple syrup; suggest 3 if using grapefruit juice)

24 ounces coconut water

1½ cups orange or grapefruit juice (can use 100% juice, bottled; 4 navel oranges; or 3 grapefruits)

½ teaspoon sea salt

*I like using hibiscus or strawberry tea, or something else fruity and refreshing. You could also use green tea, if you want a little caffeine boost.

In a small sauce pot, combine water, tea bags, and honey. Set heat to medium and bring to a simmer. As soon as mixture is simmering, remove from heat and set aside. Allow to steep 5 minutes, then remove tea bags. At this point, you can allow tea to cool as much or as little as you like before the next step—I suggest choosing based on whether or not your pitcher is heatproof.

In a large pitcher or other container, combine tea and all remaining ingredients. Refrigerate 2 hours, or until completely chilled through, before serving. Beverage will last for 1 week in the refrigerator.

ll's daily green smoothie

Ⓥ Ⓥ₉ ⒼⒻ ⒹⒻ Ⓟ   HANDS-ON TIME: *5 min*   TOTAL TIME: *6 min*   YIELD: *1 serving*   🕐

*A*ny health blogger worth his or her salt—er, kale?— has a go-to green smoothie. After years of experimenting with different combinations, I struck smoothie gold! I enjoy this green smoothie multiple times every week and sometimes daily. Banana + almond butter + cinnamon + vanilla reminds me of freshly baked banana bread. And there is absolutely no hint of "green" taste to be found. My trick is using frozen greens, which minimizes the taste even more than fresh. Plus, they last longer. This smoothie hits all the nutritional bullet points—fat, fiber, protein, vitamins, minerals, and yumminess.

Place all ingredients together into a high-powered blender in the order listed; this makes it easier to blend. Puree until smooth, adding extra tablespoons of water as necessary to reach desired consistency.

SMOOTHIE BOWL VERSION:

Add only 2 tablespoons of coconut water or milk to your blender or food processor, along with the rest of the ingredients. Blend, using a tamper, or stop and run a spatula around the edge of your food processor, until mixture forms a frozen yogurt consistency. If you're having difficulty blending, add a few more tablespoons of liquid until it starts moving.

LOW-SUGAR VERSION:

Don't fear the sugar in bananas—when you enjoy them with fat and protein in moderation, they're a great natural source of fuel, as well as important nutrients such as potassium. However, feel free to substitute the 1 banana (about ½ cup mashed) for ½ large avocado (should also be about ½ cup) and replace sweetener with 4 drops stevia. You might need to play around with it a few times to figure out what sweetness level is best for you.

½ cup coconut water or coconut milk

¾ cup water

1 frozen banana (approximately ¾ to 1 cup chunks)

1 tablespoon almond butter (sub other nut/seed butter)

1 cup frozen chopped spinach or ¾ cup frozen chopped kale

1 tablespoon chia seeds

1 medjool date or 2 teaspoons maple syrup (or to taste)

¼ teaspoon vanilla extract

¼ teaspoon cinnamon

note

I always have a bunch of bananas ripening on the counter. When they are dotted with brown spots, I peel and slice them into 1-inch pieces. I then add them to a plastic food storage bag and lay the bag flat, horizontally in my freezer. They'll freeze in a layer that's easy to break apart. Approximately 6 banana pieces equals 1 medium-sized banana.

blueberry ginger breakfast smoothie

V **GF** | HANDS-ON TIME: *5 min* | TOTAL TIME: *4 h, 5 min* | YIELD: *1 serving* | ● | OPTIONS: **Vg** **DF**

*T*his recipe is a bonanza of my favorite breakfast flavors, and it never fails to make me feel nourished and satisfied. Tangy, cool yogurt is a lovely contrast to juicy blueberries and honey, and a zip of ginger brings it all to life. This smoothie is great for your digestion, and I love to make this when I've had a heavy meal the night before. Add a tablespoon of almond butter if you want some extra protein for a satisfying on-the-go meal. I find myself absolutely craving this smoothie, and I hope you feel the same way.

Place all ingredients together into a high-powered blender in the order listed; this makes it easier to blend. Puree until smooth.

note

I am picky when it comes to the liquid in my smoothies. I use coconut water when I want something light and refreshing and canned full-fat coconut milk for a creamier result. The coconut flavor is barely detectable with either. Most boxed almond milks are filled with junk ingredients, so I avoid them. I've made my own nut milk in the past, but I honestly prefer the ease of something store-bought. Feel free to substitute whatever milk or liquid you prefer, but note that I can't guarantee the outcome will be the same.

¼ cup rolled oats, soaked in ¼ cup water 4 to 8 hours*

⅓ cup coconut water

⅓ cup plain yogurt (**Vg** **DF** sub non-dairy yogurt or full-fat coconut milk)

1 teaspoon honey (plus more to taste) (**Vg** sub maple syrup)

1-inch piece ginger root

1 tablespoon chia seeds

1 cup frozen blueberries

1 frozen banana (approximately ¾ cup)

*Place oats in a small bowl and add room-temperature water. Cover and refrigerate at least 4 hours, or ideally overnight— I just do this right before bed.

mocha smoothie

Ⓥ Ⓥg ⒼⒻ ⒹⒻ Ⓟ   **HANDS-ON TIME:** *10 min* | **TOTAL TIME:** *2 h, 10 min* | **YIELD:** *1 serving*   ❄

This scrumptious smoothie is like a DIY healthy version of your favorite coffeehouse drink. I'm actually not a coffee drinker, so I drink the Fauxcha version with something called Dandy Blend. Dandy Blend is made primarily from chicory root, so it has a coffee-like flavor without the jittery compounds. I purchase it in bulk on Amazon, and it dissolves instantly in hot or cold water. But my favorite way to enjoy Dandy Blend is definitely in this creamy divine smoothie, which I make whenever I want to feel spoiled in the morning. At half the cost and packed with nutrition, there's zero reason to drink those fake-ingredient and refined-sugar-filled store-bought versions again.

Place all ingredients together into a high-powered blender in the order listed; this makes it easier to blend. Puree until smooth.

FAUXCHA VERSION:

Increase to ⅓ cup coconut milk, and replace coffee with ⅔ cup water and 1 tablespoon Dandy Blend or other coffee substitute. Keep remaining ingredients the same.

1 cup strong coffee, chilled

¼ cup canned full-fat coconut milk

1½ frozen bananas
(approximately 1¼ cup)

2 tablespoons unsweetened
cocoa powder

1 to 2 pitted medjool dates (sub
2 teaspoons maple syrup or honey)

2 tablespoons almond butter
(sub other nut/seed butter)

½ teaspoon vanilla extract

strawberry shortcake smoothie bowl

V **GF** **DF** **P**   HANDS-ON TIME: *10 min* | TOTAL TIME: *11 min* | YIELD: *1 serving*   OPTIONS: **Vg**

*C*ruciferous vegetables (cabbage, broccoli, Brussels sprouts) are a wonderful part of a healthy diet, but I can't say I crave them first thing in the morning. This recipe is a way to get your cruciferous benefits, including vitamins K, A, and C, while enjoying a cool, creamy strawberry shortcake flavor. I promise you won't taste the purple cabbage a bit. It is important to use a really good blender for this recipe to make sure you break down the cabbage completely.

Place all ingredients together into a high-powered blender in the order listed and blend, using a tamper or stopping to run a spatula around the edge as necessary until mixture reaches frozen yogurt consistency. Add splashes of water or coconut water as necessary if you are having trouble blending. If you have a small 2- to 4-cup food processor, you could use that as well.

Add to a bowl and top with desired garnishes before enjoying immediately.

¼ cup canned full-fat coconut milk

¼ cup water

1 cup tightly packed purple cabbage, sliced into ¼-inch-thick ribbons

1¼ frozen bananas (approximately 1 rounded cup of pieces)

1 rounded cup frozen strawberries

¼ teaspoon vanilla extract

1 pitted date or 1 teaspoon honey (optional) (**Vg** omit honey)

1 to 2 tablespoons nut butter or chia seeds for protein (optional)

Fresh strawberry slices, fresh banana, freeze-dried strawberries, toasted coconut flakes, and cacao nibs (optional garnish)

---

ideas for

LEFTOVER PURPLE CABBAGE

Cabbage will last for several weeks in the refrigerator, so you can buy a head and enjoy this smoothie for quite some time. However, you can also freeze leftover cabbage so it keeps longer, and add it to the smoothie frozen. Just note that you might need a splash more liquid.

You could also make my Carrot Ginger Cabbage Slaw (page 182) or Refried Black Bean Enchiladas with Sweet Potato "Cheese" Sauce (page 281).

note

When I indicate a rounded cup measurement, I mean there are a few pieces of fruit above the cup line.

power c sunshine smoothie

Ⓥ ⒼⒻ ⒹⒻ Ⓟ | HANDS-ON TIME: *5 min* | TOTAL TIME: *6 min* | YIELD: *1 serving* | 🕐 | OPTIONS: ⓋⒼ

*F*eeling under the weather and looking for the perfect light breakfast or snack to get you back on track? This Power C Sunshine Smoothie is your one-way ticket. As much as I love my Green Immuni-Tea (page 106), it's not my preference in warmer months, and it doesn't fill me up. This cold, creamy, and stunningly beautiful smoothie radiates health and energy, and it never fails to nourish my spirit as well as my immune system. This smoothie is abundant in vitamins A and C, as well as anti-inflammatory turmeric and ginger. It is also gentle on your belly and an aid for digestion—especially if you throw in some fresh mint leaves.

⅓ cup canned full-fat coconut milk

⅓ cup water

½ fresh large navel orange or 1 small orange, peeled

1 tablespoon fresh lemon juice

1¼ frozen bananas (approximately 1 rounded cup)

1-inch-piece ginger root

¼ teaspoon turmeric

1 teaspoon honey or maple syrup for added sweetness (optional) (ⓋⒼ omit honey)

Place all ingredients in a high-powered blender in the order listed and blend until smooth. Serve immediately.

cherry almond bedtime smoothie

(V) (Vg) (GF) (DF) (P)   **HANDS-ON TIME:** *5 min*   **TOTAL TIME:** *6 min*   **YIELD:** *1 serving*

*T*wo things about me: 1) I sometimes have insomnia when I'm stressed. 2) I sometimes crave a light snack before bed, since I usually eat an early dinner. Cherry Almond Bedtime Smoothie to the rescue! Cherries are actually a source of melatonin, the hormone that helps us get sleepy as night falls. In this smoothie, I combine cherries with healthy fat from almond butter and avocado, which help keep my blood sugar balanced. The electrolytes in coconut water make me feel relaxed and calm. Almond extract is totally optional; however, the flavor pairs beautifully with cherries, and I think you'll find yourself making this more than once.

¾ cup coconut water

¼ teaspoon almond extract (optional)

1 cup frozen cherries

¼ ripe avocado (¼ cup mashed)

1 tablespoon almond butter

2 pitted dates

3 to 4 ice cubes

Place all ingredients together into a high-powered blender in the order listed; this makes it easier to blend. Puree until smooth. Add more water as necessary to reach desired consistency.

blender green juice

V Vg GF DF P   HANDS-ON TIME: *5 min* | TOTAL TIME: *6 min* | YIELD: *1 to 2 servings*

You might have noticed an absence of juice in this section. While I'm not anti-juicing, I personally prefer drinking blended whole foods that still have their fiber. Juices tend to leave me hungry and searching for carbs, whereas smoothies or this "blender juice" are satisfying. I often make this juice alongside oatmeal, avocado toast, or eggs. It's a way to get tons of green-veggie nutrition without having to eat a salad at 7 am (no judgment if that's your thing!). You could absolutely sub out watermelon for any fruit, but I suggest sticking to citrus, green apple, peaches, pineapple, or mango to retain the vibrant green color. We eat with our eyes, and I don't like muddying my green drinks with berries, plums, or other dark fruits. The next time you're craving a refreshing, instant health boost, try this simple Blender Green Juice instead of an expensive pressed juice.

1½ cups fresh seedless watermelon (sub 1½ to 2 cups fruit of choice)

1 cup cucumber or zucchini, chopped into 1-inch pieces (peel if not organic or if you don't have a strong blender)

2 cups tightly packed baby spinach

¼ cup tightly packed basil, cilantro, mint, or parsley

2 tablespoons fresh lime juice or lemon juice

1-inch-piece ginger root (sub ¼ teaspoon ground ginger)

1 cup ice

Place all ingredients together into a high-powered blender in the order listed; this makes it easier to blend. Puree until smooth. Enjoy immediately. Feel free to add water or another liquid base as you like.

OTHER VERSIONS:

Keep spinach, ginger, and ice in all versions:

- Watermelon, cucumber, basil, lime
- Orange, zucchini, mint, lemon
- Pineapple, cucumber, cilantro, lime
- Green apple, zucchini, parsley, lemon

aloha smoothie bowl

(V) (GF) (DF) (P)   HANDS-ON TIME: *10 min*   TOTAL TIME: *11 min*   YIELD: *1 serving*   🕐   OPTIONS: (Vg)

*Y*earning for a beach vacation? Whip this Aloha Smoothie Bowl together, and you'll be transported to an exotic island! okay, not quite, but it will definitely brighten your day and feel like a refreshing, tropical treat. Besides my Daily Green Smoothie (page 90), this is my favorite way to start the day in warmer months. It is hydrating, and the zing of pineapple and lime help combat sluggishness from heat and humidity. The additions of avocado and coconut oil add more than healthy fats; they act as emulsifiers, creating the most incredibly silky texture.

Place all ingredients together in a blender in the order listed and blend, using a tamper or stopping to run a spatula around the edge as necessary until mixture reaches frozen yogurt consistency. Add splashes of water or coconut water as necessary if you are having trouble blending. If you have a small 2- to 4-cup food processor, you could use that as well.

Add to a bowl and top with desired garnishes before enjoying immediately.

½ cup coconut water

1 cup frozen spinach

¼ fresh ripe avocado

1 frozen banana (approximately ¾ to 1 cup chunks)

1 cup frozen pineapple chunks (approximately 1-inch pieces)

1 tablespoon fresh lime juice

1 teaspoon coconut oil

1 teaspoon honey or maple syrup (optional) ((Vg) omit honey)

Fresh pineapple, toasted coconut flakes, toasted cashew pieces, or an extra drizzle of lime juice or honey (optional garnish)

note

To make toasted coconut flakes, heat a skillet to medium and add ¼ to ½ cup unsweetened coconut flakes. Cook, stirring, until flakes have just started to turn golden brown around the edges. Remove pan from the heat and keep stirring. Flakes will continue to toast. When most of the flakes are golden, empty them into a heatproof dish and allow to cool completely. Store leftovers in a tightly sealed container at room temperature.

green immuni-tea

V GF DF P HANDS-ON TIME: *5 min* | TOTAL TIME: *10 min* | YIELD: *1 serving* | OPTIONS: Vg

*N*o matter how much we try to take care of ourselves, sometimes a little cold or virus sneaks its way into our system, sidelining us for days or even weeks. This Green Immuni-Tea can help prevent illness by bolstering the immune system and cooling inflammation. Whenever I feel the slightest little throat tickle or notice I'm sniffling, I make this tea every single morning. Each ingredient is specifically chosen for its healing properties, and it tastes absolutely amazing. The addition of black pepper might sound strange, but you can't taste it, and it increases the effectiveness of turmeric. This is such a cozy way to stay well in the winter, but it can also be refrigerated and iced. You can also double or triple the recipe and enjoy it throughout the week.

1¾ cups filtered water

1 green tea bag

1 teaspoon grated ginger root (sub pinch ground ginger)

1 tablespoon fresh lemon juice

Pinch cinnamon

Pinch turmeric

Pinch black pepper

1 teaspoon honey (Vg sub maple syrup)

Splash coconut or almond milk (optional)

Add water to a small sauce pot, turn heat to medium-low, and bring the water to a simmer. Add remaining ingredients except milk, if using, and stir to evenly distribute ingredients. Simmer 3 minutes, then remove pot from heat and strain through a fine-mesh strainer into a mug. Stir in milk, if using. Enjoy immediately.

peanut butter apple pie smoothie

(V) (GF) | HANDS-ON TIME: *5 min* | TOTAL TIME: *6 min* | YIELD: *1 serving* | (clock) | OPTIONS: (Vg) (DF)

I mean . . . just . . . YUM! This smoothie is for those mornings when nothing sounds good, and you don't feel like being healthy, but you know you should try. This smoothie is autumn apple pie meets milkshake meets America's favorite condiment (and mine, as you'll see in this book). But it's also full of healthy fats, beneficial probiotics, antioxidants, and metabolism-boosting spice. This smoothie is also a crowd-pleaser with adults and kids alike. Want to up the nutrition even more? Throw in a few handfuls of spinach—it won't affect the flavor.

Place all ingredients together into a high-powered blender in the order listed; this makes it easier to blend. Puree until smooth.

note

This smoothie will seem hard to blend at first. Resist the temptation to add more liquid—keep blending, or let it sit out for 10 minutes before blending. Or just embrace the thickness and enjoy it as a smoothie bowl!

¼ cup canned full-fat coconut milk

¼ cup plain whole milk yogurt
   ((Vg) (DF) sub non-dairy yogurt)

¼ cup filtered water

1 to 2 tablespoons peanut butter
   (I use 2)

¼ teaspoon vanilla extract

½ teaspoon cinnamon

1 medjool date, pitted (sub 2
   teaspoons maple syrup or honey)

1 cup frozen chopped red apple*
   (approximately 1 small apple,
   I use Honeycrisp or Pink Lady)

1 frozen banana (approximately
   ¾ cup pieces)

*You could use a fresh apple, but I think
frozen is better for texture and makes it
feel like a milkshake.

recipes

4

BREAKFAST

· ·

*A*h, breakfast, my absolute favorite meal of the day! I love
nothing more (okay, a few things more) than waking up
hungry for a wholesome and delicious breakfast—bonus if it's been
made in advance and I don't have to do any work. I don't subscribe
to the notion that breakfast is the "most important" meal of the day,
because I don't think any one meal or snack pulls rank or hierarchy
over the other: they are all important, and a less than "perfect"
meal isn't going to make or break your health. However, breakfast
does set the tone for the day because, well, it's the first thing we eat.
For that reason, I emphasize a nourishing morning meal to provide
energy, satiation, and blood sugar balance.

I also particularly love breakfast because it's often the only
meal we enjoy in peace and quiet. Lunches play second fiddle to
the computer, and dinners are usually (hopefully) accompanied
by lively family conversation—and sometimes chaos. So I try to
put a little extra TLC into my breakfasts, making them special
and worth savoring.

· ·

blueberry coconut morning porridge

V Vg GF DF   HANDS-ON TIME: *20 min* | TOTAL TIME: *4 h, 20 min* | YIELD: *1 serving* ❄

This is one of the first recipes I ever put on LL Balanced, back when I was living with my parents right after moving to Nashville from New York. I remember uncovering this chilled, creamy bowl of overnight oats each morning and enjoying it on the back patio. I'd watch summer steam rising from the wet grass and feel so grateful to be home. This was a magical time, when the juxtaposition of my old and new life was fresh and strong. I still make this recipe when the weather begins to warm, as it is the perfect no-fuss, cooling way to start the day. If you're not familiar with the concept of overnight oats, it's as simple as this: oats + milk + yummy additions of choice, refrigerated overnight. Feel free to play with your flavorings and fruit, but know that you can always come back to this reliable combination.

Place all ingredients in a small bowl except blueberries and whisk to incorporate. Stir in blueberries. Whisk every 2 minutes for 10 minutes to prevent chia seeds from clumping.

Cover bowl and refrigerate at least 4 hours or overnight.

YOGURTY VERSION:

Sometimes I add 2 tablespoons or ¼ cup yogurt to the mix. When I use ¼ cup, I reduce the water by 2 tablespoons.

¼ cup rolled oats

1 tablespoon plus 1 teaspoon chia seeds

2 teaspoons unsweetened coconut flakes (toasted is even better)

Pinch cinnamon

Pinch sea salt

¼ teaspoon almond extract (sub ½ teaspoon vanilla extract)

¼ cup canned full-fat coconut milk

¼ cup to 6 tablespoons filtered water (suggest ¼ cup if using frozen berries, 6 tablespoons if using fresh)

Maple syrup to taste (sub honey)

⅓ cup fresh or frozen blueberries

SERVING SUGGESTIONS

Try topping with almond butter and extra blueberries (my favorite).

green overnight oat pudding

V Vg GF DF   HANDS-ON TIME: *15 min*   TOTAL TIME: *4 h, 15 min*   YIELD: *1 serving*   ❄

*A*s you know by now from my smoothie chapter, I try to sneak veggies into breakfast whenever I can. I wanted something I could prepare the night before that included some kind of green. This lovely recipe is the result. You cannot taste a bit of greenness, but you receive the nutritional benefits, such as fiber, folate, vitamins A, C, E, and K, calcium, and magnesium. I make this pudding at least once per week, usually as a parfait with layers of granola and fresh fruit.

Place all ingredients in a blender in the order listed. Puree until smooth, then pour into a bowl, or make a parfait in a mason jar. Cover and refrigerate at least 4 hours or overnight. This won't look like a lot of pudding, but it is very filling. Feel free to double it if you like.

¼ cup canned full-fat coconut milk

¼ cup water (sub more coconut milk or another milk of choice)

¾ cup chopped frozen spinach* (the bagged kind from the grocery) (sub 1 packed cup fresh baby spinach leaves)

¼ cup rolled oats

1 tablespoon plus 1 teaspoon chia seeds

1 tablespoon almond butter (sub sunflower seed butter, cashew butter, or peanut butter)

⅛ teaspoon cinnamon

¼ teaspoon vanilla extract

Maple syrup to taste (sub honey)

Pinch cinnamon

*If using frozen spinach leaves, crush them into small pieces before measuring.

SERVING SUGGESTIONS

Try these as toppings or parfait layers: fresh or frozen berries (the latter will thaw and mix some juice into the pudding, which I like), Apricot & Olive Granola Clusters (page 150), toasted coconut flakes, 20-Minute Chia Berry Jam (page 118), sliced bananas, or a dollop of yogurt.

note

I don't suggest other greens besides spinach, as the taste will become too noticeable.

peanut butter breakfast cookies

V GF DF   HANDS-ON TIME: *20 min*   TOTAL TIME: *40 min*   YIELD: *10 cookies*

*T*hese cookies took on a life of their own as soon as the first batch came out of the oven. I shared them with friends and family, and very quickly they became a breakfast staple in many households. My husband was asked to list his top five favorite things about Nashville for an interview, and these cookies were included! It's not hard to understand their appeal. Peanut butter will forever and always evoke cozy, childhood memories for me, and I know I'm not alone. Here, peanut butter combines with protein, fiber, and natural sweetness to create a cookie that is satisfying and nourishing from the inside out. These breakfast cookies are sturdy and portable, making them a life-saver on busy mornings, and they freeze well to boot.

Preheat oven to 350° F. Line a baking sheet with parchment paper.

In a food processor, combine oats and dates. Pulse to combine until the mixture forms a chunky crumble, approximately 30 seconds. Add remaining ingredients, and pulse until evenly incorporated. This will be a very sticky paste with small bits of oats and dates still visible.

Grab a spatula, a fork, and a medium-sized bowl of room temperature water. Remove the food processor from its base. Carefully remove blade, scraping off dough with a damp spatula into a mixing bowl. Then scrape remaining dough into bowl.

Dampen your fingers in the water bowl to prevent sticking, and roll dough into approximately 10 2½-inch balls. Place them on your prepared baking sheet with at least 2 inches between each ball. Wet your fork and use the tines to gently press down on each cookie until it is approximately 1-inch thick. You can turn the tines in opposing directions to create a cross-hatched look.

Bake for 11 minutes, or until cookies are just set on top; not firm. They will still look a little raw on top. Allow to cool 10 minutes before enjoying. Cookies can be stored in a tightly sealed container in the refrigerator up to 1 week, or in the freezer up to 3 months.

1 cup rolled oats

1 packed cup medjool dates, pitted

¾ cup runny peanut butter*
(sub nut/seed butter of choice)

2 eggs, whisked in a separate bowl

¼ teaspoon sea salt

½ teaspoon cinnamon

1 teaspoon vanilla extract

*If you have drier or not runny nut or seed butter, scoop out a few tablespoons less than the recipe calls for and add to a mixing bowl with the missing amount of tablespoons of very hot water. Stir to combine, then allow mixture to sit 10 minutes. Then stir everything together thoroughly and measure out for the recipe.

SERVING SUGGESTIONS

Try making sandwiches with the cookies and some jam.

customizable oat johnnycakes
with 20-minute chia berry jam

V GF DF | **HANDS-ON TIME:** *25 to 30 min* | **TOTAL TIME:** *25 to 30 min* | **YIELD:** *16 Johnnycakes*

As much as I love a fluffy pancake, I also adore Johnnycakes, also called "hoecakes" or "Journey cakes," among others. Dubbed the "original" pancake, Johnnycakes are a traditional cornmeal flatbread with roots in various cultures, including the South. Their slightly dense, gritty texture and nutty flavor are downright addicting. To keep things simple and stick to my pantry staples, I made a version of Johnnycakes using oat flour, and it worked! My oat Johnnycakes are hearty but tender, and they're completely customizable. I usually enjoy them with my 20-Minute Berry Chia Jam, but they're also incredible eaten the classic way, with a pat of melted butter and a drizzle of honey. You could even go savory with cheese and crispy chopped bacon.

If making the 20-Minute Berry Chia Jam, place berries and water in a small sauce pot, turn to medium-high heat, and bring to a boil. Boil for 12 to 15 minutes, or until most of the liquid is absorbed and the fruit has started to break down. Stir every minute or so. Use your spoon/spatula to break up the fruit as much as you like.

Remove pan from heat and stir in maple syrup (if using) and chia seeds. Whisk every minute or two for 10 minutes to ensure chia seeds don't clump. You can use the jam immediately, or place in a tightly sealed container in the fridge for at least an hour if you want it set to a thicker consistency. Will keep for 5 days. The recipe makes approximately ¾ cup.

To make Johnnycakes, start with making oat flour by pulsing 1 cup rolled oats in a high-powered blender or food processor until it forms a flour consistency, similar to corn meal. Empty oat flour into a medium-sized mixing bowl and whisk in salt.

(continued on next page)

20-MINUTE BERRY CHIA JAM (OPTIONAL):

2 rounded cups frozen mixed berries

¾ cup water

1 to 2 tablespoons maple syrup, to taste (optional; I use 1 tablespoon)

1 tablespoon chia seeds

JOHNNYCAKES:

1 cup rolled oats (see page 17 for oat flour instructions)

¼ teaspoon salt

2 large eggs

½ cup canned full-fat coconut milk

¼ cup water

1 tablespoon plus 1 teaspoon maple syrup

3 tablespoons nut/seed butter of choice

1 teaspoon vanilla extract

note

These Johnnycakes can be made the night before and reheated in the oven at 300° F for 5 to 10 minutes, and they also freeze well, tightly sealed, up to 1 month. Thaw in the refrigerator overnight then reheat as above.

customizable oat johnnycakes
with 20-minute chia berry jam *(continued)*

In a blender, puree eggs, coconut milk, water, maple syrup, nut/ seed butter, and vanilla extract. You can also whisk these ingredients together by hand in a mixing bowl. Pour wet mixture into dry and stir to combine.

Heat a cast-iron skillet to medium heat. If you do not have cast-iron or another nonstick pan, add 1 tablespoon butter or coconut oil to your pan and turn to medium heat. Drop a small spoonful of batter onto your skillet; if you hear a slight sizzle, it is ready for your Johnnycakes.

Pour 2 tablespoons of batter per Johnnycake onto skillet (I can usually get about 4 that I can comfortably flip). I use a ¼ cup measure and fill it half way. Johnnycakes are ready to flip when bubbles have formed in the surface, approximately 2 minutes. Use a thin, rigid spatula to gently peek under the cakes to ensure a golden brown color. Flip and cook another 2 minutes.

Repeat with remaining batter. If you are not using a cast-iron skillet or other nonstick pan, you might need to add more fat to prevent sticking as you continue to cook.

Johnnycakes will keep tightly sealed in the refrigerator up to 4 days. Allow to cool completely before refrigerating. I like to reheat mine in the microwave for 20 to 30 seconds, but you can also heat them in a 300° F oven until they are warm to touch.

note

Your batter might look really thin at first. If so, let it set up for another 5 minutes before making cakes.

note

Cast-iron skillets get hotter the longer they are on the stove. You will likely have to turn the heat down to low after you have made the first 1 to 2 batches of Johnnycakes to prevent burning.

grilled sweet potato avocado toast

V **GF** **DF** **P**   HANDS-ON TIME: *15 to 20 min*   TOTAL TIME: *30 to 45 min*   YIELD: *4 to 5 toasts*   OPTIONS: **Vg**

*T*alk about a balanced dish! This breakfast is a little sweet, a little spicy, and a perfect mixture of tradition and whimsy. Avocado toast has taken the food (and social media) world by storm, and I wanted to offer my own creative take. Here, grilled sweet potato "bread" takes the place of its yeasty counterpart, and it's an ideal vehicle for creamy avocado and drippy egg yolk. This dish is a nutrient powerhouse, filled with vitamins A, B, and C, potassium, fiber, and protein. I love to make these Grilled Sweet Potato Avocado Toasts when I have a really busy, stressful day ahead, because they help me feel even-keeled and relaxed.

1 medium sweet potato, rinsed and sliced vertically into ½-inch-thick slices (should get 4 to 5)

4 eggs (match to number of sweet potato slices) (**Vg** omit)

1 teaspoon white vinegar or apple cider vinegar

¼ teaspoon sea salt

Pinch black pepper

Pinch cayenne

1 ripe avocado

1 tablespoon lemon juice

2 teaspoons prepared horseradish (optional)

2 teaspoons extra-virgin olive oil

Chives and red pepper flakes for garnish (optional)

Prepare a colander in the sink. Add sweet potato slices to a 4-quart (or larger) sauce pot and cover with cold water. Bring to a boil, then boil 3 to 5 minutes, or until sweet potatoes can be pierced with a fork but are still firm. Quickly but carefully use tongs to pull slices out of the water and into your colander. Run cold water over slices for 30 seconds. Set aside.

(continued on next page)

grilled sweet potato avocado toast *(continued)*

To soft-boil eggs, set a timer for 5 minutes. Place eggs and vinegar in a small sauce pot and cover with 1 inch of water. Bring to a boil, then reduce to a simmer. Start timer, and as soon as it goes off, use a large spoon to immediately scoop eggs into a mixing bowl filled with ice water. Allow eggs to sit in ice water for 5 minutes before peeling.

While water is coming to a boil, combine ¼ teaspoon sea salt, pinch black pepper, cayenne, avocado, lemon juice, and horseradish (if using) in a mixing bowl. Mash ingredients together to form a chunky spread. Taste for more salt and add accordingly. Set aside.

Heat a grill to medium-high heat. Brush with olive oil. When grill is heated, add sweet potato slices running perpendicular to the grill marks. Sprinkle with a pinch of salt and pepper. Grill for approximately 2 to 3 minutes, or until there are nice grill marks on the face-down side (you can gently peek). Flip sweet potato slices and repeat on remaining side.

Top each sweet potato toast slice with a generous spread of avocado mixture and 1 soft-boiled egg. Add any desired garnish.

SERVING SUGGESTIONS

To enjoy these during a busy week, grill the sweet potato slices and soft-boil the eggs in advance. To assemble, add a slice to the toaster or oven until warmed through. While toast is warming, mash ¼ of an avocado with pinches of salt, pepper, lemon juice, and horseradish. Put layers together as directed.

note

Old eggs peel better than fresh, so I wait a week after buying to make hard- or soft-boiled eggs (use within expiration date, though).

chocolate chia avocado pudding

V **Vg** **GF** **DF** **P** | HANDS-ON TIME: *15 min* | TOTAL TIME: *4 h, 15 min* | YIELD: *6 servings* ❄

*T*his could easily pass as dessert—it is so luscious and decadent. But the great news is, it is healthy enough to enjoy as a nourishing breakfast when you want something to satisfy a sweet tooth. Avocado and cocoa powder might sound like a strange combo, but there's zero avocado flavor—just creamy, chocolatey goodness. Plus, you get a hit of antioxidants from the cocoa. Almond butter and chia seeds add protein and fiber. You can absolutely double this recipe and enjoy it throughout the week as a snack or post-dinner treat!

Place all ingredients in the order listed in a high-powered blender or food processor. Puree until smooth. Empty mixture into a bowl or storage container and refrigerate at least 4 hours or overnight before serving. Pudding will keep for up to 5 days in a tightly sealed container in the fridge.

1 cup canned full-fat coconut milk

1 cup water

¼ cup chia seeds

½ cup maple syrup (can sub honey, but it will have a noticeable honey flavor)

1 cup mashed avocado (approximately 2 small or 1½ medium)

¼ cup almond butter (sub peanut or sunflower seed butter)

½ cup cocoa powder

2 teaspoons vanilla extract

½ teaspoon cinnamon

SERVING SUGGESTIONS

I love topping this with fresh berries or banana slices and a sprinkle of coconut flakes before enjoying.

10-minute whipped banana almond porridge

V **Vg** **GF** **DF** | HANDS-ON TIME: *10 min* | TOTAL TIME: *10 min* | YIELD: *1 serving* 🕐

*I*f it's a chilly morning and I'm craving cozy comfort food, I'm making this 10-minute porridge. It probably graces my table at least 3 times per week in the winter, as it's so easy, nourishing, and satisfying. The special trick in this recipe is really whipping the frozen banana, almond butter, and coconut oil into the oats. This creates an unbeatable, creamy, fluffy texture. Bonus: mini morning arm workout! My mom always adds almond extract to her oats, and I love the pop of flavor, but feel free to leave it out if you prefer.

In a small sauce pot, combine oats, chia seeds (if using), and water. Whisk to prevent chia seeds from clumping. Turn heat to medium. When mixture is simmering, add almond extract (if using), sea salt, and cinnamon. Cook, stirring, 3 to 4 minutes, until most of the water is absorbed and the oats have a porridge-like consistency. Add banana chunks and whisk vigorously until banana has completely melted into the oats. Turn heat to low and whisk in almond butter and coconut oil. Taste and add more cinnamon, sea salt, or almond extract if you like.

Serve immediately with desired garnishes.

⅓ cup rolled oats

1 tablespoon chia seeds (optional; increase oats to ½ cup if not)

1¼ cups water

¼ to ½ teaspoon almond extract (start with ¼ and add to taste or sub vanilla) (optional)

Pinch sea salt, plus more to taste

Pinch to ¼ teaspoon cinnamon, to taste

½ cup frozen banana chunks (approximately ½ medium to large banana)

1 tablespoon almond butter

1 teaspoon coconut oil

SERVING SUGGESTIONS

I've garnished this with coconut flakes, sliced almonds, a dollop of yogurt or drizzle of full-fat coconut milk, an extra spoonful of almond butter, cinnamon, cacao nibs, fresh or frozen berries, and fresh banana slices.

note

You could also use fresh banana instead of frozen, but I prefer the way the frozen banana melts into the mixture. Either way, make sure your banana is very ripe.

grain-free cinnamon waffles

Ⓥ ⒼⒻ Ⓟ | HANDS-ON TIME: *20 min* | TOTAL TIME: *30 min* | YIELD: *2 standard-sized Belgian waffles* 🕐 | OPTIONS: ⒹⒻ

*T*here is something about waffles that makes me feel like I'm on vacation, or like I've snuck away to a little cafe for some "me" time. Now, with the magic of affordable waffle makers, you can recreate this experience at home. Most restaurant waffles are made with refined flour and sugar, then doused with fake maple syrup and powdered sugar. Read: food coma and energy crash. These Grain-Free Cinnamon Waffles are low in sugar and high in both fiber and protein, so they're a hearty *and* healthy way to start the day. It might seem like a pain to separate your eggs and whip the whites, but trust me—it is 100% worth the fluffy, tender inside, and light crispy edges.

If your waffle maker *doesn't* have a nonstick surface, grease with 1 teaspoon melted butter or coconut oil. Heat according to manufacturer directions.

In a medium mixing bowl, whisk together almond flour, arrowroot starch, cinnamon, baking powder, and sea salt.

In a separate smaller bowl, whisk together egg yolks, melted butter, coconut milk, maple syrup, and vanilla extract.

With a handheld or stand mixer, beat the egg whites until they form soft peaks, approximately 1 minute. Soft peaks hold for a second, then fall back onto themselves. This will looks like a light white foam.

Stir egg yolk mixture into dry ingredients. Gently fold in egg whites until just incorporated.

Add half of your batter to waffle maker and cook for 2½ to 3 minutes, until edges are lightly golden brown. Gently remove and repeat with remaining batter. Serve immediately.

Waffles will keep tightly sealed in the refrigerator for 2 days. I reheat them in the oven at 300° F until they are softened and warm to touch. You can also freeze them up to 1 month.

2 tablespoons melted butter, plus 1 teaspoon for waffle maker if necessary (ⒹⒻ sub coconut oil)

1 cup almond flour

¼ cup arrowroot starch (sub non-GMO cornstarch)

2 teaspoons cinnamon

1½ teaspoons baking powder

¼ teaspoon sea salt

3 large eggs, separated into yolks and whites

½ cup canned full-fat coconut milk

2 tablespoons maple syrup

1½ teaspoons vanilla extract

SAVORY VERSION:

Omit the cinnamon and serve with my Coconut-Crusted Baked Chicken Tenders (page 242) for a healthy take on chicken n' waffles.

pumpkin spice protein pancakes

Ⓥ ⒼⒻ ⒹⒻ | HANDS-ON TIME: *25 to 30 min* | TOTAL TIME: *8 h, 25 to 30 min* | YIELD: *4 servings* 💧

*T*hese pancakes were inspired by the success of my quinoa lentil pizza crust (page 219). I was pleasantly surprised by the chameleon quality of red lentils to mimic bread, and they offer ample protein and fiber. My pumpkin spice stacks taste nothing like lentils and everything like pillowy, lightly spiced-n'-sweetened goodness. Enjoying them feels decadent and festive, especially when they're drizzled with maple syrup and sprinkled with toasted chopped pecans. At the same time, these pancakes are chock-full of nutrition that will keep you energized and satisfied until lunch. Don't hold off 'til autumn to make these — they're amazing year-round!

⅓ cup dried red lentils

⅔ cup water

3 large eggs

2 tablespoons maple syrup

1 teaspoon vanilla extract

½ cup canned full-fat coconut milk

6 tablespoons pumpkin puree

½ cup blanched almond flour

1 teaspoon cinnamon

¼ teaspoon ground ginger (I do not recommend fresh ginger here)

½ teaspoon baking soda

Combine lentils and water in a bowl and place on the counter away from the sunlight. Allow lentils to soak overnight or 8 hours. In the morning, drain and rinse lentils (there will only be a little excess water). Add lentils and all remaining ingredients to a blender, in the order listed. Puree until smooth. This should be a fairly runny batter.

Heat a cast-iron or other nonstick skillet to medium heat. Holding your batter close to the pan, pour approximately 2 tablespoons of batter per pancake. It is really important to use a small amount of batter per pancake, or they will not cook through. Start testing pancakes to flip when they are dotted with air bubbles and the edges have begun to turn golden brown. You can use your flat spatula to gently peek underneath. Flip pancakes and cook approximately 1 to 2 minutes on remaining side.

Continue with remaining batter. Note that you might need to lower the heat as you continue to cook, as the pan will get hotter. Also note that you might have to add a tablespoon or two of butter or coconut oil to the pan if you're not using a nonstick or cast-iron skillet. Serve pancakes immediately.

SERVING SUGGESTIONS

We love these with maple syrup, coconut cream (refrigerate coconut milk can overnight, unopened; coconut cream will solidify and separate from the coconut water), butter, extra cinnamon, toasted coconut flakes, or sliced banana.

note

I often double this recipe and freeze leftover pancakes (don't top them with anything). Take a few servings out the night before you want to enjoy them, and then just lightly reheat in a pan the next morning.

crispy fried egg power breakfast
with ll's special spice mixture

V **GF** **P** | HANDS-ON TIME: *10 min* | TOTAL TIME: *15 min* | YIELD: *1 serving* | 🕐 | OPTIONS: **DF**

*T*his is my go-to breakfast when I'm in a savory mood and I want something that will keep me full, focused, and squelch any sugar cravings for the rest of the day. These eggs take less than 10 minutes total, but my Special Spice Mixture makes them taste completely gourmet and unique. Not only are the spices tasty together, but they're packed with anti-inflammatory compounds, adding to the megadose of nutrition provided in this dish. My mom had two fried eggs every morning for 8 years while running an all-girl's middle school . . . 'nuf said!

Combine spices in a small bowl. Spice mixture will keep tightly sealed at room temperature up to 2 months. This recipe makes enough for 4 servings of eggs.

Heat a small sauté pan to medium and add oil and butter (if using). When oil is slightly shimmering and butter has tiny bubbles, crack eggs into pan side by side. When cracking, hold the eggs very close to the pan to prevent the yolk from breaking. Sprinkle a thin, even layer of my Special Spice Mixture over the eggs. Cook eggs until the whites are completely opaque, then use a thin rigid spatula to turn them over. If they have cooked into one giant fried egg, separate them with the edge of your spatula before trying to flip them. If the pan starts smoking, lower the heat.

Season the second side of your eggs with another thin, even layer of spice mixture. Cook eggs to desired doneness. Gently touch the yolk to determine: If the yolk wiggles easily, they're over-easy (very runny); if it wiggles just a little, they're over-medium (somewhat runny); if they don't wiggle much, they're over-hard (not runny at all).

LL'S SPECIAL SPICE MIXTURE:

1 teaspoon sea salt

½ teaspoon paprika

½ teaspoon onion powder

½ teaspoon turmeric

¼ teaspoon black pepper

EGGS:

1 teaspoon olive oil

½ teaspoon butter
   (optional but recommended)
   (**DF** omit)

2 large eggs

SERVING SUGGESTIONS

My Special Spice Mixture is also amazing with poultry, seafood, and vegetables. I'll double or triple the batch and keep it around for when I want to amp up basic ingredients.

SERVING SUGGESTIONS

I love adding avocado, pesto, roasted tomatoes, sautéed greens, or mushrooms, or having these eggs over a piece of toast.

mexican spaghetti squash breakfast casserole

GF | HANDS-ON TIME: *40 min* | TOTAL TIME: *1 h, 45 min to 2 h* | YIELD: *6 to 8 servings* | ⊕ DF

*A*s soon as my husband finished his first portion of this breakfast casserole, he asked when I'd be making it again. Although I think most people could get 6 to 8 servings out of the dish, my husband and I usually dominate it over the course of 24 hours. Spaghetti squash is a low-calorie, water-rich vegetable that doesn't leave you feeling sluggish or heavy, so this is a great recipe if you're craving a big ole' portion. Once you whip up my Taco Spice Mixture (page 215) (or purchase some taco seasoning), this is an easy recipe to throw together, and it's a total crowd pleaser. I often make this dish when I have guests or family in town and I need to feed a lot of mouths. Prepare the casserole the night before, then bake it off in the morning. You can also make a double batch and freeze the second after cooking it, making holidays that much more relaxed.

Prepare Simple Spaghetti Squash (page 207), but do not season it.

Turn oven heat to 350° F. Prepare a 13 x 9 x 2-inch casserole dish by greasing with ½ teaspoon olive oil. Use fork to scrape the "noodles" off each spaghetti squash half into the casserole dish.

In a mixing bowl, whisk together eggs and 1 cup grated cheese. Set aside.

Heat a large sauté pan to medium heat and add 2 teaspoons olive oil. When oil moves easily around the pan, add turkey. Cook for 3 to 4 minutes, stirring and breaking into small pieces with a spatula until no pink remains. Turn off heat. Add turkey to a heatproof bowl and set aside.

(continued on next page)

1 batch Simple Spaghetti Squash (page 207), unseasoned

1 tablespoon plus ½ teaspoon olive oil

4 large eggs

1½ cups grated cheddar cheese (or more to taste)

1 pound ground turkey (recommend a mix of dark and white meat)

½ yellow onion, diced into ½-inch pieces

1 green bell pepper, diced into ½-inch pieces

1 batch Taco Spice Mixture (page 215) or 1 packet store-bought taco seasoning

1 cup low-sodium tomato-based salsa, plus more for serving

Sea salt, to taste

note

It is better to slightly underbake the squash than overbake so that the noodles hold shape in the casserole.

mexican spaghetti squash breakfast casserole *(continued)*

Add remaining teaspoon olive oil to the pan and heat again to medium. When oil is lightly shimmering, add onion and bell pepper. Cook 5 to 6 minutes or until softened and the onion is translucent, stirring every minute. Add a tablespoon or two of water as needed to prevent sticking.

Add turkey back to pan, along with the Taco Spice Mixture. Stir to mix seasoning in evenly. Turn off heat and stir in salsa. Taste for sea salt and add accordingly.

Add turkey mixture to the casserole dish and stir into spaghetti squash. Don't overflow the dish with squash; you may not need all of the noodles. Just use enough to fill up the dish. Pour in whisked egg and cheese and stir to incorporate everything together. Top evenly with remaining ½ cup cheese, or more to taste.

Bake for 1 hour, or until golden brown around the edges and the top springs back when gently pressed. Allow to cool 10 minutes before serving. Casserole will keep tightly sealed in the refrigerator up to 4 days.

note

If you have leftover spaghetti squash, you can freeze it or season with a little salt, pepper, and butter and enjoy as a side dish for other meals.

pesto chicken & spinach frittata

GF | **HANDS-ON TIME:** *20 min* | **TOTAL TIME:** *50 min* | **YIELD:** *6 servings* | ⏱ ⊕ | **OPTIONS: DF P**

I wasn't sure which chapter this frittata was best for: breakfast or entrees? Frittatas are wonderfully versatile—equally appropriate for breakfast, lunch, or dinner and delicious cold, room temperature, or warm. Plus, they're portable. Frittata—you never cease to amaze me! Pesto is one of my favorite condiments, and it pairs beautifully with chicken and spinach in this dish. Every year around December, I host a potluck brunch at my house, and I always contribute this beloved frittata.

Preheat oven to 375° F. In a large mixing bowl, whisk together eggs, milk, and pepper until fully incorporated.

Heat a large cast-iron or nonstick skillet to medium heat and add olive oil. When oil is lightly shimmering, add onion and cook, stirring every minute or so, until onion is softened and slightly golden brown around the edges—approximately 3 to 4 minutes. Add garlic powder and cook another 30 seconds, stirring.

(continued on next page)

6 large eggs

¼ cup full-fat canned coconut milk

Pinch black pepper

1 tablespoon olive oil

½ yellow onion, chopped into ½-inch pieces (approximately 1 cup onion)

½ teaspoon garlic powder

1 8-ounce bag organic baby spinach

½ cup Arugula Walnut Pesto (page 286) (sub store-bought or another homemade version)

1½ cups shredded rotisserie chicken

Sea salt, to taste

⅓ cup crumbled feta cheese (optional) (**DF** **P** omit)

note

You might have a messy skillet on your hands after this. I suggest soaking it in hot water for 20 minutes, then scrubbing with a stiff brush (but not a metal brush). If there's more residue, dry the skillet and sprinkle in ¼ cup salt to cover the surface. Use a rag to scrub salt into the skillet; this should loosen up remaining debris. Throw salt mixture away and rinse skillet with warm water, then dry.

pesto chicken & spinach frittata *(continued)*

Add spinach; turn heat to low and allow spinach to wilt. Stir every 30 seconds or so to prevent burning. You can place a lid on the skillet to help steam spinach more quickly. Wilting should only take 1 to 2 minutes, and you want the spinach to retain a bright green color but have reduced in size to where you can stir it into the onion mixture.

When spinach has wilted, add pesto (page 286) and shredded chicken. Stir to incorporate. Taste for sea salt and add accordingly (I usually add ½ teaspoon). Add egg mixture and stir carefully until evenly distributed. Sprinkle with feta cheese, if using.

Place skillet in the oven, uncovered, and bake for 20 minutes or until the top is set (bouncy but firm to the touch) and the edges are golden brown. Remove and allow to cool 10 minutes before slicing and serving. I find a flat metal spatula is best for this: I run the spatula around the rim of the frittata to loosen the edges, and then I cut it into 6 wedges. I make sure to use gentle force to scrape underneath each slice to get all the goods.

Frittata will keep up to 4 days in a tightly sealed container in the refrigerator.

OTHER VERSIONS:

Frittatas are a great for whatever you have laying around that needs to be used up. Keep the ratios of 6 eggs to ¼ cup milk to approximately 2½ cups mixed veggies and/or protein.

sweet potato & kale eggy muffin cups

Ⓥ Ⓖⓕ | HANDS-ON TIME: *35 min* | TOTAL TIME: *1 h, 10 to 15 min* | YIELD: *12 pieces* | OPTIONS: Ⓓⓕ Ⓟ

*W*hen I really love an ingredient, I make a point to use it multiple times over. Peanut butter, chocolate, avocado, and sweet potatoes are all high on my list, so they're rotating stars throughout this cookbook. Here, sweet potatoes show up as the base for these savory, portable, high-protein muffin cups. They're moist, tender, and light, and they look beautiful when served on a platter. The key to this recipe is sautéing the aromatics, spices, and sweet potato before mixing them with the eggs, because it adds a depth and richness of flavor. These cups freeze well, and I enjoy two at a time for an energizing breakfast, or one as a snack.

3 cups sweet potato, peeled and chopped into 1-inch pieces (approximately 1 medium potato)

1 tablespoon coconut oil (sub olive oil)

⅓ cup minced shallot (approximately 1 medium shallot)

3 cloves garlic, minced

1½ teaspoons sea salt

½ teaspoon black pepper

1 teaspoon sweet smoked paprika

1 teaspoon fresh rosemary, minced

2 cups fresh kale, stemmed and chopped into 2-inch pieces

12 eggs, whisked

¼ cup grated parmesan cheese (Ⓓⓕ Ⓟ sub ¼ cup nutritional yeast)

Preheat oven to 375° F and line a 12-cup cupcake tin with paper liners.

Place sweet potato pieces in a food processor and pulse until they are the texture of rice.

Heat a large sauté pan to medium heat and add coconut oil. When oil is shimmering, add shallots and garlic. Cook, stirring, until fragrant and translucent (approximately 2 minutes). Add sweet potato, salt, pepper, paprika, and rosemary. Cook, stirring, another 4 to 5 minutes, until sweet potato is soft and tender. Add kale and turn to medium-low heat. Cover pan with a lid for 2 minutes and allow kale to soften.

Remove pan from the heat and allow to cool 15 minutes. While potato mixture is cooling, whisk together eggs and cheese in a large bowl. Add cooled sweet potato mixture and whisk to combine all ingredients.

Divide mixture evenly into cupcake liners and bake for 20 to 25 minutes, or until the edges have started to pull away and a toothpick comes out clean, but the top is still moist and springy. Allow to cool 15 minutes before removing.

crispy potato, rosemary & goat cheese frittata

V **GF** | HANDS-ON TIME: *25 to 30 min* | TOTAL TIME: *40 to 45 min* | YIELD: *6 to 8 servings* | OPTIONS: **DF** **P**

I made this frittata one morning because we had a few leftover potatoes and smidgens of leftover rosemary and goat cheese. Little did I know I'd be creating one of my husband's favorite dishes — and he doesn't even like cheese! The frittata turned out so well, I knew I had to include it in the cookbook. Pan-frying the potatoes before cooking adds decadence and texture, making this recipe particularly special. As I noted with my pesto frittata, my love of this impossible-to-mess-up egg dish knows no bounds. I often make this for dinner, and sometimes I'll throw in some cooked sausage or bacon for a little extra heartiness.

Preheat oven to 350° F.

In a large mixing bowl, whisk together eggs, coconut milk, Dijon mustard, sea salt, onion powder, and black pepper. Gently stir in goat cheese (if using) and set bowl aside.

Heat a cast-iron skillet to medium-high heat and add olive oil. When oil is lightly shimmering and coats the surface of the skillet, add potato slices, trying not to overlap as much as possible.

Allow to cook without stirring for 4 minutes, or until the face-down sides have turned golden brown (you can start peeking around 3 minutes). Carefully flip potatoes and repeat on remaining side — this side should only take 2 to 3 minutes.

Add garlic and rosemary and stir into potatoes. Cook, stirring, until garlic and rosemary are fragrant and softened, approximately 1 minute. Turn heat to medium-low and pour in egg mixture. Stir to incorporate ingredients evenly, then allow frittata to cook until the sides are starting to puff and pull away from the edge of the skillet, approximately 3 minutes.

Turn off the stove and place frittata in the oven to bake for 15 to 18 minutes, or until the middle springs back when gently pressed (start checking at 15 minutes). Allow to cool 10 minutes before slicing and serving.

10 large eggs

½ cup canned full-fat coconut milk (sub unsweetened unflavored milk of choice, preferably something creamy)

1 tablespoon Dijon mustard

1½ teaspoons sea salt

1 teaspoon onion powder

¼ teaspoon black pepper

½ cup crumbled goat cheese (**DF** **P** omit, adjust seasoning to taste)

2 tablespoons olive oil

¾ pound Yukon Gold potatoes, sliced into ¼-inch-thick rounds, with larger slices split into half-moons. (I choose small potatoes because I like more skin)

5 cloves garlic, minced

1½ tablespoons fresh rosemary, minced

note

Depending on the size of your potato slices, you might need to cook them in two batches. If so, place the first round of potatoes on a plate nearby, and then add back to the pan before adding garlic and rosemary.

tempeh pecan breakfast "sausage"

V Vg | **HANDS-ON TIME:** *35 min* | **TOTAL TIME:** *1 h* | **YIELD:** *12 patties* | ⏱ DF

*T*his recipe was inspired by one of my favorite healthy spots in Nashville—The Post East. I was thrilled when I discovered that The Post East serves brunch, with items like locally sourced whole grain quiches, matcha lattes, green smoothies, and a vegetarian "sausage" patty that completely blew my mind! I ordered this "sausage" on a whim and loved it so much, I ordered two to go. I have no clue what goes into their version, but I think mine is a strong rival. Hearty, nutty, cheesy, with just a hint of sweetness, these patties are a wonderful substitute for animal protein–based sausage. My husband, the consummate carnivore, loves them as well. Rosemary always reminds me of autumn, and I particularly enjoy making my Tempeh Pecan Breakfast "Sausage" as the weather cools.

1 cup raw pecans

1 tablespoon fresh rosemary, roughly chopped

1 tablespoon plus 1 teaspoon olive oil

8 ounces tempeh, cut into 1-inch cubes

½ cup yellow onion, diced into ½-inch pieces

½ teaspoon sea salt

1 teaspoon onion powder

1 teaspoon garlic powder

½ teaspoon paprika

1 tablespoon plus 1 teaspoon low-sodium tamari

1 tablespoon maple syrup

1 cup grated semi-sharp cheese (I've used a grass-fed cheddar and a grass-fed Manchego)

1 egg

Preheat oven to 350° F and toss pecans, rosemary, and 1 teaspoon olive oil on baking sheet, ensuring that pecans do not overlap. Roast for 10 minutes, remove, and set aside to cool.

Heat a large sauté pan to medium heat and add remaining 1 tablespoon olive oil. When oil is lightly shimmering, add tempeh cubes and onions. Cook, stirring every minute or so, until onion is softened and fragrant and tempeh has a light golden color (approximately 5 minutes). You can add splashes of water if tempeh is sticking. Turn heat to low and add spices, tamari, and maple syrup. Cook, stirring another minute, until spices are fragrant and ingredients are evenly mixed.

(continued on next page)

note

I haven't made this with any other type of pan, but if you want to try, be sure to add some olive oil or other fat to the pan to prevent sticking.

tempeh pecan breakfast "sausage" *(continued)*

Allow tempeh mixture to cool 15 minutes. Add grated cheese to a large mixing bowl. When tempeh has cooled, add it to mixing bowl and stir to incorporate cheese. In a food processor, combine tempeh mixture, pecans and rosemary, and egg. Pulse until ingredients are evenly incorporated into a thick paste with texture.

Carefully remove blade from food processor. Place a small bowl of room temperature water next to your stove and heat a cast-iron or nonstick skillet to medium heat.

When you hover your hand a few inches above the skillet and feel heat, dampen your fingers with water and roll the tempeh mixture into balls approximately 2½ inches in diameter. Place balls on the skillet and flatten with a dampened spatula or your fingers to ½-inch thickness. Space balls (great movie) several inches apart so you can flip them (I only do about 4 to 5 patties at a time). Cook patties for 2 to 3 minutes on each side, until golden brown. I know they're ready to flip when the spatula slides easily under them.

Repeat with remaining balls. Serve patties immediately. Leftover patties will keep tightly sealed in the refrigerator for 4 days.

note

Cast-iron skillets get increasingly hot, so I usually end up turning the heat down to medium-low or even low after my first batch.

recipes

5

BAKERY

· ·

I am an introvert by nature. I love time with my friends and
family, but I recharge best through alone time. A few solo
hours in my kitchen (her name is Felicity), with my beloved cherry-
red pots and pans, is my idea of total relaxation. In particular,
baking is my favorite rejuvenating kitchen activity. Baking is cozy
and indulgent, all wrapped up with memories of laughter, snow
days, and weekends. My childhood was punctuated by Mom's gooey
chocolate chip cookies and her fudgy double-chocolate Bundt
cake coated in powdered sugar. I've held onto the magic of baking,
but I have updated the recipes with healthier flours, more whole-
food ingredients, and natural sugar. Each recipe in this book is a
wonderful gesture of love for yourself and your dear ones. Whether
or not you're an introvert like me, I think these decadent but
nourishing baked goods will result in deep breaths and smiles.

NOTE: Just a reminder that eggs should be room temperature
and large; if desired, you can sub chia "eggs" (see page 51), but note
that I have not tested them in all recipes.

· ·

apricot & olive oil granola clusters

(V) (GF) (DF) | **HANDS-ON TIME:** *20 min* | **TOTAL TIME:** *2 h, 5 to 20 min* | **YIELD:** *5 cups clusters; 10 servings* | **OPTIONS:** (Vg)

*T*his recipe is my take on Melissa Clark's granola from a 2009 *New York Times* Dining feature. I couldn't believe her granola featured olive oil, but after one bite I was a loyal convert. Good olive oil has a grassy, savory quality that's wonderful with the nutty and sweet granola flavors. My recipe differs from Melissa's in two main ways: 1) I use much less sugar and 2) mine is full of crunchy clusters. I prefer chunky granola over the kind you can sift between your fingers, so that each bite contains all the flavors and textures. I love enjoying my granola clusters in a yogurt parfait, or drowning in milk with fresh fruit. It's one of few recipes in this book that I almost can't stop eating when I make it—and I am A-okay with that!

Preheat oven to 275° F and line a baking sheet with parchment paper.

Add ½ cup oats to a food processor and blend until oats turn the consistency of a flour. Add nuts and pulse to roughly chop, 5 to 6 pulses.

Add oat/nut mixture to large mixing bowl, then add remaining dry ingredients, except apricots.

Add wet ingredients to a blender and puree, or whisk together in a mixing bowl.

Pour wet into dry and mix to thoroughly combine. Stir in apricots.

(continued on next page)

DRY INGREDIENTS:

2 cups rolled oats (see page 17 for oat flour instructions)

½ cup roughly chopped raw hazelnuts*

½ cup roughly chopped raw walnuts*

½ cup roughly chopped raw cashews*

2 teaspoons cinnamon

¼ teaspoon ground ginger

½ teaspoon sea salt

¾ cup dried unsulphured apricots, chopped into ½-inch pieces (can sub another dried fruit; if using something small like cherries or cranberries, use ½ cup)

WET INGREDIENTS:

¼ cup extra-virgin olive oil

2 tablespoons runny tahini paste (sub almond, peanut, or sunflower butter)

1 teaspoon vanilla extract

¼ cup honey ((Vg) sub maple syrup)

1 egg ((Vg) sub chia "egg," page 51)

*Feel free to substitute preferred nuts of choice. Just keep the total to 1 1/2 cups.

note
If you don't have a food processor, you can make oat flour in a blender and hand-chop the nuts.

apricot & olive oil granola clusters *(continued)*

Spread mixture onto parchment-lined baking sheet in an even layer. Do not leave gaps—make sure everything is touching and use the palm of your hand to press firmly down all along the surface.

Bake granola for 55 to 60 minutes if using maple syrup, or 45 to 50 minutes if using honey, until edges are golden brown and the center feels firm when pressed. Remove and allow to cool for at least 1 hour before breaking it up into chunks. Granola will keep tightly sealed on the counter for 2 weeks or in the refrigerator for 1 month.

OTHER VERSIONS

Try switching out the nuts, fruits, and sweetener with the below suggestions. Otherwise, follow the original recipe.

- Peanuts instead of hazelnuts, dried strawberries, maple syrup

- Pecans instead of hazelnuts, dried cranberries, maple syrup

- Double cashews instead of hazelnuts, dried cherries, ⅓ cup cacao nibs added to dry ingredients, honey

note

TO MAKE CLUSTERY GRANOLA:

1. Press granola together so there are no gaps and the ingredients fuse as they bake.

2. Turn some of the oats into oat flour to create extra binder.

3. Use eggs, which firm as they bake, making them a natural source of structure.

4. Allow granola to cool thoroughly.

energizing oatmeal cookies

V **GF** **DF** | **HANDS-ON TIME:** *20 min* | **TOTAL TIME:** *40 min* | **YIELD:** *18 bites*

*T*hese Energizing Oatmeal Cookies snuck into the cookbook as I was sealing up my outline. I was on my hundredth trip to Publix that week when I discovered Healthy Vegan Bite cookies from a company called Alyssa's (see note below). I purchased them out of curiosity and fell in love! I immediately set about creating something similar, which I did after six separate trials. These are one of the most beloved recipes in our home now. They're lightly sweetened, full of warming spices, sturdy with a tender crumb, and just filling enough: I have two for breakfast with a hard-boiled egg, or one spread with almond butter for a snack. I've also made ice cream sandwiches with them and my Banana Peanut Butter Elvis Ice Cream (page 333).

Preheat oven to 350° F. Line a large baking sheet with nonstick parchment paper.

Place 1 cup rolled oats and all of the oat bran in a food processor. Process until mixture forms a fine flour.

In a large mixing bowl, whisk together the flour you just made, along with remaining rolled oats, cinnamon, sea salt, baking soda, and baking powder. In a separate mixing bowl, whisk together all wet ingredients until smooth.

Pour wet ingredients into dry and gently fold with a spatula to mix evenly. Stir in chopped fruit. Keeping a bowl of room temperature water next to you, use a dampened 2 ounce ice cream or cookie scoop to form blobs of dough. Place them on the baking sheet at least 1 inch apart. If you don't have a scoop, use approximately 2 tablespoons of dough per cookie. Continually dip the scoop in water and shake off excess to help prevent dough from sticking, as this is a wet batter.

Lightly dampen fingertips and use to smooth the surface and edges of cookies. Bake for 12 to 15 minutes, until cookies are slightly firm when touched, but still soft. Cookies will be a light golden brown color. Allow to cool 5 minutes before enjoying.

Store cookies tightly sealed on the counter for 48 hours, or in the fridge for 1 week. If using out of the refrigerator, I suggest microwaving for 10 to 12 seconds, or allowing to sit on the counter for 20 minutes before enjoying.

DRY INGREDIENTS:

1½ cups rolled oats

½ cup oat bran

2 teaspoons ground cinnamon

¼ teaspoon sea salt

¼ teaspoon baking soda

½ teaspoon baking powder

WET INGREDIENTS:

6 tablespoons coconut sugar

¼ cup coconut oil, melted
(can sub olive oil; bites will have a slightly nutty flavor)

1 large egg

1½ teaspoons vanilla extract

½ plus ⅓ cup unsweetened applesauce
(I know this is a weird amount, but trust me!)

MIX-INS:

⅓ cup medjool dates, pitted and chopped into ¼-inch pieces*

⅓ cup dried apricots, chopped into ¼-inch pieces*

*Sub 2/3 cup chocolate chips or chopped chocolate for the dried fruit.

SMALLER VARIATION

These cookies are bigger than Alyssa's. If you want the nutrition to be more similar to those cookies, make them half the size (watch for a shorter baking time) and use half of the dried fruit.

fig jam crumble bars

V GF DF | HANDS-ON TIME: *30 min* | TOTAL TIME: *5 h, 15 min* | YIELD: *16 square bars*

I think this is my husband's favorite recipe from the entire cookbook, despite not being a dessert person. The classic Fig Newton combination of a barely sweet crust with the pop and crunch of fig jam is unbeatable. This recipe also took multiple rounds of testing, but as with a spouse—when you know, you know. My husband and I enjoy one or two of these bars for breakfast, as they're full of good healthy fats and relatively low in sugar. My only caveat with making these is that you might have a mutiny on your hands when they run out.

1½ cups dried Mission figs

1½ plus ½ cups rolled oats

1 plus ½ cups raw walnuts

3 plus 1 tablespoons melted coconut oil

1 large egg

4 plus 4 teaspoons maple syrup*

¼ teaspoon sea salt

½ packed cup medjool dates, pitted

1 tablespoon lemon juice

¼ cup water

1½ teaspoons vanilla extract

*Sorry for the odd number! I didn't want these bars to be very sweet, in homage to the classic Fig Newton, and this tasted perfect. Feel free to add a little more sweetener, knowing you might have to adjust the baking time.

Add figs to a bowl and cover with room temperature water. Soak 4 hours in the refrigerator, covered. Drain figs and pull off any stems. Preheat oven to 350° F and line an 8 x 8-inch baking dish with parchment paper, making sure that the paper hangs over the edges an inch or two.

In a food processor, combine 1½ cups rolled oats, 1 cup walnuts, 3 tablespoons coconut oil, egg, 4 teaspoons maple syrup, and sea salt. Process until mixture forms a dough and you can barely detect separate oat pieces (this will be sticky). Turn dough out into baking dish and pat firmly into an even layer. I dampen my fingers with water to help prevent sticking.

In food processor (no need to clean), add remaining ½ cup rolled oats, remaining ½ cup walnuts, remaining 1 tablespoon coconut oil, and remaining 4 teaspoons maple syrup. Pulse several times until mixture forms a chunky crumble. Empty in a bowl and set aside.

Wash and dry food processor. Combine figs, dates, lemon juice, water, and vanilla extract. Process until mixture forms a thick paste. Wet a rubber spatula and spread paste on top of dough, in an even layer. Top with crumble; press crumble lightly into the paste.

Place dish on the middle rack and bake for 35 minutes. Remove from the oven and allow to cool 15 minutes before removing from baking dish. Cool another 10 to 15 minutes before slicing into shapes of choice.

Bars will keep tightly sealed on the countertop for 2 days, or in the refrigerator for 5 days. Allow to sit out 20 minutes after removing from the fridge before enjoying.

SERVING SUGGESTIONS

We love these best straight from the fridge. The chill adds a delectable density and extra chew we adore.

bananas foster walnut muffins

V GF DF P | HANDS-ON TIME: *20 min* | TOTAL TIME: *1 h, 10 min* | YIELD: *12 muffins*

One of my favorite childhood desserts was Bananas Foster. Brown sugar, creamy bananas, and a splash of rum are brought to their fullest potential in a screaming hot skillet, where everything gets gooey and caramelized. These muffins are Bananas Foster in a portable, healthier form. As with any good banana bread, it is absolutely crucial to use bananas that are overly ripe. Dark and spotty is the name of the game, and don't skimp on umami-rich walnuts. I gave these muffins to my publishers to get them extra excited for the cookbook, and it worked.

Preheat oven to 350° F and line a 12-cup cupcake tin with paper liners.

Place walnuts on a baking sheet and bake 10 to 12 minutes, or until fragrant and slightly darkened in color. Remove and set aside to cool.

In a large mixing bowl, whisk together flours, baking powder, cinnamon, and sea salt.

In a separate mixing bowl, mash banana, vanilla, coconut sugar, eggs, and coconut milk until almost completely combined with very small banana pieces. You can also puree the bananas in a blender to avoid chunks in the muffins—this will yield approximately 1¼ cups banana puree.

Add wet ingredients to dry and mix thoroughly until incorporated. Chop cooled walnuts and stir them into batter. Scoop a rounded ¼ cup batter into each tin. If there is leftover batter, distribute it evenly into cupcake molds. This is a thicker batter, so use dampened fingers to even out the tops of each mold for even baking.

Bake for 25 minutes or until a toothpick comes out clean and tops are golden brown. Allow to cool 15 minutes before enjoying.

Muffins will keep tightly sealed on the countertop for 2 days or refrigerated for 5 days. If enjoying out of the refrigerator, allow to sit for 20 minutes, or microwave 30 seconds.

1 cup raw walnuts

1½ cups blanched almond flour

½ cup coconut flour

2 teaspoons baking powder

1½ teaspoons ground cinnamon

½ teaspoon sea salt

1½ cups mashed ripe banana
   (or 4 small bananas or 3½ medium)

1 teaspoon vanilla extract

½ cup coconut sugar

3 large eggs

¼ cup canned full-fat coconut milk

pumpkin spice pecan bread

V GF DF P   HANDS-ON TIME: *15 min* | TOTAL TIME: *1 h, 10 min* | YIELD: *10 slices*

*A*s soon as I started experimenting with almond and coconut flours, I knew pumpkin bread had to be on my testing list. I simply refuse to do autumn without thick slices of tender, spiced, nutty pumpkin bread. My version is even more delicious than traditional recipes, but you can feel good eating it any time of the day. My favorite way to devour this cozy loaf is toasted in the oven for a few minutes, then lashed with butter and a sprinkle of sea salt. My sweet 3-year-old niece Vivian loves this bread plain, and I respect her no-nonsense approach!

Preheat oven to 350° F and line a standard (8½ x 4½ x 2¾-inch) loaf pan with parchment paper, allowing 1 inch of parchment to hang over the sides.

In a mixing bowl, whisk together pumpkin puree, coconut milk, maple syrup, and eggs.

In a large mixing bowl, stir together almond flour, coconut flour, baking soda, cinnamon, nutmeg, and sea salt.

Add wet ingredients into dry and stir to incorporate. Stir in pecans. Empty batter into loaf pan and bake for 45 to 50 minutes or until a toothpick comes out clean. Allow to cool 10 minutes before slicing. Bread will keep in a sealed container on the counter for 24 hours, or refrigerated for 5 days.

¾ cup pumpkin puree

¼ cup canned full-fat coconut milk

½ cup maple syrup

4 large eggs

1½ cups blanched almond flour

½ cup coconut flour

½ teaspoon baking soda

4 teaspoons cinnamon

½ teaspoon ground nutmeg

½ teaspoon sea salt

⅔ cup pecans, roughly chopped

apple cinnamon coffee cake

V GF P   HANDS-ON TIME: *25 min*   TOTAL TIME: *2 h*   YIELD: *16 squares*   OPTIONS: DF

*H*ere you have all the pleasure of buttery, crumbly coffee cake, but none of the guilt. I developed this recipe on a chilly October morning, and it is truly a herald of autumn. I tune into my body as the seasons change, and I make food accordingly. That morning, my body needed something slightly indulgent and warming using my favorite fall food: crisp sweet apples. I have a square of this coffee cake for breakfast topped with yogurt, fresh chopped apples, and cinnamon. Because of the protein and fiber from coconut and almond flours, this Apple Cinnamon Coffee Cake is satisfying, and one piece does the trick.

Preheat oven to 350° F. Line an 8 x 8-inch baking dish with parchment paper, allowing 1 inch of parchment to hang over each side.

In a large mixing bowl, whisk together flours, sea salt, cinnamon, and baking powder. In a small mixing bowl, whisk together vanilla extract, maple syrup, coconut milk, and eggs. Add wet ingredients to dry and stir to combine. Fold in apple pieces.

In a food processor, combine crumble ingredients. Pulse until you reach the consistency of tiny pebbles. If you don't have a food processor, you can finely hand-chop the walnuts and mix everything together.

Empty ½ of your apple batter into the baking dish and smooth evenly with a spatula. Sprinkle half of the crumble on top. Add remaining batter and smooth, then add the remaining crumble.

Bake for 1 hour or until a toothpick comes out clean. Allow to rest for 30 minutes before removing from baking dish by pulling up sides of the parchment paper. Cut into 16 squares.

CAKE:

1¼ cups blanched almond flour

½ cup coconut flour

½ teaspoon sea salt

2½ teaspoons cinnamon

1 teaspoon baking powder

1 teaspoon vanilla extract

½ cup maple syrup

½ cup canned full-fat coconut milk

4 large eggs

2 cups red apples, peeled and chopped into 1-inch pieces

CRUMBLE:

2 cups raw walnuts

6 tablespoons coconut sugar

2 tablespoons softened butter (DF sub coconut oil)

½ teaspoon cinnamon

sylvia's blueberry bran muffins

V GF DF **HANDS-ON TIME:** *15 m* | **TOTAL TIME:** *50 min* | **YIELD:** *12 muffins*

*E*veryone needs a blueberry muffin recipe in their repertoire, and this one fell in my lap. The original version of these muffins belongs to my mother-in-law by way of her mother, and they've been a family staple for decades. In fact, my MIL has two of these muffins every single morning for breakfast! She allowed me to "balance" her recipe by switching olive oil for vegetable oil, using whole eggs instead of whites, and substituting coconut milk for skim dairy. The result is a wholesome, lightly sweetened, and tender muffin: the perfect hybrid of tradition and modern nutritional knowledge.

2¼ cups oat bran (sub oat flour, see page 17)

½ teaspoon sea salt

1½ teaspoons ground cinnamon

1½ teaspoons baking powder

3 large eggs

½ cup unsweetened applesauce

¼ cup maple syrup

¾ cup canned full-fat coconut milk (any unsweetened milk will work)

2 tablespoons extra-virgin olive oil

1 teaspoon vanilla extract

2 cups fresh or frozen blueberries

Preheat oven to 325° F and line two 6-cup or one 12-cup cupcake tin with paper liners.

In a large mixing bowl, whisk together oat bran, sea salt, cinnamon, and baking powder.

In a blender, combine eggs, applesauce, maple syrup, coconut milk, olive oil, and vanilla. Puree until smooth. You can also whisk by hand in a mixing bowl.

Pour wet mixture into dry and stir to incorporate. This is a thin batter, so expect that! Stir in blueberries. Scoop a generous ¼ cup batter into each cupcake tin, then evenly distribute any leftover batter. The cups will be almost completely full.

Bake for 23 to 25 minutes, or until muffins are mostly set but still give a little when touched (closer to 23 minutes with fresh blueberries, and 25 with frozen). Cool for 10 minutes before enjoying. Muffins keep in a tightly sealed container in the refrigerator for 5 days or in the freezer up to 2 months.

cashew tahini blender bread

V GF DF P | HANDS-ON TIME: *15 min* | TOTAL TIME: *1 h, 5 min* | YIELD: *10 to 14 slices*

*T*his recipe was actually inspired by my acupuncturist. He is from Israel, where tahini is a staple ingredient, and he ran across a grain-free tahini bread in a magazine. He didn't recall the recipe, so I promised him I'd try to make something similar. And I was smitten with the result! This is a beautifully risen, sturdy loaf with a mild nutty flavor. I treat this bread like sandwich bread, and it's incredibly versatile. You can go sweet with butter and my 20-Minute Chia Berry Jam (page 118), savory with my Arugula Walnut Pesto (page 286) and avocado, or a combination with a swipe of Whipped Goat Cheese Spread and my Fig & Olive Tapenade (page 68).

6 large eggs

¼ cup olive oil

½ cup runny tahini paste (should not be thick)

1 tablespoon maple syrup

1 teaspoon apple cider vinegar or white vinegar

1½ cup raw cashews

½ teaspoon sea salt

1¼ teaspoon baking soda

Sesame seeds (optional garnish)

Preheat oven to 350° F and line a standard (8½ x 4½ x 2¾-inch) loaf pan with parchment paper, leaving an inch overhanging the sides.

To a high-powered blender or food processor, add ingredients in the order listed. Blend, scraping the sides as necessary to incorporate ingredients thoroughly. This forms a very thick batter, so I suggest using a food processor if your blender isn't strong or doesn't come with a tamper to help the mixture move.

Empty mixture into your prepared loaf tin. Wet a rubber spatula to help smooth to an even thickness without sticking. Top with sesame seeds, if using. Bake for 35 minutes, cool 5 minutes, then use overhanging parchment to lift loaf out of the tin. Cool another 10 minutes before slicing. I personally like to slice it thinly, making about 14 slices, but slice to whatever thickness you prefer.

Allow loaf to cool completely before storing. Loaf will keep tightly sealed on the counter for 2 days or in the refrigerator for 1 week. When enjoying leftovers out of the fridge, allow to sit at room temperature for 20 minutes or warm in the oven at 300° F for a few minutes to soften.

sunflower superseed flatbread

V **Vg** **GF** **DF** HANDS-ON TIME: *15 min* | TOTAL TIME: *1 h, 10 min* | YIELD: *8 servings*

*T*here are a lot of "superfood" bread recipes out there, which are usually versions of The Life-Changing Loaf of Bread by Sarah Britton of My New Roots. But these recipes require something called psyllium husk, which I don't keep in my pantry staples. Mine is the busy/basic gal's version of Sarah's bread. It uses just seven ingredients and comes together in 10 minutes. The primary ingredient is nutritious chia seeds, because they're fantastic binding agents. This bread is amazing for your digestion, and I always have some in my freezer that I can toast up for a quick meal or snack. Energizing, nutty, hearty, and versatile, this is easily one of my favorite recipes in the book.

Preheat oven to 350° F and line a large baking sheet with parchment paper. Place oats in a food processor or blender and blend into a flour consistency. Add walnuts and process until broken down into small pieces, approximately 20 seconds.

In a large mixing bowl, whisk together oat flour/walnut mixture, chia seeds, sunflower seeds, and sea salt. In a small bowl, whisk together maple syrup and water.

Add wet ingredients to dry and quickly stir to incorporate. Use a dampened rubber spatula to spread dough into an even layer on baking sheet, approximately ¼-inch thickness. Try to form as close to rectangular shape as possible.

Bake flatbread for 40 minutes, or until the edges are golden brown and the center is firm to touch. Allow to cool 15 minutes before slicing and serving.

SuperSeed Flatbread will keep tightly sealed on the counter for 2 days, or in the refrigerator for 1 week.

1 cup rolled oats (see page 17 for oat flour instructions)

½ cup walnuts

⅔ cup chia seeds

½ cup sunflower seeds

¾ teaspoon sea salt

1 tablespoon plus 1 teaspoon maple syrup

1 cup water

SERVING SUGGESTIONS

This bread toasts beautifully. Here are my favorite ways to enjoy it:

1. Toasted with pesto, mashed avocado, and basil

2. Toasted with almond butter, my 20-Minute Chia Berry Jam (page 118), and coconut flakes

3. Spread with 1-Minute Ganache (page 341) and topped with banana slices, cacao nibs, toasted pecans, and toasted coconut flakes

chocolate banana ponderosa cake

V **GF** | HANDS-ON TIME: *25 to 30 min* | TOTAL TIME: *2 h, 15 min* | YIELD: *16 squares*

*A*nother friend-inspired recipe. My gorgeous Canadian friend Katherine mentioned a recipe from the University of British Columbia called the UBC Ponderosa Cake. This is a heavenly hybrid of banana bread and chocolate cake, and I couldn't resist creating a healthier version. It only took me one shot, where I swapped white flour for oat, refined sugar for coconut sugar, and used a mixture of butter and coconut oil. Now I understand why the UBC cake is so popular! Criminally moist and rich with layers of chocolate-cinnamon filling, I love this best on a chilly afternoon with a cup of steaming herbal tea.

Preheat oven to 350° F and line an 8 x 8-inch baking dish with parchment paper, leaving an inch overhanging the sides.

In a small bowl, combine ¼ cup coconut sugar and cinnamon. Mix and set aside.

In a large mixing bowl, whisk together oat flour, sea salt, and baking soda.

In a blender, combine coconut milk, vanilla extract, remaining coconut sugar, coconut oil, butter, egg, and banana in the order listed. Blend until smooth. Pour wet mixture into dry ingredients and use a whisk to incorporate ingredients until smooth.

Pour ½ of the batter into your prepared baking dish. Spread in an even layer. Sprinkle with ½ of your coconut sugar/cinnamon mixture, and top with ½ of your chocolate pieces. Add remaining batter to your dish, spread in an even layer, and repeat with remaining toppings.

Bake for 50 minutes, or until a toothpick comes out clean. Allow cake to cool for 20 minutes before removing from the pan. Cool another 30 minutes before slicing. I suggest cleaning your knife with a damp towel between slices to keep it from sticking and getting messy.

Cake will keep tightly sealed on the counter for 2 days, or in the refrigerator up to 4 days. To enjoy out of the refrigerator, microwave individual squares for 12 seconds, or heat in the oven at 300 ° F for 5 minutes.

¼ plus ¾ cup coconut sugar

1 teaspoon cinnamon

1½ cups rolled oats (see page 17 for oat flour instructions)

¼ teaspoon sea salt

1 teaspoon baking soda

½ cup canned full-fat coconut milk

1 teaspoon vanilla extract

¼ cup coconut oil, melted

¼ cup butter, softened

1 large egg

1 cup mashed very ripe bananas (2 large or 3 small)

1 cup semi-sweet chocolate chips

note

If you double this recipe, you might need to add an extra cup of oat flour to the dry to get the right consistency.

recipes

6

SIDES

When I'm assembling my dinner plate, I try to practice the notion of "condi-meat," where I treat meat as a condiment instead of the main attraction. Not only does this help me moderate my meat consumption, it also makes room for an array of nutrient-dense veggies, fruits, beans, and grains. I haven't quite gotten my husband on the "condi-meat" train, but it's a lot easier when he's excited about whatever else I'm making. So I make an extra effort to create flavorful, creative, and craveworthy side dishes.

Using a mixture of the spices and seasonings in my pantry staples section (page 37), I've created colorful sides to appeal to every palate, as well as something for every season: Pan-Seared Beets with Pumpkin Crumble & Lemon Yogurt (page 181), Turmeric & Tahini Roasted Cauliflower (page 189), and Grilled Asparagus with Basil Walnut Vinaigrette (page 193), to name a few. I love making a few sides on Sunday and mixing and matching them for meals during the week, topped with chickpeas, avocado, or hard-boiled eggs.

perfect oven fries two ways

(V) (Vg) (GF) (DF) (P)   HANDS-ON TIME: *15 to 20 min*   TOTAL TIME: *50 to 55 min*   YIELD: *6 servings*

J'm immediately suspicious of anyone who doesn't like fries, but I definitely prefer them homemade, when I can be sure they're not cooked in vegetable oils. The key to perfect oven-baked fries is to start them on parchment paper, then remove the parchment halfway, which helps them really puff and turn golden brown. This method never fails, and I easily make a batch of my Oven Fries twice per week. I'm an equal-opportunity potato lover, so I had to share my seasonings for both Yukon Gold and sweet potatoes. If you decide you prefer one over the other, simply make a double batch of your favorite.

Preheat oven to 400° F and line two large baking sheets with parchment paper.

In one mixing bowl, combine Yukon potatoes and Yukon seasoning and toss to coat evenly. Repeat in a separate bowl for sweet potatoes and their seasoning.

Spread Yukon potatoes evenly onto one baking sheet, sweet potatoes on the other. Bake for 20 minutes, then remove from the oven and pull out the parchment paper. Flip potatoes and bake another 15 to 20 minutes until golden brown and crispy (time will depend on the size of your fries).

FRIES:

1 pound small Yukon Gold potatoes, sliced into 1-inch-thick wedges*

1 pound small sweet potatoes, sliced into 1-inch-thick wedges*

YUKON GOLD SEASONING:

1 teaspoon olive oil

1 teaspoon sea salt

1 teaspoon dried oregano

½ teaspoon onion powder

¼ teaspoon garlic powder

SWEET POTATO SEASONING:

1 teaspoon coconut oil

1 teaspoon sea salt

¼ teaspoon cinnamon

¼ teaspoon paprika

*To cut wedges properly, start with small potatoes, which makes the process easier. Slice potatoes in half lengthwise, then place the flat sides facing down on cutting board. Cut in half again vertically, then repeat with each new half.

SERVING SUGGESTIONS

I love dipping my sweet potato wedges in my Curried Honey Mustard (page 258), and my Yukon wedges taste great in my When in Doubt Sauce (page 278) or Sesame Horseradish Mayonnaise (page 222).

crispy garlic smashed potatoes

Ⓥ ⒼⒻ Ⓟ　　HANDS-ON TIME: *25 min*　│　TOTAL TIME: *2 h*　│　YIELD: *6 servings*

𝒫otatoes + high heat + a little fat + garlic = all the good things in life. I used this magical formula when my husband and I were first dating, and he was entranced by my potato sorcery. This recipe is still one of my go-to side dishes, especially for a cozy couch date night. Classic LL Balanced comfort food at its best, the trick to this recipe is coating the potatoes in roasted garlic. Roasted garlic is truly transformative, so I suggest making it regularly to use with other cooked vegetables, meat, or rubbed onto toast with a little butter.

2 pounds baby Yukon Gold potatoes (you can use other colors, but watch boiling and baking time for slight differences)

2 plus 1 teaspoons olive oil

1 plus ¼ teaspoons sea salt

¼ teaspoon black pepper

1 large or 2 small heads garlic, ¼ inch of the pointy top sliced off to reveal all of the cloves

1 tablespoon melted butter

Preheat oven to 450° F and line two large baking sheets with parchment paper.

Bring 4 quarts (16 cups) water to a boil. Add potatoes, let water come to a boil again, and then boil 10 to 14 minutes, or until potatoes can be easily pierced with a knife (will depend on size and type of potato). Drain potatoes into a colander and allow to cool 5 minutes.

Place potatoes in a mixing bowl and toss to coat with 2 teaspoons olive oil, 1 teaspoon salt, and pepper. One by one, use a potato masher or meat mallet (or another heavy blunt object) to lightly smash each potato until it splits open but doesn't completely break apart. Place on baking sheets without overlapping. Place heads of garlic on baking sheet, exposed side up. Drizzle exposed cloves with remaining teaspoon of olive oil.

Roast potatoes and garlic for 35 to 40 minutes, or until crispy and dark golden brown around the edges. Switch the oven position of each baking sheet after 20 to 25 minutes if on different racks. You want your potatoes to be deeply golden brown, with some burnt bits around the edges. Remove from oven and carefully place garlic head(s) in a small bowl and refrigerate for 10 minutes, or until you can handle with your fingers. Squeeze cloves out of their skin into a small bowl and mash with melted butter and remaining ¼ teaspoon sea salt. Use a pastry brush or fingers to spread garlic mixture evenly over potatoes. Place potatoes back in the oven for 5 minutes, then serve immediately with dip of choice. I love them best with my When in Doubt Sauce (page 278) or Sesame Horseradish Mayonnaise (page 222).

Potatoes will keep tightly sealed in the refrigerator for 4 days.

tahini ginger mashed sweet potatoes

V GF DF P | HANDS-ON TIME: *15 to 20 min* | TOTAL TIME: *25 to 40 min* | YIELD: *6 to 8 servings* | OPTIONS: Vg

The first time I tried this unique twist on traditional mashed potatoes, I found myself saying "oh my gosh" out loud . . . and repeatedly dipping my tasting spoon back into the pot. I served it to my family that night with my Apricot & Rosemary Glazed Pork Tenderloin (page 229), and the pairing quickly became a holiday staple. Sweet potatoes, earthy tahini, and creamy coconut milk are a trifecta of nourishing awesomeness, and the result is comforting and satisfying. Although this puree tastes completely decadent, it's full of nutrition from beta-carotene, vitamin C, and calcium.

- 4 medium sweet potatoes, peeled and chopped into 2-inch pieces (approximately 7 to 8 cups)
- 1 15-ounce can full-fat coconut milk
- ¼ cup tahini paste
- ¾ teaspoon ground ginger
- 1 tablespoon plus 1 teaspoon honey (Vg sub maple syrup)
- 2 teaspoons sea salt
- ¼ teaspoon black pepper

Add sweet potatoes to a large sauce pot and cover with water completely by 1 inch. Bring to a boil and boil until sweet potatoes are fork-tender, approximately 10 to 13 minutes (from the start of boiling). Drain potatoes and place back in sauce pot.

Add remaining ingredients and blend with an immersion blender. If you do not have an immersion blender, allow mixture to cool 15 minutes, then add to a food processor in batches and puree until smooth. Add back to pot.

Turn heat to low and warm mash through, stirring, before serving. This will keep in a tightly sealed container in the refrigerator for 4 days. Potatoes will thicken as they chill. Reheat in a sauce pot with splashes of water, stirring until you achieve desired consistency and mash is warmed through.

SERVING SUGGESTIONS

I love these mashed sweet potatoes with my Curried Honey Mustard Salmon (page 258), Marinated Skirt Steak (page 222), and Perfect Marinated Chicken Breasts (page 251).

pan-seared beets *with*
pumpkin crumble & lemon yogurt

V GF | HANDS-ON TIME: *35 to 40 min* | TOTAL TIME: *55 min to 1 h* | YIELD: *4 servings* | ⏱ | OPTIONS: **Vg DF P**

I cannot do justice to the amazing flavor of this dish . . . other than to insist that you make it. Coating the beets in a pumpkin seed "flour" lends a nuttiness and crunch that is a perfect foil for tangy lemon yogurt. This recipe is so easy to make, but it truly looks like a restaurant dish—an extremely healthy one! Gorgeous ruby beets are packed with antioxidants and are used in Chinese medicine to cleanse the liver. Pumpkin seeds are a fantastic source of zinc, a common mineral deficiency, and plain, full-fat yogurt can help with digestion.

Place pumpkin seeds, sea salt, black pepper, garlic powder, and ground ginger in a high-powered blender or food processor. Pulse until seeds turn into a coarse flour. Set aside.

In a mixing bowl, whisk together yogurt, lemon zest, and maple syrup. Refrigerate.

Heat a large sauté pan to medium heat and add olive oil. When oil is shimmering, add beets in an even layer. Allow beets to sear without stirring, approximately 4 minutes, until bottoms have lightly golden edges. Flip beets to sear another side (it's okay if you don't flip them all perfectly, you just want to try to turn most of them). Cook another 3 to 4 minutes. Turn heat to its lowest possible setting and cover pan. Cook until beets are easily pierced with a fork, approximately 20 to 25 minutes.

Uncover pan and stir pumpkin seed crumble into beets. Cook another 2 minutes, stirring, or until crumble is fragrant with some golden-brown edges. You can add a splash of water to the pan to prevent sticking. Taste for salt and add accordingly. Turn beets out into your serving dish.

Remove yogurt from the refrigerator and dollop on beets. If you think you'll have/want leftovers, I suggest only putting yogurt on the individual servings instead of the whole batch, so you can reheat easily. Beets and yogurt will store tightly sealed in the fridge for 3 days.

½ cup pumpkin seeds

1 teaspoon sea salt, plus more to taste

¼ teaspoon black pepper

¼ teaspoon garlic powder

¼ teaspoon ground ginger

6 ounces plain, full-fat yogurt (approximately a rounded ⅓ cup) (**Vg DF P** sub non-dairy yogurt)

2 teaspoons lemon zest (approximately 1 medium lemon)

½ teaspoon maple syrup

2 tablespoons extra-virgin olive oil

4 cups beets, peeled and diced into ¾-inch pieces (approximately 3 medium or 2 large beets)

carrot ginger cabbage slaw

Ⓥ Ⓖ𝐅 Ⓓ𝐅 Ⓟ   HANDS-ON TIME: *15 min* | TOTAL TIME: *1 h and 15 min* | YIELD: *4 servings*   ❄   OPTIONS: Ⓥ𝗀

*T*his slaw is the perfect hybrid of classic creamy coleslaw, with modern flavors and healthier ingredients. It is nourishing and satisfying, and the flavor profile goes with any of my Asian-inspired recipes. I originally created this recipe for my teriyaki fish tacos (page 265), but it was so yummy that I decided it needed a whole page to itself. One of my favorite quick ways to enjoy this slaw is over a grilled Applegate Farms organic hot dog . . . just trust me!

Place grated cabbage and carrots in a large dish towel (one you don't mind staining). Wrap veggies and twist towel over sink to squeeze out as much excess liquid as possible—use some serious elbow grease here! Add vegetables to a large mixing bowl.

In a small mixing bowl, whisk together mayonnaise, tahini, vinegar, honey, ginger, sea salt, ginger powder, onion powder, and turmeric. Add to cabbage and carrots; add scallions, and stir everything together to evenly coat vegetables with sauce. Want it a little creamier? Stir in another tablespoon of mayonnaise and/or tahini to taste. Cover and refrigerate at least 1 hour before serving.

Slaw will keep tightly sealed in the refrigerator for 3 days. Before serving, drain any excess liquid.

2 cups grated purple cabbage*
(approximately ¼ large head)

2 cups grated carrot*
(approximately 2 medium carrots)

2 tablespoons mayonnaise
(Ⓥ𝗀 sub vegan mayonnaise)

2 tablespoons tahini paste

3 tablespoons white balsamic vinegar

2 teaspoons honey
(Ⓥ𝗀 sub maple syrup)

1 tablespoon freshly grated
ginger root

¼ teaspoon sea salt

¼ teaspoon garlic powder

¼ teaspoon onion powder

¼ teaspoon turmeric

½ cup scallions, sliced into ⅛-inch
slices (as thin as you can!)

*You can grate with a box grater, which is
a little messy but works fine, or use the
grater attachment on your food processor—
I prefer the latter.

sesame maple brussels sprouts bits

V **Vg** **GF** **DF** **P** | HANDS-ON TIME: *25 min* | TOTAL TIME: *45 min* | YIELD: *4 to 6 servings*

*R*aise your hand if you're always picking the crispy bits out of roasted veggies and hoarding them for yourself. Guilty as charged over here. When I roast Brussels sprouts, I often find myself picking out all of the crispy "shells" that have fallen onto the pan. So I decided to make a Brussels sprouts recipe that is allll about the bits. Each bite has golden-brown edges and a slightly sweet toasted sesame flavor that will have you running back for seconds.

Preheat oven to 400° F and line two baking sheets with parchment paper.

Trim the base off Brussels sprouts and slice them in half vertically, discarding/composting any outer leaves with brown spots or holes. Slice larger Brussels sprouts into quarters.

Place Brussels sprouts in a food processor and pulse until the Brussels sprouts pieces are the size of blueberries—not completely minced. It's okay if there are still some larger pieces. You might need to do this in two batches, depending on the size of your food processor.

Empty Brussels sprouts into a large mixing bowl and toss with coconut oil, sea salt, and pepper. Split mixture onto each baking sheet and spread in an even layer.

Roast Brussels sprouts for 18 to 20 minutes, or until edges are golden brown; you could roast for 25 minutes for extra-crispy. While roasting, whisk together maple syrup, sesame oil, and tamari.

When Brussels sprouts come out of the oven, drizzle each pan with ½ of the sesame oil mixture. Use a spatula to gently stir to coat evenly. Garnish as desired and serve immediately. Brussels sprouts will keep tightly sealed in the refrigerator for 3 days, but they will not be as crispy.

2 pounds Brussels sprouts, rinsed and patted dry

2 teaspoons coconut oil or olive oil

1 teaspoon sea salt

¼ teaspoon black pepper

2 teaspoons maple syrup

2 teaspoons toasted sesame oil

2 teaspoons low-sodium tamari

Sesame seeds, red pepper flakes, finely minced fresh mint, or lemon zest (optional garnish)

lemon parmesan cauliflower steaks

V **GF**   HANDS-ON TIME: *15 min*   TOTAL TIME: *40 min*   YIELD: *4 steaks*

*S*eriously . . . what can't cauliflower do? Not only can this chameleon vegetable show up as rice or pizza or "chicken" wings (ask Google), it also tastes incredible with a vast array of flavors. Here, cauliflower becomes hearty, meaty "steaks" that you can cut into with a knife and fork— incredibly satisfying. You can't go wrong with the classic combo of lemon zest and sharp, melty parmesan. This is an ideal recipe to serve a group, as it can double for a vegetarian entree, and it looks stunning. I also adore sprinkling capers or chopped black olives onto the cauliflower steaks.

2 tablespoons extra-virgin olive oil

1 teaspoon sea salt

¼ teaspoon black pepper

1 large head cauliflower

1 to 2 tablespoons lemon zest (more if you like a strong lemon flavor; approximately 1 tablespoon zest per medium lemon)

¼ pound parmesan

Preheat oven to 425° F and line a large baking sheet with parchment paper. In a small bowl, whisk together oil, salt, and pepper.

Slice off the green parts of your cauliflower stem, but leave all of the white stem intact—you need this for your cauliflower steaks to hold together. Turn the cauliflower so it is sitting on the base and slice it vertically into approximately 4 1-inch-thick steaks. Place steaks and leftover florets on your baking sheet, making sure pieces do not overlap.

Use a pastry brush to brush half of the olive oil mixture on the face-up surface of the cauliflower. Gently flip cauliflower pieces over and repeat on remaining side. No pastry brush? Just use a paper towel, or your fingers.

Roast for 25 minutes, remove from the oven, and immediately sprinkle with lemon zest and grate on copious amounts of parmesan—I let the first layer melt, then add two more layers. Cauliflower will keep tightly sealed in the refrigerator for 3 days. Note that when reheated, it won't be as crispy as the first time.

ideas for
LEFTOVER PARMESAN

Grate over my Crispy Fried Egg Power Breakfast (page 133) or into scrambled eggs.

Make parmesan cheese crisps: Lightly grease a baking sheet and spread grated parm over sheet in a thin layer. Bake 8 to 10 minutes until golden and crispy. Cool and break into pieces.

note

If all of your steaks fall apart, don't worry! Sometimes this happens, and you'll still have delicious roasted cauliflower.

turmeric & tahini roasted cauliflower

(V) (Vg) (GF) (DF) (P) | HANDS-ON TIME: *10 min* | TOTAL TIME: *40 min* | YIELD: *4 servings*

One of the most popular recipes on my blog to date, this cauliflower has become a staple in our home and in others. When calcium-rich tahini and nutritional yeast are baked, the result is a cheese-like crust that is downright addicting. I love the addition of earthy turmeric, which also adds extra anti-inflammatory power. If you love this combination as much as I do, feel free to play with the amount of tahini and nutritional yeast, after trying it once as written.

Preheat oven to 400° F and line a large baking sheet with parchment paper. In a mixing bowl, whisk together tahini, olive oil, turmeric, sea salt, nutritional yeast, and water. Add cauliflower florets and use clean hands to toss to coat evenly.

Turn florets out onto baking sheet and spread in an even layer. Roast for 30 minutes, or until fork-tender with golden-brown edges. Cool a few minutes before enjoying.

Cauliflower will keep tightly sealed for 3 days, but note that it will not be as crispy when reheated.

1½ to 2 tablespoons tahini paste (more if you want a thicker "cheese" crust)

2 teaspoons olive oil

1½ teaspoons turmeric

1 teaspoon sea salt

1 tablespoon nutritional yeast

2 tablespoons water

1 large head cauliflower, stem removed and chopped into 1½-inch florets

SERVING SUGGESTIONS

Drizzle this with sriracha to really take it to the next level.

pinewood social roasted broccoli
with almond dipping sauce

V Vg GF DF P | **HANDS-ON TIME:** *20 min* | **TOTAL TIME:** *40 min* | **YIELD:** *6 servings*

*I*t's difficult to play favorites with Nashville restaurant dishes, but Pinewood Social's broccoli appetizer is undeniably at the top of the list. It's a menu staple, and I notice it on almost every table when I'm there. Their version uses delicately fried broccoli, which of course tastes amazing, but the real magic is the addicting almond dipping sauce. This recipe was created by chef Randall Prudden, and he generously shared so I could make an LL Balanced version. Instead of frying the florets, I roast them quickly at high heat, which produces a similar crispness. I suggest eating them while hot (without burning yourself), completely smothered in sauce. If you find yourself in Nashville, you must check out Pinewood Social and order the broccoli . . . then go home and make mine!

To make Almond Dipping Sauce, combine all ingredients in the order listed in a blender. Puree until mostly smooth, but with some small pieces of almond left visible. Add to a sealable container and refrigerate.

Preheat oven to 415° F. Line a baking sheet with parchment paper.

In a large mixing bowl, toss together broccoli ingredients until evenly coated. Add to baking sheet and roast for 20 minutes, or until edges are golden brown and crispy.

Enjoy broccoli immediately with dipping sauce. Broccoli will keep for 2 to 3 days tightly sealed in the refrigerator; sauce for 1 week.

ALMOND DIPPING SAUCE:

¼ cup water

3 tablespoons white balsamic vinegar

¼ cup olive oil

1 tablespoon lemon juice

1 tablespoon plus 1 teaspoon Dijon mustard

2 cloves garlic, minced

3 tablespoons shallots, minced (scant ¼ cup)

¼ cup pitted medjool dates (approximately 3 large dates)

½ teaspoon sea salt

½ cup roasted unsalted almonds

BROCCOLI:

10 cups broccoli florets (approximately 2 crowns)

1½ tablespoons olive oil

½ teaspoon sea salt

Pinch black pepper

---

ideas for

LEFTOVER ALMOND DIPPING SAUCE

If you have leftover sauce, you can use it as a dip for any roasted or raw veggies, as a pasta sauce when thinned with some water, or even as a coating for baked chicken or fish.

grilled asparagus *with* basil walnut vinaigrette

(V) (VG) (GF) (DF) (P)   **HANDS-ON TIME:** *35 min*   **TOTAL TIME:** *45 min*   **YIELD:** *6 servings*

*T*his dish is a stunning herald to the magic of spring, with its vibrant shades of green and siren call for the grill. It is equally at home next to a big ole' steak or a delicate plate of fish, and we often make this at my family's farm to celebrate warmer days. The Basil Walnut Vinaigrette is fresh and rich, and I always save leftovers to use as a salad dressing or as a dip for raw carrots.

Preheat oven to 375° F and place walnuts on a baking sheet. Bake for 8 to 10 minutes, or until fragrant and slightly darker in color. Remove walnuts from oven and allow to cool completely, then roughly chop.

Combine all vinaigrette ingredients except ¼ cup of the walnuts in a blender and puree until smooth. Pour vinaigrette into a small bowl and refrigerate. Note that vinaigrette will thicken significantly once refrigerated. I like the thicker texture, but feel free to thin with a little water and add seasoning to taste. Makes approximately 1 cup.

In a large mixing bowl, toss together asparagus, olive oil, and sea salt. Heat a grill pan to medium-high heat and add asparagus, placing them perpendicular to the ridges on the grill (this will create nice grill marks). You will probably have to grill in two batches.

Allow asparagus to grill for 3 to 4 minutes before using tongs to flip.

Plate asparagus and garnish with remaining ¼ cup walnuts, torn basil leaves, and vinaigrette. Asparagus will keep tightly sealed in the refrigerator for 3 days, but it will not retain the same crisp texture.

ideas for
LEFTOVER BASIL

Sub basil for part of the greens in my Arugula Walnut Pesto recipe (page 286).

Add to hot tea.

Add to a pitcher of water with fresh strawberries and refrigerate overnight before straining and serving.

Toss with cherry tomatoes, sliced mozzarella, and a drizzle of balsamic vinegar.

BASIL WALNUT VINAIGRETTE:

½ cup raw walnuts

2 teaspoons Dijon mustard

¼ cup white balsamic vinegar

1 packed cup basil leaves, plus more for optional garnish

1 clove garlic, minced

½ teaspoon sea salt

¼ teaspoon black pepper

⅓ cup extra-virgin olive oil

¼ cup water

ASPARAGUS:

2 pounds asparagus, prepared (see note)

2 teaspoons olive oil

1 teaspoon sea salt

note

To get only the tender part of the asparagus, hold each end of a stalk with one hand. Bend stalk, and it will break where it becomes woody. Discard the woody end.

note

The grilling time will depend on the width/size of the asparagus and your particular grill. If you are unsure when to flip, test a few spears—turn them over and look for golden brown grill marks. Repeat on other side. Asparagus is ready when it can be easily pierced with a fork but isn't completely soft.

simple spicy garlicky greens

Ⓥ ⒼⒻ Ⓟ   HANDS-ON TIME: *15 min* | TOTAL TIME: *15 min* | YIELD: *4 servings*   🕐   OPTIONS: ⓋⒼ ⒹⒻ

*J*n my opinion, there is no more reliable side dish than properly
sautéed greens. I use kale in this particular recipe, but you
could apply the same cooking technique to Swiss chard, collards,
or dandelion or mustard greens. All boast vitamin K, a nutrient that
is crucial for proper blood clotting, fiber, antioxidants, B vitamins,
and calcium. These greens are all considered "bitter" vegetables,
which help clear detoxification pathways, stimulate metabolism
and immune function, and aid in digestion. Hints of butter, garlic,
spice, and acidity soften the astringency of leafy greens and
enhance their lovely earthiness. Whenever I'm at a loss deciding
on a side dish, I turn to these Simple Spicy Garlicky Greens.

Heat a large sauté pan to medium-low heat and add olive oil and
butter (if using). Swirl to coat pan evenly. When butter has melted
and is slightly bubbling, add garlic and red pepper flakes (if using).
Cook, stirring, until garlic is softened and fragrant, approximately
1 minute.

Add kale, reduce heat to low, and cover pan (you might have to
squish the kale in there). Allow to cook 4 to 5 minutes, or until kale
is almost completely wilted but still has some body. Uncover and
add remaining ingredients. Stir to incorporate everything together,
then remove pan from heat. Serve immediately. Kale will keep in
the refrigerator up to 3 days.

1 tablespoon olive oil

1 teaspoon butter (ⓋⒼ ⒹⒻ omit)

3 cloves garlic, minced

¼ teaspoon red pepper flakes
  (can omit)

10 ounces kale (approximately
  1 bunch), stems removed and
  leaves torn into 2- to 3-inch
  pieces (I prefer lacinato/Tuscan
  kale for this)

Scant ½ teaspoon sea salt (or start
  with ¼ teaspoon and add to taste)

Pinch black pepper

1 tablespoon fresh lemon juice

1 teaspoon balsamic vinegar

note

You could use spinach for this, but
it will cook much more quickly, so
watch your timing.

lightened-up green pea guacamole

V Vg GF DF | HANDS-ON TIME: *25 min* | TOTAL TIME: *1 h, 25 min* | YIELD: *4 to 6 servings* | ❄

We are competition-grade guacamole eaters in our household. Although I'm huge proponent of healthy fats and avocado-everything, there is such a thing as too much (with everything!). This lightened-up version is exactly how it sounds: all the flavor of guacamole but lighter, because I add lil' green peas to provide volume without extra avocado. I also use shallots and cherry tomatoes as personal tweaks that result in a brighter and slightly sweeter guacamole than you typically find. My husband tried this and immediately declared it his favorite ever.

In a large mixing bowl, combine shallot, jalapeño, tomatoes, lime juice, maple syrup, garlic powder, cumin, sea salt, and black pepper. Stir to incorporate.

Add green peas and avocado to a food processor. Pulse to form a chunky paste, or, if you like a smoother guacamole, pulse to reach desired consistency.

Empty pea/avocado mixture into bowl with tomato mixture. Stir to incorporate. Cover and refrigerate at least 1 hour before serving.

Guacamole will keep tightly sealed in the refrigerator for 2 days.

⅓ cup shallot, minced (approximately 1 large or 2 small shallots)

¼ cup jalapeño, minced (approximately 1 medium jalapeño)

1 cup sweet cherry tomatoes, quartered

3 tablespoons fresh lime juice

½ teaspoon maple syrup

¼ teaspoon garlic powder

¼ teaspoon cumin

½ teaspoon sea salt

Pinch black pepper

1 cup frozen green peas, thawed and drained of excess water

1 medium-sized ripe avocado

Thinly sliced scallions or cilantro (optional garnish)

ideas for

LEFTOVER FROZEN PEAS

Substitute for spinach or other greens in a green smoothie (seriously).

Stir into any of my soups or stews.

Toss with my Mushroom & Arugula Walnut Pesto Pasta (page 286).

Heat in a saucepan with a pat of butter, salt, and pepper and cook through for a simple, delicious side dish.

creamy green bean casserole

GF **DF** **P**   HANDS-ON TIME: *45 to 50 min*   TOTAL TIME: *1 h, 35 to 45 min*   YIELD: *6 to 8 servings*   OPTIONS: **V** **Vg**

*L*ike it or not, cream of anything soups are a Southern staple. These gloopy mixtures appear most notoriously in casseroles, as a binder and a way to add flavor without a lot of work. These cream-of-casseroles used to taste wonderful to me, but now all I taste is salt. Plus, I know that lurking within are harmful vegetable oils and modified ingredients. Two holiday seasons ago, I decided to make a healthy twist on green bean casserole, using a homemade cream of mushroom base. This casserole was so instantly popular, it has already become a staple on festive family menus throughout the year. Pops of Dijon mustard and nutritional yeast add richness, and my almond flour "crust" is a wonderful, nutty alternative to breadcrumbs.

Preheat oven to 350° F. Prepare an 11 x 8 x 2-inch casserole dish.

Fill a large stock pot with water (approximately 5 to 6 quarts or 20 to 24 cups) and bring to a boil. Add green beans and boil for 90 seconds, then drain in a colander and rinse with cold water for 1 minute. Spread green beans evenly into casserole dish.

Prepare almond crust by mixing all ingredients in a bowl.

Heat a large sauté pan (see note) to medium heat and add 1 tablespoon olive oil. When oil is lightly shimmering, add mushrooms in an even layer. Cook, stirring only once or twice, until mushrooms are starting to turn golden brown, approximately 8 to 10 minutes.

Remove mushrooms from pan and set aside on a plate. It's okay if the mushrooms have left some brown bits in the pan. Add remaining tablespoon olive oil to pan and add onions. Cook, stirring every minute or so, until softened and fragrant, approximately 3½ to 4½ minutes. Turn off heat, add minced garlic and cook, stirring, for 30 seconds.

(continued on next page)

GREEN BEANS:

1 pound green beans, trimmed of stems

1 plus 1 tablespoons extra-virgin olive oil

10 ounces sliced baby portabella mushrooms, wiped of dirt with a damp cloth

1½ to 2 cups yellow onion, chopped into ½-inch pieces (approximately 1 medium onion)

3 cloves garlic, minced

1½ cups canned full-fat coconut milk

2 cups low-sodium chicken stock (**V** **Vg** sub vegetable stock)

2 tablespoons Dijon mustard

2 teaspoons sea salt

¼ teaspoon black pepper

1 teaspoon garlic powder

1 teaspoon onion powder

1 teaspoon dried oregano

2 tablespoons arrowroot starch (sub non-GMO cornstarch)

6 tablespoons water

Chopped roasted almonds, fried onions, or garlic (optional garnish)

ALMOND CRUST:

½ cup blanched almond flour

½ teaspoon sea salt

½ teaspoon onion powder

½ teaspoon garlic powder

½ teaspoon oregano

2 tablespoons nutritional yeast

creamy green bean casserole *(continued)*

Add mushrooms back to pan, along with coconut milk, chicken stock, mustard, salt, pepper, garlic powder, onion powder, and oregano. Stir gently to combine and bring to a simmer on medium heat. Simmer for 15 minutes or until the liquid has reduced by approximately half, stirring every minute or so.

Whisk arrowroot starch with 6 tablespoons water and add to sauté pan. Stir to incorporate and cook another minute, until liquid has thickened. Remove pan from heat.

Pour mushroom mixture over green beans in the casserole dish. Stir to incorporate evenly. Top with almond crust. Bake for 30 minutes, until the crust is golden brown and the mixture is bubbling. Broil if you would like a golden crust, watching carefully to prevent burning. Allow casserole to cool 5 minutes before serving.

Casserole will keep tightly sealed in the refrigerator for 4 days.

note

Because of the amount of liquid in this recipe, you want a sauté pan that has sides at least 2½ inches high, not a shallow pan. You can also use a stock or soup pot, but watch the cook times, as they might be slightly different.

GO-TO ROASTED VEGGIES

· ·

(V) (Vg) (GF) (DF) (P)

Although most of my sides are easy to whip up, sometimes I want to keep things as simple as possible. On those days, I'll roast two large baking sheets full of veggies for the week: one for non-starchy veg and one for starchy veg. The process takes less than an hour, and I know I have flavorful, nutrient-dense additions to my meals.

When shopping, pick up approximately 1½ pounds of non-starchy veggies and 1½ pounds of starchy veggies. Each category requires its own baking sheet, as roasting times vary.

NON-STARCHY CATEGORIES

Cruciferous veg: Brussels sprouts, cauliflower, broccoli (20 to 30 minutes)

Soft veg: onions, eggplant, bell peppers, zucchini, squash, asparagus, green beans (15 to 25 minutes)

Mushrooms* (30 to 40 minutes)

STARCHY CATEGORY
(35 TO 50 MINUTES)

White potatoes

Sweet potatoes

Beets

Parsnips

Carrots

Chop all veggies into uniform-sized pieces, usually 2 inches.

Preheat the oven to 400° F. Line 2 to 3 baking sheets with parchment paper, depending on how many categories you are roasting. Add vegetables to baking sheets accordingly and in an even layer. Drizzle each sheet with olive oil (I usually use approximately 2 teaspoons per sheet), then season with salt and pepper. Use a spatula or clean hands to gently toss veggies in oil and seasoning to coat evenly, then spread in an even layer, trying to keep a little space between each vegetable.

Roast veggies until they are fork-tender and golden brown around the edges. Start checking on the early ends of the suggested times above. To reheat leftovers throughout the week, I add veggies to a baking sheet in an even layer and place in a 300° F oven for 5 to 10 minutes, until warmed through. They won't be as crispy as the first day, but they're still delicious.

asian marinated cucumber zucchini salad

V Vg GF DF P | HANDS-ON TIME: *30 min* | TOTAL TIME: *1 h, 20 to 25 min* | YIELD: *4 servings* ❄

*T*his easy and hydrating salad is one of my absolute favorites in the summer. The cool crunch of vegetables with a subtle sesame marinade is dreamy! Cucumbers and zucchinis have a high water content and are low in calories. As a result, you can eat a whole mess of 'em and feel full without feeling weighed down. These veggies are also anti-inflammatory, rich in nutrients, and can help freshen your breath.

In a large colander, combine cucumbers, zucchini, and sea salt. Toss to coat, then set aside for 20 minutes. Use clean hands to gently squeeze excess liquid out of vegetables and transfer them to a dry mixing bowl. Pat with paper towels to remove any leftover moisture.

In a small mixing bowl, whisk together remaining ingredients, except for garnishes. Pour over vegetables and toss to coat. Refrigerate mixture for 30 minutes before serving. Liquid will gather in the bottom of the bowl; drain before serving. Dish will keep tightly sealed in the refrigerator for 2 days.

2 cups thinly sliced cucumbers*
 (approximately 1 medium cucumber)

2 cups thinly sliced zucchini*
 (approximately 1 large zucchini)

1 teaspoon sea salt

1½ teaspoons maple syrup

1½ teaspoons low-sodium tamari

2 teaspoons toasted sesame oil

1 tablespoon white balsamic vinegar

1 clove garlic, finely minced

1-inch piece ginger root, finely minced

Toasted sesame seeds, scallions, or
 red pepper flakes (optional garnish)

*I use a mandolin set to 1/8-inch.

note

If your cucumber has a thick, chewy skin, you can peel it. The best cucumbers for this recipe are English cucumbers, which are sweeter with small seeds and thin skin. They usually come individually wrapped at the grocery.

note

To make toasted sesame seeds, add 2 tablespoons sesame seeds to a small sauté pan and heat to medium. Stir constantly until the seeds start to turn golden brown. Remove from the heat immediately and continue stirring, as they will continue to darken and cook.

ambrosia fruit salad *with* oat crumble

V GF | HANDS-ON TIME: *40 min* | TOTAL TIME: *10 h* | YIELD: *10 servings* ❄ | OPTIONS: Vg DF

*A*mbrosia salad is a classic Southern dessert masquerading as a side dish, as it is typically prepared with heavy cream, sour cream, and marshmallows. It tastes fabulous, but somewhat defeats the purpose of enjoying a fresh bowl of fruit. I remade this traditional dish with much less sugar, using just a touch of honey, and with hint of brightness from lemon juice and ginger. Instead of marshmallows, I made a quick crumble topping that provides wonderful texture and contrast. My mother had a few bites of my Ambrosia Fruit Salad and proclaimed, "This is going to be a hit!" Fingers crossed you agree.

Refrigerate coconut milk can overnight, unopened.

Preheat the oven to 300° F. Line a baking sheet with parchment paper. Make the crumble by adding all ingredients to a food processor and pulsing until mixture forms a crumble consistency. You should only be able to see tiny pieces of dates.

Spread crumble in a solid even layer onto your baking sheet. The less gaps you have in the mixture, the more crumble "clusters" you'll get.

Bake for 18 to 22 minutes, checking at 18, until edges are golden brown. Allow to cool while you make fruit mixture by combining fruit and lemon juice in a large mixing bowl. Toss to coat and refrigerate.

(continued on next page)

OAT CRUMBLE:

1 cup rolled oats

½ cup unsweetened coconut flakes

½ cup medjool dates, pitted

1 tablespoon coconut oil

¼ teaspoon vanilla extract

¼ teaspoon cinnamon

Pinch sea salt

FRUIT MIXTURE:

3½ cups nectarines, chopped into 1-inch pieces (approximately 3 nectarines)

2 cups mandarin orange segments (approximately 5 to 6 oranges)

3 cups pineapple, chopped into 1-inch pieces (approximately ⅔ whole pineapple—I freeze the rest for smoothies)

2 tablespoons fresh lemon juice

COCONUT CREAM MIXTURE:

1 15-ounce can full-fat coconut milk

½ cup plain whole milk yogurt (Vg DF sub dairy-free yogurt)

1½ tablespoons honey (Vg sub maple syrup)

1 teaspoon freshly grated ginger

ambrosia fruit salad *with* oat crumble *(continued)*

Now begin the coconut cream mixture. Open refrigerated canned coconut milk. The coconut cream should have solidified and separated from the coconut water. Scoop out coconut cream into a blender. Save coconut water for smoothies. Add yogurt, honey, and ginger to blender as well. Puree until smooth.

Remove fruit from refrigerator and pour coconut cream mixture over fruit. Toss to coat evenly. Stir in crumble topping. Cover bowl and refrigerate 1 hour before serving. Salad will keep tightly sealed in the refrigerator for 3 days, but note that the crumble will soften over time.

note

The crumble will soften over time, which I actually like. If you want it to maintain a crunchy texture, keep crumble separate and add at the time of serving.

OTHER VERSIONS:

Alternatively, use 8½ cups of any fruit mixture you like. Try strawberries, peaches, grapes, mango, and apples.

easiest fluffy quinoa

GF DF HANDS-ON TIME: *5 min* TOTAL TIME: *20 to 25 min* YIELD: *4 servings* OPTIONS: V Vg

*Q*uinoa is my go-to when I want to add nutritious, fiber-rich carbohydrates to a dish. It is also a fantastic source of plant protein, containing all nine essential amino acids. Properly cooked quinoa is light and fluffy, with just slight textural bite. It soaks up flavors beautifully, and it pairs with almost anything. Often, I double this recipe and keep a batch of quinoa handy to nosh on throughout the week with whatever else I can find. The key to perfectly cooked quinoa is patience and a super-low heat setting. Feel free to get creative with this basic recipe and add whatever spices and seasonings you love best.

1 cup quinoa

2 cups water or low-sodium chicken stock (V Vg sub vegetable stock)

½ teaspoon sea salt

To rinse quinoa, place quinoa in a mesh strainer or colander and run under water, using your hand to make sure bottom layer of quinoa is rinsed as well. You want to run the water until there are no small foamy bubbles and the water runs clear, approximately 1 to 2 minutes. Allow to drain.

Add quinoa and water or stock into a sauce pot (at least 2 quarts in size). Stir in salt. Bring to a boil and then reduce to a simmer on the lowest possible setting. Cover pot with a lid and simmer for 15 to 22 minutes, or until the liquid has evaporated. Remove pot from the heat but keep covered. Allow to sit 5 minutes, then uncover and fluff with a fork.

Leftovers will store tightly sealed in the refrigerator for 4 days.

simple spaghetti squash

V GF P HANDS-ON TIME: *15 min* TOTAL TIME: *55 min to 1 h, 20 min* YIELD: *4 servings* OPTIONS: Vg DF

*S*paghetti squash is a delicious low-carb, grain-free alternative to noodles, and a great side dish in its own right. Plus, it's incredibly versatile, taking on whatever flavors you choose to pair it with. Give this easy preparation a try and find out for yourself!

1 medium spaghetti squash

1 teaspoon sea salt, plus more to taste

½ teaspoon black pepper, plus more to taste

2 tablespoons butter (Vg DF sub olive oil)

Preheat oven to 400° F. Carefully, slice squash in half lengthwise, and place flesh side down on a baking sheet. Bake for 25 minutes, or until the skin gives slightly to the touch, then allow to cool 15 minutes. Using a fork, scrape out the seeds on the inside of each half. Alternatively, if you're having trouble slicing your squash in half, bake for around 45 minutes, then allow to cool 20 minutes before slicing.

After seeds are removed, use fork to scrape the remaining "noodles" off each half into a large bowl. Add salt, pepper, and butter and stir until butter is incorporated throughout. Taste and add salt and pepper as you like. Set aside.

baked coconut rice

(V) (GF)   **HANDS-ON TIME:** *10 to 15 min* | **TOTAL TIME:** *1 h, 15 to 20 min* | **YIELD:** *6 to 8 servings* | **OPTIONS:** (Vg) (DF)

*C*onfession—cooking rice is not my strong suit. For some reason, I never quite get the ratios and timing right when I make rice in a sauce pot. Thus, I developed this foolproof method that avoids common rice pitfalls. Baking rice in liquid, covered, ensures that every single grain is moist, tender, and fluffy. This flavor version is my absolute favorite, as coconut milk infuses a rich, slightly sweet flavor into every grain.

Preheat oven to 375° F. Grease an 8 x 8-inch baking dish with coconut oil or butter. Add rice to dish.

In a small sauce pot, combine coconut milk, water, and sea salt. Stir to combine. Cover and heat to medium-high. Check every minute or so, and as soon as liquid comes to a rapid simmer (more than small bubbles but less than a rolling boil), pour over rice. Stir and cover dish tightly with aluminum foil. It is key to make sure the dish is wrapped tightly.

Bake rice for 65 minutes. Remove and uncover, fluffing with a fork. Stir in toasted coconut flakes and serve immediately. Be mindful of the hot dish. Use a butter knife to scrape off any rice that sticks to the sides and mix it in—these are the best pieces! Rice will keep tightly sealed in the refrigerator for 5 days.

1 teaspoon softened butter
  ((Vg) (DF) sub coconut oil)

1½ cups medium grain white
  rice, uncooked

1½ cups canned full-fat coconut milk

1 cup water

1 teaspoon sea salt

⅓ cup toasted coconut flakes
  (see note)

note

To make toasted coconut flakes, add coconut to a small saucepan and heat to medium. Stir constantly. As soon as flakes start turning a golden brown, remove pan from heat and continue stirring 30 seconds, before scraping flakes into a heatproof container.

LUNCH & DINNER ENTREES

······························

*T*hese recipes are authentic representations of what I cook
at home. I love using 100% grass-fed ground beef—when it
goes on sale, I stock up and throw anything I won't use that week
into the freezer. I've also recently started using ground lamb,
and my Lamb Burgers with Addictive Tahini Sauce (page 230)
are easily one of my favorites from the book. Using a free-range
rotisserie chicken is another great shortcut to help busy cooks
get a meal on the table. I keep my seafood recipes bright and
rich, with ingredients like citrus, honey, and garlic, and focus
on classics with an LL Balanced twist; the seafood section is
full of unique but familiar flavors, making perfect icebreakers
for those who might be more hesitant about seafood. Lastly, the
veggie entrée section is for everyone, even carnivores. I am a fan
of tempeh, a fermented whole-foods form of soy, so you'll see it
appear. Here's hoping a few of these easy and flavorful recipes
become household staples for your family!

······························

red meat

....

When I cook red meat, I rarely use fancy cuts like rumps or roasts. As I mentioned, I use grass-fed ground beef often, as it is incredible versatile. I love having a repertoire of recipes that start with the same ingredient but yield different results. In this chapter, ground beef turns into tacos, meatballs, and a Mexican-flavored Bolognese.

Grass-fed and pasture-raised meat is, quite literally, a different animal from its industrial counterpart. As a result, it requires its own cooking techniques. Slapping pasture-raised steak on the grill will leave you with a chewy mess, but a few hours of marinating will transform it. Try my Marinated Skirt Steak with Sesame Horseradish Mayonnaise (page 222) or Beef & Veggie Stir Fry (page 225) to see for yourself!

I am particularly proud of this section, and I hope you enjoy incorporating these recipes into your dinner rotation as much as I enjoyed creating them.

....

the best 15-minute taco meat

GF **DF** | **HANDS-ON TIME:** *15 min* | **TOTAL TIME:** *15 min* | **YIELD:** *4 servings* | 🕐 | **OPTIONS:** **P**

*G*rowing up, my mom's tacos were a regular in the dinner rotation. What made them so special? I'm convinced it was the heavy hand Mom used with that packaged seasoning. At first, the meat looked like it was drowning in spices, but slowly it began to absorb the flavors, creating a rich, satisfying filling. I wanted to share this taco experience with my husband, but with a homemade seasoning free from excess sodium and preservatives. This recipe is also super versatile—we enjoy it over salads, pasta, or tossed with rice.

Combine all ingredients for Taco Spice Mixture in a small bowl and whisk to incorporate. You can double or triple the batch and store leftovers in a tightly sealed container up to 1 month.

Begin preparing the taco meat. Heat a large skillet to medium heat and add olive oil (you can also use a cast-iron or nonstick skillet and eliminate the oil). When oil flows easily over the pan, add ground beef. Use a turner spatula to break up the beef into small pieces. Cook, stirring occasionally, until meat has only a small amount of pink remaining (approximately 3 minutes).

Add Taco Spice Mixture, turn heat to low and carefully stir to incorporate seasoning onto the meat. Cook another minute to remove any remaining pink. Turn off heat, take pan off stove, and allow to cool 2 to 3 minutes before scooping into tacos.

SERVING SUGGESTIONS

Top with shredded lettuce, sliced cherry tomatoes or salsa, avocado, cilantro, lime juice, plain full-fat yogurt (a delicious substitute for sour cream), black beans, or shredded cheese. We also love to make taco salads with this meat. Chop up a bunch of romaine lettuce, toss with a little bit of olive oil and white balsamic or apple cider vinegar, and top with taco meat and other garnishes of choice.

TACO SPICE MIXTURE:

2¼ teaspoons paprika

2¼ teaspoons chili powder

2 teaspoons onion powder

1 teaspoon garlic powder

1¼ teaspoons cumin

1 teaspoon dried oregano

1½ teaspoons sea salt

1 tablespoon coconut sugar (sub light brown sugar)

MEAT:

2 teaspoons extra-virgin olive oil

1 pound ground beef (recommend 85/15 meat/fat ratio)

ASSEMBLY:

Taco shells (**P** omit)

Toppings of choice

SUGGESTED SIDES

Lightened-Up Green Pea Guacamole (page 197)

Asian Marinated Cucumber Zucchini Salad (page 203)

meatloaf meatballs & simple spaghetti squash

| GF DF | HANDS-ON TIME: *40 min* | TOTAL TIME: *1 h, 10 min* | YIELD: *6 servings* | ⊕ | OPTIONS: P |

I can't say this is the most glamorous-sounding recipe in the world, but oh my is it good! This is also a little more labor-intensive than some other dishes, but it makes a lot of food and freezes beautifully. Plus, there is always leftover sauce in the pot that I save for when I need a quick pasta sauce. These are beloved by men and women, young and old alike. There's never a meatball left standing when I make them for a group. This is everything LL Balanced is about—flavorful comfort dishes made with quality whole foods.

To make the sauce, combine all ingredients in a blender and puree until smooth. Set aside. Prepare Simple Spaghetti Squash (page 207).

To make meatballs, in a large mixing bowl, combine bread with almond milk. Allow to soak 10 minutes, then drain remaining almond milk.

While bread is soaking, heat a sauté pan to medium and add 1 tablespoon olive oil. When oil moves easily around the pan, add onion and sauté 4 to 5 minutes, stirring, until translucent and fragrant. Add garlic and sauté another 30 seconds, stirring. Remove from heat and set aside to cool at least 5 minutes (they must be cool enough to touch so they can be mixed into the meatball mixture.

(continued on next page)

SAUCE:

1 28-ounce can organic crushed tomatoes in sauce

1 6-ounce can tomato paste

2 tablespoons molasses

2 tablespoons coconut sugar

1 tablespoon Dijon mustard

1 teaspoon sea salt

2 tablespoons low-sodium tamari

1 cup water

MEATBALLS:

1 batch Simple Spaghetti Squash (page 207)

3 slices sandwich bread (don't use something really dense and grainy) (P sub paleo bread)

¾ cup unsweetened almond milk (sub milk of choice)

1 plus 2 tablespoons olive oil

2 cups onion, diced into ½-inch pieces (approximately 1 medium sweet onion)

3 cloves garlic, minced

2 pounds grass-fed ground beef (I use 85/15)

2 large eggs

1½ teaspoons dried oregano

2 teaspoons dried basil

2 teaspoons sea salt

1 teaspoon black pepper

meatloaf meatballs & simple spaghetti squash *(continued)*

In the bowl that contains the bread, add beef, eggs, oregano, basil, sea salt, and pepper. Add onion/garlic mixture. Use clean hands to incorporate everything together well.

Heat a large wide pot to medium-high heat and add remaining 2 tablespoons olive oil. When oil begins shimmering, use hands to form meatballs approximately 2½ inches in diameter, placing them in the pot as you go. Pack them tightly in your palm so they don't fall apart. Place meatballs in pot side-by-side and allow to sear, approximately 3 to 4 minutes. Flip using a spatula and sear other side. You might need to sear the meatballs in two batches, depending on the size of your pot. If so, place several paper towels on a large plate. Place first batch of seared meatballs on the plate while you sear the rest.

If you seared in two batches, place first batch gently back into the pot. Add sauce to pot, cover, and simmer for at least 20 minutes and up to 1 hour. Serve over my Simple Spaghetti Squash noodles. Meatballs will keep in a tightly sealed container in the refrigerator for 4 days or frozen for 1 month. You can also save leftover sauce and freeze separately for when you need a quick pasta sauce.

SUGGESTED SIDES

Pinewood Social Roasted Broccoli with Almond Dipping Sauce (page 190)

Simple Spicy Garlicky Greens (page 194)

Husband-Favorite Salad with Cucumber Mint Dressing (page 303)

note

After you have seared meatballs, you can take them all out and drain excess fat. I personally keep the fat in the pot for flavor, but draining is an option.

quinoa lentil pizza crust two ways *with* 10-minute new york chunky pizza sauce

(V)* (GF)* (DP)* | HANDS-ON TIME: *25 min* | TOTAL TIME: *7 h* | YIELD: *2 pizzas* | ⊕ ◊ | OPTIONS: (Vg)*

Symbols apply to crust and sauce recipes only.

This pizza crust is just everything. It holds together perfectly, is easy as (pizza) pie to make, and it tastes incredible. I'll never forget the night I nailed this recipe. I took the pizzas out of the oven, tingling with anticipation to photograph them. All of a sudden, a thunderstorm swept over Nashville and my lighting disappeared. Undaunted, I flung open the porch door and turned our stone patio into my "set." And the pictures turned out wonderfully! Feel free to play around with whatever toppings you like best; the crust holds up well to most veggies and meat.

To make the crust, add quinoa and lentils to a large bowl and cover with at least 1 inch of water. Soak 6 to 8 hours, then drain in a fine-mesh colander (one that the quinoa won't fall through), rinsing thoroughly with cold water until the water runs clear.

To make the pizza sauce, heat a large sauté pan to medium heat. Add olive oil and garlic and cook, stirring constantly, until garlic is fragrant (approximately 20 seconds). Add remaining ingredients and turn heat to low. Cook, stirring, 3 to 4 minutes to heat ingredients thoroughly. Taste for salt and pepper. Will keep refrigerated in a tightly sealed container for 1 week, or frozen for 3 months. This recipe makes approximately 2 cups. Double the sauce recipe if you want both pizzas to be pepperoni, or you like a lot of sauce on your pizza.

Preheat oven to 425° F and line two baking sheets with parchment paper. Grease each piece of parchment paper with 1 teaspoon olive oil.

Now, complete the crust. Add quinoa, lentils, ½ cup water, remaining ¼ cup olive oil, salt, and pepper to a food processor and puree until completely smooth, approximately 5 minutes. Scrape down the sides as necessary with a spatula.

Turn half of your dough (2 rounded cups per pizza) onto the center of each baking sheet. Use a spatula to spread in a thin, even layer, approximately ¼-inch thick.

(continued on next page)

QUINOA LENTIL PIZZA CRUST:

1½ cups quinoa

1 cup dry red lentils

½ cup water

¼ cup plus 2 teaspoons extra-virgin olive oil

1½ teaspoons sea salt

¼ teaspoon black pepper

10-MINUTE NEW YORK CHUNKY PIZZA SAUCE:

2 tablespoons extra-virgin olive oil

2 to 3 cloves garlic, minced

1 15-ounce can diced tomatoes

1 6-ounce can tomato paste

1 teaspoon sea salt

¼ teaspoon black pepper

½ teaspoon red pepper flakes

1 tablespoon dried oregano

1 teaspoon onion powder

2 teaspoons honey
((Vg) sub maple syrup)

⅓ cup fresh basil, roughly chopped, or 1 teaspoon dried basil (optional)

note
I have an 11-cup food processor. If yours is smaller, you may need to puree in batches.

note
This is more of a batter than a dough, and it should be liquidy.

quinoa lentil pizza crust two ways *with* 10-minute new york chunky pizza sauce *(continued)*

Bake crust for 18 minutes, or until it is solid to touch and golden brown around the edges. Remove from the oven and turn heat to 450° F. Allow crust to cool 5 minutes, then add pizza toppings (see versions). Bake for 13 to 15 minutes, or until the cheese is melted completely and bubbling. Remove from oven and allow to cool another 5 minutes before slicing. Pizza will keep tightly sealed in the refrigerator for 3 days.

SUGGESTED SIDES

Perfect Oven Fries Two Ways (page 174)

Grilled Asparagus with
Basil Walnut Vinaigrette (page 193)

PEPPERONI VERSION:

Amounts are for 1 pizza; double if you want both to be pepperoni.

10-Minute New York Chunky Pizza Sauce to taste

8 ounces fresh mozzarella, sliced into ¼-inch-thick rounds

1 cup grated grass-fed cheddar cheese

3 ounces pepperoni

¼ cup black olives, sliced into ¼-inch-thick rounds

Red pepper flakes, to taste

Spread a thin layer of pizza sauce on crust, leaving 1 inch open around the edges. Hand-shred mozzarella slices and place over sauce, then sprinkle on grated cheddar. Top with an even layer of pepperoni, olives, and red pepper flakes (if using). There might be some liquid on top of the pizza from the fresh mozzarella after pizza is finished baking; just dab it off with a few paper towels.

PROSCIUTTO ARUGULA VERSION:

Amounts are for 1 pizza; double if you want both to be prosciutto.

1 batch Arugula Walnut Pesto (page 286)

¾ cup shredded mozzarella

4 ounces goat cheese

4 ounces prosciutto

1 cup fresh arugula

Spread a thin layer of pesto on crust, then sprinkle on mozzarella. Dollop with goat cheese and add prosciutto slices to taste. Add fresh arugula after pizza is finished baking.

marinated skirt steak *with* sesame horseradish mayonnaise

GF DF P | HANDS-ON TIME: *25 min* | TOTAL TIME: *2 h, 35 min* | YIELD: *4 to 6 servings* ❄

My husband is a classic carnivore, and we joke that he could happily subsist on meat, bourbon, and fruit (go figure). For his birthday every year, Max requests steak and a baked potato, so I decided to use his recent birthday to create something cookbook-worthy. The marinade and sauce for this skirt steak were inspired by delectable recipes my mother used throughout my childhood, and they are completely foolproof. The result is deeply flavorful meat, and the Sesame Horseradish Mayonnaise would taste good on a boot (do not try this at home!). Needless to say, my husband was a happy birthday boy, and I have a feeling this will be repeated next May.

Combine the steak and the marinade ingredients in a gallon food storage bag and squeeze out excess air. Seal tightly and shake to mix everything together. Refrigerate for 2 to 4 hours.

Make the Sesame Horseradish Mayonnaise by whisking ingredients together in a mixing bowl. Cover and refrigerate for at least 1 hour before serving. Mayonnaise will keep tightly sealed in the refrigerator up to 3 days. Recipe makes approximately ½ cup.

When meat has finished marinating, heat a grill pan to high heat and brush with coconut oil. When oil is lightly smoking, pull meat out of the bag with tongs, shaking the excess marinade off. Discard marinade. Place meat on grill perpendicular to grill marks.

Grill steak for 4 to 6 minutes on each side, or until it reaches desired doneness. Gauge doneness by using the finger test (see note).

Allow meat to rest 10 to 15 minutes before slicing against the grain into ¼-inch-thick slices. Serve with Sesame Horseradish Mayonnaise.

note

To use the finger test for meat doneness, start by opening a hand and relaxing it. Press the ball of your thumb with a finger from your other hand. See how soft that feels? That is what a raw steak feels like. For all donenesses, you will be testing by touching the indicated fingers together, then pressing the ball of the thumb with your other hand's index finger. **Rare:** Thumb and index finger; **Medium-rare:** Thumb and middle finger; **Medium:** Thumb and ring finger; **Well-done:** Thumb and pinky

STEAK:

1½ pounds flank steak (sub skirt or flat iron steak)

1 teaspoon coconut oil (sub butter)

ANY MEAT MARINADE:

6 tablespoons low-sodium tamari

6 tablespoons fresh lime juice (approximately 3 to 4 limes)

3 tablespoons coconut sugar

5 cloves garlic, peeled and roughly chopped

SESAME HORSERADISH MAYONNAISE:

¼ cup mayonnaise

1 tablespoon low-sodium tamari

1 tablespoon honey or maple syrup

1 clove garlic, minced

1 tablespoon horseradish

½ teaspoon freshly grated ginger root (optional)

1¼ teaspoons toasted sesame oil

SUGGESTED SIDES

Crispy Garlic Smashed Potatoes (page 177)

Turmeric & Tahini Roasted Cauliflower (page 189)

beef & veggie stir fry

GF DF | HANDS-ON TIME: *40 min* | TOTAL TIME: *1 h, 40 min* | YIELD: *4 to 6 servings* ❄ | OPTIONS: P

I've made this stir fry more than almost any recipe in this entire book. It's often requested in the classes I teach, and it's also a hit during our Sunday night family dinners. This stir fry covers all of the bases—savory, a touch sweet, indulgent-tasting, but packed with veggies. I always feel like I've treated myself to something special after a bowl of my Beef & Veggie Stir Fry. It's also a one-pot meal, which is always a bonus. My favorite way to serve this stir fry is with my Baked Coconut Rice (page 208). So good! I could go for a bowl right now . . .

Combine sauce ingredients in a mixing bowl. Whisk to combine. Place sirloin slices in a large plastic food storage bag and add half of the sauce. Seal and shake. Marinate for 1 to 3 hours.

Heat a large sauté pan or wok to medium-high heat. Add coconut oil. When oil is shimmering, use tongs to add sirloin from bag to pan, saving the marinating juice. Allow to sear, approximately 1 minute per side. Remove sirloin from pan and deglaze with a few tablespoons of water, scraping the brown bits at the bottom of the pan. Turn heat to medium-low heat.

Add vegetables to the pan, as well as marinating juice, remaining ½ batch of sauce, and sea salt. Stir to combine and cook for 4 to 5 minutes or until veggies are al dente, retaining some crispness. Add sirloin back into pan and cook mixture another 2 to 3 minutes. Turn heat to the lowest setting. In a small bowl, whisk together arrowroot starch and 1 tablespoon water. Add to pan and stir until liquid thickens, approximately 1 minute.

Serve stir fry over my Baked Coconut Rice (page 208), or whatever else you like. Top with desired garnish. Stir fry will keep tightly sealed in the refrigerator for 4 days, or frozen up to 2 months.

SAUCE:

3 cloves garlic, minced

1 teaspoon freshly grated ginger root

¼ cup toasted sesame oil

6 tablespoons low-sodium tamari

3 tablespoons maple syrup

¼ cup apple cider vinegar

¼ cup peanut butter
　(P sub tahini or almond butter)

½ cup water

BEEF:

1½ pounds sirloin, sliced against the grain into ½-inch-thick pieces (sub flank, skirt, or flat iron steak)

2 tablespoons coconut oil

VEGGIES:

2 cups purple cabbage, sliced into 1-inch ribbons (sub green cabbage, kale, collards, or bok choy)

2 cups sliced bell peppers of choice

1 red onion, sliced into ¼-inch-thick half-moons (sub thinly sliced carrot)

½ teaspoon sea salt

1 tablespoon arrowroot starch (sub non-GMO cornstarch)

Sliced scallions (optional garnish)

SUGGESTED SIDES

Tahini Ginger Mashed Sweet Potatoes (page 178)

Baked Coconut Rice (page 208)

mexican slow cooker bolognese

GF DF P | HANDS-ON TIME: *5 min* | TOTAL TIME: *3 or 6 h* | YIELD: *4 servings*

This recipe is a dinner Hail Mary if there ever was one. Five ingredients, one dish: set it and forget it. And the outcome is a supremely tender, flavorful, and versatile meat sauce. This "Bolognese" is just as comfortable Italian-style over pasta as it is heading south of the border into a taco. In the winter, I make this at least once per week for my husband, who loves to sneak little bites from the slow cooker and the fridge. This dish is also freezer-friendly, so it's a great recipe for new moms or busy anybodies. I hope this dish makes your life a little easier and tastier!

Add all ingredients to a slow cooker and mash together to incorporate. Cover and cook on low for 6 hours or high for 3 hours. Stir every few hours if possible (not mandatory). Taste for salt and add as you like. If there is excess liquid/fat pooling around the sides, drain this into a glass container and allow to cool before throwing away (do not pour grease down sink drain). Serve over pasta, rice, vegetable noodles, in tacos, or on a salad.

Mexican Bolognese meat will keep tightly sealed in the refrigerator for 4 days. This also freezes for up to 2 months.

VEGGIE VERSION:

Sometimes I'll mix in vegetables in the last hour to 30 minutes of cooking, such as fresh kale or spinach, zucchini, thinly sliced carrots, or small broccoli florets. Check every 15 minutes to test doneness.

1 pound 90/10 ground beef

1½ cups low-sodium tomato-based red salsa

1 teaspoon paprika

½ teaspoon onion powder

1 tablespoon molasses

Salt to taste (optional)

> **SUGGESTED SIDES**
> Lemon Parmesan Cauliflower Steaks
> (page 186)

apricot & rosemary glazed pork tenderloin

GF DF P | HANDS-ON TIME: *15 to 20 min* | TOTAL TIME: *55 min to 1 h* | YIELD: *6 to 8 servings*

*T*enderloin is a tricky meat to work with, because it's so lean that it dries out in a snap. When it's cooked correctly, though, it is an absolute dream to enjoy—especially when it is coated with my apricot, rosemary, and garlic glaze, which I could happily eat with a spoon. With this recipe, a meat thermometer is your only surefire way to have a successfully tender-loin, as each is a different thickness. Don't want to add another gadget to the mix? Your best bet is to slice into one of the end pieces around minute 30. This will cook faster than the middle, so when it's completely cooked through, you probably need another 3 to 4 minutes for the center. Whatever method you choose, this recipe is WORTH IT! The glaze bubbles and caramelizes, creating the perfect sweet-savory coating for this simple cut of meat. Everything about this dish exclaims holiday, family, and contentment.

- ¼ cup plus 1 teaspoon olive oil
- 2 pounds pork tenderloin, silver skin removed (ask your butcher to do this)
- ½ cup dried apricots, soaked in hot water for 10 minutes then drained
- 10 cloves garlic, roughly chopped
- ¼ cup fresh rosemary leaves (pulled off the stems)
- 2 tablespoons low-sodium tamari
- ¼ teaspoon sea salt
- ¼ teaspoon black pepper

Preheat oven to 350° F and grease a shallow baking dish with 1 teaspoon olive oil. Place tenderloin in the baking dish; if you have more than one, place them side by side, lengthwise.

In a food processor, combine apricots, garlic, rosemary, tamari, sea salt, black pepper, and remaining ¼ cup olive oil. Pulse until mixture forms the consistency of a thick jam. Make sure to pulse well; you don't want to see any visible pieces of rosemary.

Use a dampened spatula to evenly coat the tenderloins with the apricot mixture.

Roast tenderloins for 30 minutes, or until your meat thermometer reads between 150 and 160° F in the thickest part of the tenderloin (start checking at 25 minutes). 150° F = medium-rare; 160° F = medium.

Allow tenderloins to rest 10 minutes before slicing (this is crucial). Meat will keep tightly sealed in the refrigerator for up to 4 days.

SUGGESTED SIDES

Creamy Green Bean Casserole
(page 198)

Roasted Fennel, Orange &
Wild Rice Salad (page 296)

SERVING SUGGESTIONS

We love the leftover tenderloin cold, sliced over arugula, with a simple mixture of white balsamic vinegar and olive oil.

lamb burgers *with* addictive tahini sauce

GF P | **HANDS-ON TIME:** *20 to 30 min* | **TOTAL TIME:** *1 h* | **YIELD:** *6 burgers* | **OPTIONS:** DF

Oh mercy, these lamb burgers. If you haven't cooked much with lamb, this is THE recipe to start with. Pasture-raised lamb is tender and mild, and it is an amazing source of valuable fatty acids and vitamin B12. It is also increasingly available at the grocery stores, if you keep an eye out for it. And you must so that you can make these lamb burgers, which are easily one of my favorite recipes in the book. They are as juicy and flavorful as burgers get, with my "secret" tricks of adding egg, almond flour, and tahini. I always double this recipe and freeze leftover patties. It's such a treat to pull two (or four) out of the freezer the night before a busy day and be excited for my pre-made dinner!

Preheat oven to 400° F. Grease a slotted baking sheet with olive oil.

If making the tahini sauce, place all ingredients in a high-powered blender and puree until smooth. After thickening in the fridge, the sauce will have a spreadable consistency similar to ketchup. Add an amount of water that creates a creamy dressing consistency when mixing everything together. Refrigerate for 30 minutes before serving. Sauce will continue to thicken in the fridge for the next day and will keep tightly sealed in the refrigerator up to 5 days. This recipe makes approximately ¾ cup.

Combine all remaining burger ingredients in a large mixing bowl. Dampen clean hands with water and use fingers to mix evenly.

Form eight balls from lamb mixture (a rounded ½ cup). Place on slotted baking sheet, then press into a patty shape approximately 3½ inches wide and ¾ inch high. Repeat with remaining lamb mixture.

Cook burgers in the oven for 23 to 25 minutes, or until they are lightly golden on top and feel semi-firm to touch. Allow to rest 5 minutes before serving. Serve with Addictive Tahini Sauce and other toppings of choice. Burgers will keep tightly sealed in the refrigerator up to 4 days.

ADDICTIVE TAHINI SAUCE (OPTIONAL):

¼ cup tahini paste

2 to 6 tablespoons water (depending on tahini thickness)

2 tablespoons lemon juice

1 clove garlic, roughly chopped

1 teaspoon honey or maple syrup

¼ teaspoon sea salt

BURGERS:

1 teaspoon olive oil

2 pounds ground lamb

2 large eggs

½ cup blanched almond flour

¾ teaspoon sea salt

¼ teaspoon black pepper

1½ teaspoons dried oregano

¾ teaspoon garlic powder

1 teaspoon onion powder

1 tablespoon low-sodium tamari

3 tablespoons tahini paste

Roasted red onions, feta cheese, sliced cucumber, tomatoes, or Fig & Olive Tapenade (page 68) (optional garnish) (DF omit cheese)

SUGGESTED SIDES

Pan-Seared Beets with Pumpkin Crumble & Lemon Yogurt (page 181)

Perfect Harvest Salad with Cinnamon Date Vinaigrette (page 295)

POULTRY

recipes

poultry

Some think poultry, and particularly chicken, is boring. I think that's what's great about it! Chicken and turkey are blank canvases for whatever flavor profile you're craving, and almost everyone enjoys them.

Before I began putting this section together, I anticipated that some people might take issue with my use of store-bought rotisserie chicken. But I also anticipated that others also find these rotisserie chickens to be a busy home cook's blessing. More importantly, I have to share recipes that reflect my real life. And should you bump into me at the market, there's a good chance an organic rotisserie chicken is in the cart. That said, I am a stickler for the quality of the bird, and if I can't get an organic chicken that has been allowed outdoor access, I'll make my own shredded chicken in the slow cooker (see page 235). Either way, this versatile and tender chicken is an ideal base for a variety of dishes.

I can promise you this: no boring birds come out of the LL Balanced Kitchen.

tarragon almond chicken salad

GF DF P | HANDS-ON TIME: *20 min* | TOTAL TIME: *1 h, 20 min* | YIELD: *6 servings* | ❄ ⊕

*T*his is hands-down one of the most popular recipes on my website, and for good reason! Everyone loves chicken salad, but traditional recipes can have up to one whole cup of mayonnaise for just a few servings. I love mayo, but too much of a good thing is, well, not. Here, avocado replaces most of the mayo, and it offers heart-healthy, nourishing monounsaturated fats. I use tarragon and almond as a nod to my sweet grandmother, who loved those flavors in her daily chicken salad lunch. The flavors are subtle but completely lovely. I enjoy this chicken salad with peppery arugula on open-faced toasted sandwiches.

Place shredded chicken in a large bowl.

Combine avocado, garlic, mustard, onion powder, honey, mayo, tarragon, lemon juice, sea salt, and pepper in a high-powered blender and puree until smooth, adding water to achieve the texture of a thick sauce.

Pour sauce over chicken and stir to incorporate evenly. Add celery and sliced almonds. Refrigerate, covered, for at least 1 hour for best taste. Store tightly sealed and refrigerated for up to 4 days.

note

The sauce can be a bit of a bear to get out of the blender, but have patience and, ideally, a skinny spatula. I may or may not occasionally resort to scooping the last bits with my (clean) fingers.

3 cups shredded plain chicken (approximately 1 whole rotisserie chicken, or use ½ batch Scratch Slow Cooker Shredded Chicken on page 235)

1 large ripe avocado

2 cloves garlic, peeled and roughly chopped

1 tablespoon Dijon mustard

1 teaspoon onion powder

1 tablespoon honey or maple syrup

2 tablespoons mayo

1½ teaspoons dried tarragon or 1 tablespoon fresh, minced*

2 tablespoons fresh lemon juice

1 teaspoon sea salt

¼ teaspoon black pepper

2 stalks celery, sliced into ¼-inch-thick pieces

½ cup roasted unsalted almonds, sliced

*No tarragon? No problem! Sub dried or fresh basil in the same amounts, or leave out altogether. It's still delicious.

SUGGESTED SIDES

Grilled Asparagus with Basil Walnut Vinaigrette (page 193)

Watermelon, Quinoa & Arugula Salad with Honey Lime Dressing (page 300)

scratch slow cooker shredded chicken

GF DF P | HANDS-ON TIME: *10 min* | TOTAL TIME: *6 h, 10 min* | YIELD: *6 cups*

Place all ingredients in a slow cooker on low for 6 to 8 hours. When chicken is finished cooking, use forks to shred chicken in the slow cooker, letting it absorb some of the liquid. After you are finished shredding, drain chicken of excess liquid in a colander. Taste for more seasoning, remembering that whatever recipe you use it in will also have seasoning. This will make enough for at least two recipes requiring 3 cups chicken each. Leftovers freeze beautifully.

4 pounds boneless skinless chicken thighs (breasts will tend to dry out)

1 cup water or low-sodium chicken stock

¼ teaspoon salt, plus more to taste

¼ teaspoon black pepper

curried cashew & lime chicken salad

GF | HANDS-ON TIME: *20 min* | TOTAL TIME: *1 h, 20 min* | YIELD: *6 servings* | ❄ ⊕ | OPTIONS: DF P

I hesitated to include two chicken salad recipes in this book when there are so many fabulous ways to enjoy chicken. But once again, I had to be authentic to me, and me is a person who can never have enough chicken salad! Plus, this version is completely different than my Tarragon Almond Chicken Salad (page 234). Instead of avocado as the creamy base, yogurt does the trick here, lending a pleasant tanginess. I make double batches of this Curried Cashew & Lime Chicken Salad whenever my husband and I have friends to our family's farm in the summer. It is a hit with everyone, and is a unique twist on a Southern classic.

In a large mixing bowl, whisk together yogurt, mayonnaise, honey, lime juice, lime zest, curry powder, turmeric, sea salt, and black pepper. Add shredded chicken and stir to incorporate evenly. Taste for more curry powder and/or sea salt and add accordingly. Add apricots or cranberries, scallion, and cashews to chicken and stir to incorporate. Refrigerate, covered, for at least 1 hour for best taste. Store tightly sealed and refrigerated for up to 4 days.

--- *ideas for* ---

LEFTOVER DRIED APRICOTS

Since you'll already have these dried apricots lying around, I suggest also making my Apricot & Rosemary Glazed Pork Tenderloin (page 229) and Apricot & Olive Oil Granola Clusters (page 150) recipes when you make this chicken salad.

½ cup plain full-fat yogurt
(DF P sub non-dairy yogurt)

¼ cup mayonnaise

2 tablespoons honey

1 tablespoon fresh lime juice

2 teaspoons lime zest (approximately 1 large or 2 small limes)

1 tablespoon curry powder, plus more to taste

½ teaspoon turmeric

1 teaspoon sea salt, plus more to taste

¼ teaspoon black pepper

3 cups shredded chicken (approximately 1 whole rotisserie chicken, or use ½ batch Scratch Slow Cooker Shredded Chicken on page 235)

⅓ cup dried apricots, chopped into ¼-inch pieces, or ⅓ cup dried cranberries

¼ cup scallion, thinly sliced

⅓ cup toasted cashews, roughly chopped

SUGGESTED SIDES

Pan-Seared Beets with Pumpkin Crumble & Lemon Yogurt (page 181)

Roasted Fennel, Orange & Wild Rice Salad (page 296)

slow cooker indian butter chicken

GF DF P | HANDS-ON TIME: *25 min* | TOTAL TIME: *8 h, 25 min* | YIELD: *6 to 8 servings*

One of my husband's and my favorite indulgences is ordering take-out Indian food on the weekends. We always get two orders of butter chicken, because we love the combination of tender meat, creamy coconut milk, and warming spices. When we moved to a new house a year ago and delivery prices skyrocketed, I decided to make my own and keep it weekend-simple with a slow cooker. Flavorful thigh meat breaks down and soaks up the other flavors. The healthy fats in coconut milk nourish our brains and bodies, and I love knowing that there aren't any added harmful vegetable oils. Next time you're planning a movie night, get this cooking in the morning, then enjoy it cozy on the couch over a generous scoop of my Baked Coconut Rice (page 208).

Add all ingredients except arrowroot/cornstarch to a slow cooker (at least 6-quart size). Stir to combine and turn to low heat. Cook for 8 hours. Taste for more salt and add accordingly. In a small bowl, mix starch with 2 tablespoons water until dissolved. Add to slow cooker and stir until mixture thickens, approximately 1 minute. Enjoy over rice or other grains, with garnish of choice.

Leftovers will keep tightly sealed in the refrigerator for 5 days, or frozen for a month.

3 pounds boneless skinless chicken thighs, trimmed of excess fat and cut into 1-inch pieces*

1 15-ounce can full-fat coconut milk

1 6-ounce can tomato paste

2 tablespoons honey or maple syrup

1 medium yellow onion, chopped into ½-inch pieces

3 cloves garlic, minced

2 teaspoons chili powder

1 teaspoon cumin

1 teaspoon paprika

1 teaspoon turmeric

1 tablespoon sea salt, plus more to taste

½ teaspoon cayenne pepper (optional, if you like spice!)

2 tablespoons arrowroot starch (sub non-GMO cornstarch)

Fresh basil or cilantro, lime juice, crushed roasted peanuts or cashews, or yogurt (optional garnish)

*I do not recommend substituting chicken breasts, as they tend to dry out.

SUGGESTED SIDES

Tahini Ginger Mashed Sweet Potatoes (page 178)

Carrot Ginger Cabbage Slaw (page 182)

Baked Coconut Rice (page 208)

turkey jalapeño meatloaf

GF **DF** | HANDS-ON TIME: *30 to 35 min* | TOTAL TIME: *1 h, 45 min* | YIELD: *10 slices*

As I write this headnote, my husband's leftover breakfast dish is sitting in the sink. What did he have? Two slices of Turkey Jalapeño Meatloaf, thank you very much! We love this loaf so much that it's always gone within 24 hours. Lentils might sound like a strange addition to meatloaf, but they add moisture and pleasant texture to each bite. Jalapeño melts into the meat as it cooks, adding more flavor than spiciness. This recipe is actually quite lean, but it feels rich and decadent. My cousin Rachel likes to make my Turkey Jalapeño Meatloaf for family Shabbat dinners, as it's a true crowd pleaser.

To make meatloaf, combine the five spices (garlic powder through sea salt) in a small bowl and set aside.

Preheat oven to 375° F and line a baking sheet with parchment paper.

Heat olive oil in a sauté pan on medium heat, until oil is slightly shimmering. Add onion and jalapeño and cook for 3 to 4 minutes, or until onion is translucent with some golden-brown edges. Turn heat to low. Add garlic and spices. Add a splash of water to prevent sticking, if needed. Stir and cook 1 minute, until garlic is fragrant and softened. Remove from heat and set aside 5 to 10 minutes.

While veggies are cooling, combine turkey, lentils, egg, tamari, and flour in a large mixing bowl. When veggies have cooled, add them to the mixing bowl. Using clean hands, mix everything together until incorporated.

Turn mixture out onto your prepared baking sheet. Shape into a loaf, approximately 6 inches wide and 2½ inches deep.

While meatloaf is baking, whisk together the glaze ingredients. After 40 minutes, remove the loaf from the oven and coat with half of the glaze. Place back in the oven for 15 minutes. Optional: Broil for 5 minutes for a darker, richer glaze. Remove and allow to rest 15 minutes before slicing.

Slice into 1½-inch-thick slices. Serve with remaining glaze. Leftovers will keep tightly sealed in the refrigerator for 4 days or frozen for 1 month.

MEATLOAF:

½ teaspoon garlic powder

1 teaspoon onion powder

1 teaspoon oregano

¼ teaspoon black pepper

1½ teaspoons sea salt

1 tablespoon extra-virgin olive oil

1 cup white onion, diced into ¼-inch pieces

⅓ cup jalapeño, seeded and minced

3 cloves garlic, minced

2 pounds organic ground turkey

1 15-ounce can organic cooked lentils, drained and rinsed

1 egg

1 tablespoon low-sodium tamari

½ cup blanched almond flour

GLAZE:

⅔ cup ketchup

2 tablespoons honey

2 tablespoons low-sodium tamari

SUGGESTED SIDES

Creamy Green Bean Casserole (page 198)

Kale Caesar with Sweet Chili Pumpkin Seed Clusters (page 299)

coconut-crusted baked chicken tenders
with sweet chili dipping sauce

GF DF P | HANDS-ON TIME: *35 to 45 min* | TOTAL TIME: *5 h* | YIELD: *4 to 6 servings* ❄

*T*his recipe is another go-to for my cooking classes, especially when I'm teaching young parents. My baked chicken tenders have just enough sophistication to feel like "adult" food, but all the crunchy, dippable goodness of classic "kid" food. Win-win! To create flavor and crunch without frying, I coat my tenders in a mixture of pecans, coconut flakes, and anti-inflammatory spices. I almost always make a double batch, because my husband will eat them for breakfast or a snack.

Add sliced chicken, milk, and apple cider vinegar to a large plastic food storage bag. Seal tightly and shake bag gently to incorporate vinegar evenly throughout. Refrigerate chicken for 4 to 8 hours. I like to wipe off the bag with a sudsy sponge before putting it in the fridge.

After chicken has finished marinating, preheat the oven to 415° F and place a slotted baking sheet on top of a solid baking sheet. Grease slotted baking sheet with olive oil.

To a food processor or high-powered blender, add coconut flakes, pecans, sea salt, paprika, onion powder, and garlic powder. Process until mixture forms a fine crumble, approximately 15 to 20 seconds. Do not over-process.

Empty coating mixture into a shallow bowl. Remove chicken from the refrigerator and place next to the bowl of coating. Place baking sheet on the other side of the bowl of coating. Open bag; it should be able to sit upright without spilling. Using clean fingers, pull each tender out, shake off excess milk into the bag, and press firmly into coating mixture. Flip the tender and coat on opposite side. Place on baking sheet. Continue with remaining tenders, making sure tenders aren't touching (they can be very close). If there's extra coating, use the rest to double-layer some of the tenders if you like.

(continued on next page)

CHICKEN TENDERS:

2 pounds boneless skinless chicken breasts, trimmed of excess fat and sliced into approximately 2-inch strips (sub chicken tenderloins)

1 cup unsweetened almond milk or other unsweetened milk

2 teaspoons apple cider vinegar

1 teaspoon olive oil

1½ cups unsweetened coconut flakes

1¾ cups raw pecans

2 teaspoons sea salt

1½ teaspoons paprika

¾ teaspoon onion powder

½ teaspoon garlic powder

SWEET CHILI DIPPING SAUCE (OPTIONAL):

1 tablespoon arrowroot starch (sub non-GMO cornstarch)

1½ teaspoons chili flakes

3 cloves garlic, minced

¼ cup apple cider vinegar

¼ cup honey or maple syrup

1 tablespoon plus 1 teaspoon low-sodium tamari

¾ cup water

coconut-crusted baked chicken tenders
with sweet chili dipping sauce *(continued)*

Bake for 25 minutes, until tenders are golden brown and crispy to touch. Allow to cool 5 minutes before enjoying.

While the chicken bakes (or ahead of time), prepare the chili sauce, if using. In a bowl, combine 2 tablespoons water and arrowroot starch. Set aside.

In a small sauce pot, combine chili flakes, garlic, apple cider vinegar, honey, tamari, and ¾ cup water. Heat to medium-high and bring to a boil, then turn heat to low/simmer. Remix arrowroot mixture with a spoon, then stir into chili sauce. Cook for another 2 minutes, stirring constantly, until sauce has reduced by approximately ⅓ and has darkened slightly in color.

Pour sauce into a heatproof dish and allow to cool at least 5 minutes before serving. Test before serving to prevent burning. Makes ¾ cup.

Note that some of the tasty chicken coating might come off while eating—this is the best part.

Leftovers will keep tightly sealed in the refrigerator for 4 days, but they won't be quite as crispy when you reheat them. You can also freeze them for up to 2 months.

SUGGESTED SIDES

Crispy Garlic Smashed Potatoes
(page 177)

Sesame Maple Brussels Sprouts Bits
(page 185)

note

Making this for kids and don't want the sauce so spicy? You can reduce the amount of chili flakes by half, or use my Curried Honey Mustard (page 258) or When in Doubt Sauce (page 278). For picky eaters, feel free to leave the spices, besides salt, out of the chicken recipe.

spicy asian chicken collard cups

GF DF | HANDS-ON TIME: *30 to 35 min* | TOTAL TIME: *30 to 35 min* | YIELD: *6 to 8 servings* | OPTIONS: P

*S*eriously, y'all, the filling that goes into these collard cups is delicious. Credit really belongs to the peanut sauce, and the rest of the ingredients are simple vehicles to carry it. These Spicy Asian Chicken Collard Cups were inspired by an appetizer at an Asian restaurant, and I wanted a version that doesn't contain excess sugar or sodium. After you give this dish a try, you'll never see a need for restaurant Chinese again . . . or at least, less often! Enjoy this filling over my Coconut Baked Rice (page 208) or pasta, or just tossed with cooked veggies. However, kudos to you if it does successfully wind up in the cups without being devoured first.

To prep Swiss chard or collard leaves, rinse and pat dry thoroughly. Place leaves face down on a cutting board. Use a sharp knife to cut out the thick, woody part of the stem, leaving a few inches at the top.

Mix the sauce. In a medium mixing bowl, whisk together peanut butter, sesame oil, honey, lime juice, garlic, sriracha (if using), tamari, sea salt, and ginger.

Cook the chicken mixture. Heat a large sauté pan or wok to medium-high heat. Add coconut oil. When oil is shimmering but not smoking, add minced chicken. Allow to pop, crackle, and brown around the edges before flipping. Turn heat down if you see smoking.

When chicken is golden brown and cooked through (approximately 4 to 5 minutes), turn heat to low and add sauce and water chestnuts. Cook for another minute, stirring, until sauce has thickened.

(continued on next page)

ASSEMBLY:

2 bunches Swiss chard or collard leaves

Shredded carrots, sliced cabbage, sliced scallions, or sesame seeds (optional garnish)

SAUCE:

¼ cup unsalted, unsweetened peanut butter (P sub tahini or almond butter)

3 tablespoons toasted sesame oil

2 tablespoons honey

2 tablespoons lime juice

2 cloves garlic, minced

2 tablespoons sriracha (can omit, add 1 more tablespoon honey)

2 tablespoons low-sodium tamari

½ teaspoon sea salt

1 packed teaspoon freshly grated ginger root (sub ¼ teaspoon ground)

CHICKEN:

1 tablespoon coconut oil (sub olive oil)

2 pounds boneless skinless chicken breast, minced into ½-inch pieces

1 cup water chestnuts, diced (approximately 1 8-ounce can, drained and rinsed; sub celery, diced jicama, or blanched almonds)

spicy asian chicken collard cups *(continued)*

Scoop ¼ cup chicken mixture onto the top of each prepared leaf. Add a little bit of each garnish if desired, then roll the mixture up in the leaf, slightly overlapping the two open sides of the leaf as you roll. Tie with string if making ahead of time, or eat as-is.

Leftover chicken mixture will keep tightly sealed in the refrigerator up to 4 days.

SUGGESTED SIDES

Turmeric & Tahini Roasted Cauliflower (page 189)

Asian Marinated Cucumber Zucchini Salad (page 203)

note

I will sometimes make this sauce and keep it around for various uses; tossed with pasta, as a dip for raw veggies, or heated with some coconut milk, stock, and chickpeas for a quick peanut curry.

bbq chicken quinoa casserole
with remarkable bbq sauce

GF | **HANDS-ON TIME:** *35 to 40 min* | **TOTAL TIME:** *1 h, 25 min* | **YIELD:** *8 servings* ⊕ **OPTIONS:** DF

*A*nother LL Balanced take on a Southern classic: the casserole. Instead of gloopy noodles or canned pastry dough, I use nutritious quinoa as the base of this chicken casserole. BBQ sauce is universally beloved, but using my Remarkable BBQ Sauce takes it to another level. This is such a cozy, warming dish, and it's perfect if you need a big-batch meal to last throughout the week.

To make BBQ sauce, combine all ingredients in a blender, in the order listed, and puree until smooth. Pour into a bowl or storage container and refrigerate at least 1 hour before serving. BBQ sauce will keep tightly sealed in the refrigerator up to 5 days, or frozen for 2 months. Recipe makes approximately 2 cups. If you just want enough for the casserole, halve the amounts.

Now, let's begin the casserole. Preheat oven to 300° F and grease a shallow 11 x 9 x 2-inch baking dish with ½ teaspoon olive oil. Heat a sauté pan to medium heat and add remaining teaspoon olive oil. When oil is lightly shimmering, add red onion. Cook, stirring, until onion is softened and lightly golden brown around the edges, approximately 5 minutes. Add splashes of water as necessary to prevent sticking. Remove from heat.

In a large mixing bowl, combine cooked quinoa, cooked red onion, garlic powder, chicken, corn, ½ cup water or stock, and ¾ cup BBQ sauce. Stir carefully to incorporate ingredients evenly. Taste for sea salt and add accordingly. Turn mixture into prepared baking dish and spread in an even layer. Drizzle or spread on remaining ¼ cup BBQ sauce (I use a pastry brush to coat evenly).

(continued on next page)

**REMARKABLE BBQ SAUCE
(SUB BBQ SAUCE OF CHOICE):**

¾ cup ketchup

¼ cup apple cider vinegar

1 tablespoon molasses

1 tablespoon sriracha (optional)

¼ cup olive oil

3 to 4 cloves garlic, minced
(sub 2 tablespoons minced shallot)

1½-inch piece ginger, peeled
and minced

2 tablespoons melted butter
(DF sub olive oil)

¼ cup Dijon mustard

2 tablespoons coconut sugar
(sub brown sugar, or omit for
lower-sugar option)

1 tablespoon chili powder

1 teaspoon sea salt

¼ teaspoon black pepper

2 tablespoons lemon juice

(continued on next page)

bbq chicken quinoa casserole
with remarkable bbq sauce (continued)

Bake casserole for 40 to 50 minutes, or until the edges are golden brown—this is a forgiving casserole and has a flexible bake time, so anywhere in the time frame is okay. Allow to cool 10 minutes before adding desired garnishes and serving. Casserole will keep tightly sealed in the refrigerator up for 4 days, or frozen for 2 months.

ADDED VEGGIES VERSION:

Want to amp up the veggie quotient? Stir in a few cups of sturdy frozen vegetables like broccoli, spinach, kale, or green peas (don't thaw, just add frozen). Increase baking time by 5 minutes or so. Also consider topping with thin half-moon slices of red onion or extra corn before baking, and add minced chives, fresh avocado, or fresh cilantro after baking.

CASSEROLE:

1 plus ½ teaspoons extra-virgin olive oil

1 cup red onion, diced into ¼-inch pieces (approximately 1 medium onion)

1 batch Easiest Fluffy Quinoa (page 207)

¾ teaspoon garlic powder

3 cups shredded chicken (1 rotisserie chicken, or use ½ batch Scratch Slow Cooker Shredded Chicken on page 235)

½ to 1 cup fresh or frozen non-GMO corn kernels (more if you really love corn)

½ cup water or low-sodium chicken stock

Sea salt, to taste (I add 1 teaspoon)

SUGGESTED SIDES

Ambrosia Fruit Salad with Oat Crumble (page 204)

Husband-Favorite Salad with Cucumber Mint Dressing (page 303)

perfect marinated chicken breasts

GF P | HANDS-ON TIME: *30 min* | TOTAL TIME: *24 h, 30 min* | YIELD: *4 servings* | ❄ ⊕ | OPTIONS: DF

*B*oneless skinless chicken breasts can be a chef's nightmare. It is no small feat to make them tender and flavorful, but using my Any Meat Marinade (page 222) does the trick. The two key steps are marinating for 24 hours, then giving them a quick, hot sear to caramelize the outside. My mom also taught me to pour deglazing liquid over the sliced chicken for increased moisture and richness. This sweet and savory chicken can be paired with almost any vegetable, grain, or sauce. Once you get in the habit of planning ahead, you will love having these chicken breasts to enjoy throughout the week!

1 batch Any Meat Marinade (page 222)

1½ pounds boneless skinless chicken breasts

1 tablespoon olive oil

1 teaspoon butter (DF sub olive oil)

1½ teaspoons coconut sugar

SUGGESTED SIDES

Pinewood Social Roasted Broccoli with Almond Dipping Sauce (page 190)

Perfect Harvest Salad with Cinnamon Date Vinaigrette (page 295)

Lay two large sheets of plastic wrap on a countertop. If using large chicken breasts, slice into two or three pieces. Place chicken breasts/pieces on the plastic wrap side by side, and lay another piece of plastic wrap on top. Using a heavy bowl or meat mallet, gently pound the chicken breasts to a 1-inch thickness. Pour marinade into a large plastic food storage bag and add chicken breasts. Toss to coat and seal tightly. Refrigerate for 24 hours.

Preheat oven to 400° F and place a slotted baking sheet over a solid baking sheet lined with parchment (to catch drippings and make cleanup easy).

Heat a large oven-safe sauté pan to medium-high heat and add olive oil and butter (if using). When oil is bubbling and popping, shake off any excess marinade from the chicken and add chicken breasts to pan. Allow to sear without touching for 3 to 4 minutes, or until they have a golden-brown crust on the bottom (you can start to peek around 3 minutes). Flip and repeat on opposite side— this should take less time, approximately 2 minutes.

(continued on next page)

perfect marinated chicken breasts *(continued)*

Use tongs to remove chicken from the pan onto your slotted baking sheet and bake for 5 minutes. Do not clean your sauté pan! While chicken is baking, heat pan to medium-low and add enough water to cover the bottom of the pan, along with coconut sugar. Deglaze the pan by using a spatula to scrape the caramelized brown bits off the pan. Cook, stirring, for 3 to 4 minutes, until the liquid has reduced to a medium-thick sauce consistency—sauce should be able to coat the back of the spatula without running off. There won't be a lot.

Remove chicken from oven and allow to rest 10 minutes. After 10 minutes, move chicken from slotted baking sheet to parchment-lined baking sheet and slice chicken into ¼-inch-thick slices. Pour deglazing liquid over chicken. Serve as-is, or with my Sesame Horseradish Mayonnaise (page 222).

Chicken will keep for up to 4 days tightly sealed in the refrigerator.

note

This recipe doubles well, and I suggest freezing a batch of sliced chicken for quick protein in a pinch.

seafood

inding high-quality, fresh seafood is a battle here in Nashville. But it is oh-so-important in a healthy diet! The omega-3 fatty acids found in cold-water fish like salmon and tuna are highly anti-inflammatory and can help with everything from brain to immune to cardiovascular health. As I mentioned in Chapter 1, I rely on Vital Choice and Thrive Market as resources for frozen seafood, and I like to order individual fillets in bulk. Although the idea of canned seafood might give some people the willies, it's actually delicious when properly prepared. I highly recommend you to try my Sunday Tuna Salad (page 257) or Shockingly Delicious Asian Salmon Cakes with Sriracha Aioli (page 266) to see for yourself. No worries though; if canned isn't your thing, I have several other options for you, such as my Curried Honey Mustard Salmon (page 258) and Orange & Ginger Seared Scallops (page 270).

sunday tuna salad

GF DF P | HANDS-ON TIME: *15 min* | TOTAL TIME: *15 min* | YIELD: *4 servings*

*T*una salad is, to me, reminiscent of childhood in the South. Typically, a mountain of mayo-saturated tuna is piled between two slices of white bread—a delicious treat, but not something to enjoy regularly. When I discovered how much my husband loves tuna salad, I knew I needed a healthier alternative . . . but I didn't know I was creating a tuna monster. I first served him my version on a Sunday afternoon 2 years ago, and he's requested it every Sunday since. I prefer mine on sourdough, sprinkled with cheese, and placed under the broiler. Max likes his in a sandwich with butter lettuce, tomato, and some crispy bacon.

In a medium-sized mixing bowl, whisk together mayonnaise, tahini, mustard, honey, lemon juice, onion powder, sea salt, and pepper. Add tuna and use a fork to mash all ingredients together thoroughly. Stir in pickle. Serve immediately or allow to refrigerate 1 hour to serve chilled (not required, but this is my preference). Tuna will keep tightly sealed in the refrigerator up to 3 days.

3 to 4 tablespoons mayonnaise
(I use 4)

1 tablespoon tahini paste
(can sub 1 tablespoon mayo)

2 teaspoons Dijon mustard

2 teaspoons honey

1 tablespoon fresh lemon juice

½ teaspoon onion powder

½ teaspoon sea salt

¼ teaspoon black pepper

2 6-ounce cans wild tuna, drained

⅓ to ½ cup dill pickle, finely chopped
(I use ½ cup)

SUGGESTED SIDES

Husband-Favorite Salad with
Cucumber Mint Dressing (page 303)

Ambrosia Fruit Salad with
Oat Crumble (page 204)

curried honey mustard salmon two ways

GF* DF* P* | HANDS-ON TIME: *10 min* | TOTAL TIME: *18 to 20 min* | YIELD: *4 servings*   ⊕ ⊘

Symbols apply to Curried Honey Mustard Salmon recipe only.

Wild salmon is one of the best sources of omega-3 fatty acids, and I always feel nourished and energized after eating this dish. In fact, I love this salmon so much that I was utterly compelled to share two ways to enjoy it: in a Strawberry, Pecan & Goat Cheese Salad, or a Sautéed Greens & Rice Bowl. Both take about 20 additional minutes to make. I often make my Curried Honey Mustard Salmon when my husband is out of town, because it's so easy to make a single serving.

Make mustard sauce by whisking all ingredients together in a bowl. Makes approximately ¼ cup. It will keep tightly sealed in the refrigerator up to 5 days.

Now, prepare the salmon. Preheat oven to 350° F. Line a baking sheet with parchment paper and add salmon fillets, leaving at least an inch between each. Season fillets evenly with salt, pepper, and olive oil. Place salmon in the oven for 8 to 10 minutes, or according to your preference. Eight minutes will make medium/medium-rare salmon; 10 minutes will be more well-done.

Remove from the oven and glaze each fillet with Curried Honey Mustard. Allow to rest 3 to 5 minutes and add another coat of glaze before serving.

(continued on next page)

CURRIED HONEY MUSTARD:

¼ cup honey

1 tablespoon plus 1 teaspoon Dijon mustard

1 teaspoon curry powder

SALMON:

4 4-ounce wild salmon fillets, skin removed

½ teaspoon sea salt, plus more for finishing

¼ teaspoon black pepper, plus more for finishing

1 tablespoon extra-virgin olive oil

note

To make 1 serving at a time, use 1 teaspoon oil, small pinches of salt and pepper, and the following ratio for the Curried Honey Mustard: 1 tablespoon honey, 1 teaspoon Dijon, and ¼ teaspoon curry powder. Follow instructions otherwise.

curried honey mustard salmon two ways *(continued)*

STRAWBERRY, PECAN & GOAT CHEESE SALAD:

¾ cup raw pecans

3 tablespoons plus ½ teaspoon extra-virgin olive oil

6 ounces baby spinach

½ cup strawberries, hulled and sliced ¼-inch thick, any direction

4 ounces goat cheese, crumbled

1½ tablespoons white balsamic vinegar

Preheat oven to 350° F. Line a baking sheet with parchment paper. In a small bowl, combine pecans and ½ teaspoon olive oil. Spread pecans in a single layer onto baking sheet and bake for 10 to 12 minutes, or until pecans are fragrant and slightly darker in color. Remove from oven and set aside to cool.

While pecans are roasting, add spinach to a large mixing bowl and top with strawberries and crumbled goat cheese.* When pecans are cooled, roughly chop them and add to salad. In a small bowl, whisk together remaining 3 tablespoons olive oil and white balsamic vinegar. Add dressing to spinach to taste, and gently toss to coat. Portion salad to individual plates and top each with a salmon fillet. Season with extra salt and pepper if you like.

*Alternatively, if you want to keep your toppings looking pretty, toss the spinach with dressing, then add cheese, strawberries, and pecans.

SUGGESTED SIDES
Perfect Oven Fries Two Ways (page 174)

SAUTÉED GREENS & RICE BOWL:

1 batch Simple Spicy Garlicky Greens (page 194) (or other veggies of choice)

1 cup white or brown rice, cooked according to package directions

¼ ripe avocado, sliced

Low-sodium tamari, to taste

Thinly sliced radishes, thinly sliced purple cabbage, toasted coconut flakes, sesame seeds, fresh lime juice, thinly sliced carrots, or chopped bell peppers (optional garnish)

To make salmon bowls, add ½ to ¾ cup rice to the bottom of the bowl. Top with Spicy Garlicky Sautéed Greens and avocado. Drizzle with tamari, to taste. Add salmon fillet and desired toppings.

bbq shrimp & quinoa grits

GF | HANDS-ON TIME: *50 min to 1 h, 5 min* | TOTAL TIME: *1 h, 40 min to 2 h* | YIELD: *4 servings* ⊕ | OPTIONS: DF

*I*f you're familiar with Southern culture, you know that shrimp n' grits is a thang. However, this dish varies wildly from state to state. Some versions are tomato-based stews, while others focus on herbs and butter. Since BBQ sauce is one of my favorite condiments, I decided to use it for a Nashville LL Balanced version. This is actually the first dish I made when I moved home from NYC to Nashville, so it holds a very dear place in my heart. And oh, these quinoa grits! They are so good that you may want to enjoy them as a separate side dish on other occasions, or as a savory breakfast.

Start by making the quinoa grits. Heat a medium (around 4 quart) sauce pot to medium-low heat and add 1 tablespoon butter. When butter has melted and is lightly bubbling (or if using olive oil, oil is lightly shimmering), add garlic. Cook, stirring, until fragrant and softened, approximately 1 minute. Add quinoa, stock, sea salt, and black pepper and stir to combine. Turn heat to medium-high and bring to a boil. As soon as mixture starts boiling, turn heat to the lowest setting possible and cover with a lid.

(continued on next page)

QUINOA GRITS:

1 plus 2 tablespoons butter
(DF sub olive oil)

4 to 6 cloves garlic, minced
(6 for a more pronounced garlic flavor, which I prefer)

¾ cup quinoa, rinsed thoroughly and drained

2 cups low-sodium chicken stock

1 teaspoon sea salt, plus more to taste
(I prefer 2 teaspoons)

¼ teaspoon black pepper

1 plus ⅓ to ½ cups canned full-fat coconut milk

3 tablespoons nutritional yeast or grated parmesan cheese (more to taste)

BBQ SHRIMP:

1 tablespoon olive oil

1 pound fresh or thawed shrimp, peeled and deveined, but tail-on (can remove, but I think they have better flavor when they cook with the tail)

¼ to ½ teaspoon sea salt
(I use ½ teaspoon)

Pinch black pepper

⅓ to ⅔ cup Remarkable BBQ Sauce (page 248) (sub BBQ sauce of choice)

bbq shrimp & quinoa grits *(continued)*

Simmer quinoa for 22 to 25 minutes, or until almost all of the liquid is absorbed, but it doesn't look dry. Stir in 1 cup coconut milk and nutritional yeast or parmesan cheese. Stir in remaining tablespoon or two of butter (1 is delicious, but I prefer the decadence of 2). Taste for more salt and add accordingly. Note that it will look too liquidy at first, but after a few minutes the mixture will thicken to a grits-like consistency. Add more coconut milk as necessary to achieve desired consistency. I usually end up adding an extra ⅓ cup.

Now prepare the shrimp. Heat a large sauté pan to medium heat and add olive oil. When oil runs easily and is lightly bubbling, add shrimp and season with salt and pepper. Shrimp should sizzle on contact. Stir to coat evenly with seasoning, then cook, stirring frequently, until shrimp is almost completely opaque and pink, approximately 3 to 4 minutes. Add BBQ sauce, starting with ⅓ cup and adding to taste; stir to coat shrimp. Cook another minute until sauce is heated through and shrimp are completely opaque (if you're not sure, cut one open and take a peek inside).

Serve immediately over quinoa grits.

Shrimp will keep up to 2 days; quinoa will keep up to 4 days. Reheat quinoa in a sauce pot with a splash of water to loosen. I don't recommend reheating shrimp, but if you insist, you can place it in a 300° F oven until just warmed through.

SUGGESTED SIDES

Simple Spicy Garlicky Greens (page 194)

Watermelon, Quinoa & Arugula Salad with Honey Lime Dressing (page 300)

teriyaki fish tacos *with* avocado crema

GF DF | HANDS-ON TIME: *30 to 35 min* | TOTAL TIME: *30 to 35 min* | YIELD: *3 to 4 servings* ⊕ 🕐 | OPTIONS: P

These teriyaki tacos look and taste like something out of an authentic taco truck. I love making them in the middle of winter with frozen wild cod, and they never fail to lift any flagging spirits. My Avocado Crema ties everything together, and you can even use it as a dip for tortilla chips on the side. This is a great recipe for seafood newbies, because cod is incredibly mild and, well, who doesn't like tacos?

Combine all ingredients for Avocado Crema in blender and puree until smooth. The recipe makes approximately 1¼ cups. Sauce will keep tightly sealed in the refrigerator up to 2 days.

Now, prepare the fish taco mixture. Heat a large sauté pan to medium-high heat and add coconut oil. When oil is lightly shimmering, add cod. Season with a pinch of sea salt. Allow to cook without stirring for 2 minutes, or until the bottom is golden. Turn the heat to low and add ⅓ cup of the teriyaki sauce, reserving the rest for garnish. Toss fish gently to coat in sauce. Cover the pan with a lid and cook until fish is completely opaque all the way through and, another 2 minutes or so.

Remove pan from the stove and serve immediately. Garnish with extra teriyaki sauce, Avocado Crema, sliced purple cabbage or my Carrot Ginger Cabbage Slaw, and whatever else you like.

I don't love fish taco leftovers, but you can gently reheat any leftover fish in a pan with a splash of water until warmed through.

note

A trick to make tortillas more pliable: Heat a skillet to medium and add tortillas. Warm for 10 seconds on each side. This should help them bend without breaking.

AVOCADO CREMA:

½ cup canned full-fat coconut milk

1 cup avocado, peeled and chopped into 1-inch chunks

2 tablespoons mayonnaise

2 tablespoons lime juice

¼ teaspoon sea salt

TACOS:

1 tablespoon coconut oil (sub olive oil)

1 pound wild cod, diced into 1-inch pieces*

¼ teaspoon sea salt, plus more to taste

⅓ plus ⅓ cup teriyaki sauce (store-bought or my homemade recipe, page 66)

Thinly sliced purple cabbage or my Carrot Ginger Cabbage Slaw (page 182)

Corn tortillas (P sub paleo tortillas)

Sriracha, lettuce, fresh lime juice, cilantro, thinly sliced raw radishes, or sesame seeds (optional garnish)

*Can use fresh or thawed from frozen.

SUGGESTED SIDES

Lightened-Up Green Pea Guacamole (page 197)

shockingly delicious asian salmon cakes *with* sriracha aioli

(GF) (DF) (P) | HANDS-ON TIME: *25 to 30 min* | TOTAL TIME: *25 to 30 min* | YIELD: *9 cakes*

Here in landlocked Nashville, I am all about recipes that transform canned seafood into something absolutely crave-worthy. Canned boneless and skinless wild salmon and tuna are staples in my pantry, and sometimes I'll simply enjoy some with a squeeze of lemon juice and sprinkles of salt and pepper. However, if you're looking to impress, this recipe is the ticket! Asian flavors are right at home with salmon, and eggs and almond flour create the most tender little cakes. My husband and I love these with a generous dollop of my Sriracha Aioli, and they're a regular in the dinner rotation, especially when I don't have a lot of time.

If making Sriracha Aioli, whisk ingredients together in a small bowl. Makes approximately ¼ cup. Aioli will keep tightly sealed in the refrigerator up to 3 days.

Prepare salmon mixture. In a mixing bowl, mash together salmon, eggs, almond flour, and sea salt. In another bowl, whisk together sesame oil, lemon juice, ginger, tamari, honey, and mayo or avocado. Add sesame oil mixture to salmon mixture and combine thoroughly.

Heat a well-seasoned cast-iron skillet or ceramic nonstick skillet to medium heat. Allow to get hot. If you don't have either of these, add 1 tablespoon olive oil to a pan.

Scoop a tightly packed ¼ cup of salmon mixture into the pan, then use fingers or a spatula to flatten to approximately ¾ inch. Repeat with the remaining salmon mixture. Cook for 3 minutes until golden brown and easily flipped with a spatula. Repeat on other side. Remove from the pan and allow to rest 5 minutes before serving with Sriracha Aioli. Cakes will keep tightly sealed in the refrigerator up to 3 days.

SRIRACHA AIOLI (OPTIONAL):

¼ cup mayonnaise

1 clove garlic, minced

2 teaspoons sriracha

1 teaspoon fresh lemon juice

SALMON:

12 ounces canned wild salmon or cooked fresh salmon

2 large eggs

½ cup blanched almond flour

1 teaspoon sea salt

1½ teaspoons toasted sesame oil

1 tablespoon fresh lemon juice

1 teaspoon freshly grated ginger root (sub ¼ teaspoon ground)

1 tablespoon low-sodium tamari

1 teaspoon honey

2 tablespoons mayonnaise or mashed avocado

SUGGESTED SIDES

Sesame Maple Brussels Sprouts Bits
(page 185)

Baked Coconut Rice (page 208)

chilled caesar shrimp & asparagus pasta salad

GF HANDS-ON TIME: *30 to 35 min*   TOTAL TIME: *1 h, 30 to 35 min*   YIELD: *6 to 8 servings*   ❄ ⊕   OPTIONS: DF P

I'm always looking for creative ways to reuse my homemade condiments, and this recipe is the result of leftover Caesar dressing from a dinner party. I decided to see how it translated to a pasta sauce, and the answer is, magnificently! With the first stirrings of a Tennessee spring, nothing sounded better than a refreshing seafood pasta salad. However, this dish is customizable to all four seasons. I like to serve it warm with chicken sausage and frozen peas instead of shrimp and asparagus in cooler months. My parents love this pasta salad as well, so I always drop some off for them.

Cook pasta according to package directions. Drain and add to a large mixing bowl. Stir in ½ cup Caesar Dressing. Cover bowl with aluminum foil and refrigerate.

Bring 2 quarts (8 cups) of water to a boil and add 1 teaspoon sea salt. Add asparagus spears and cook until tender but not mushy— this will depend on the thickness of the stalks, but it usually takes about 1 minute for me.

Drain asparagus in a colander and immediately rinse with cold water for 1 minute to stop the cooking. Chop asparagus into 1-inch pieces and stir into your pasta salad. Place back in the fridge.

Heat a large sauté pan to medium heat and add butter. When butter is melted and slightly bubbling, add shrimp. Sprinkle with sea salt and black pepper. Cook, stirring every 30 seconds or so, until shrimp is opaque all the way through. Add shrimp to a plate and allow to cool until you can handle with your fingers. Dice shrimp into small pieces (I usually get three pieces per shrimp).

Stir shrimp into pasta. Toss pasta with more dressing, salt, and pepper to taste. I usually end up adding another ½ cup dressing. Cover bowl once more and refrigerate 1 hour before serving. Pasta will keep tightly sealed in the refrigerator for 2 days.

8 ounces pasta of choice
(I like shells or elbow macaroni)
(P sub paleo pasta)

1 double batch Caesar Dressing
(page 299) (½ cup plus more to taste, but note there will be a bit extra; sub 1 cup store-bought)

1 teaspoon sea salt, plus more to taste

1 pound asparagus,
woody stalks removed

1 tablespoon butter (DF sub olive oil)

½ pound fresh or thawed
shrimp, peeled and deveined (approximately 15 medium-sized shrimp)

Black pepper to taste

HEARTIER VERSION:

Feel free to double the amount of shrimp if you want a heartier dish with more protein.

SIMPLER VERSION:

Too many steps? Don't mess with asparagus and toss frozen peas into the hot pasta along with the Caesar Dressing. Delicious!

SUGGESTED SIDES

Lemon Parmesan Cauliflower Steaks
(page 186)

Roasted Fennel, Orange & Wild Rice
Salad (page 296)

orange & ginger seared scallops

GF P | HANDS-ON TIME: *25 min* TOTAL TIME: *25 min* YIELD: *3 to 4 servings* ⏱ OPTIONS: DF

I used to have a mental barrier with scallops, convinced that they were difficult to prepare and reserved for dining out. When I finally tiptoed reluctantly into the world of home-cooked scallops, I was surprised by how quick and simple they actually are! This is my favorite preparation, as the brightness of orange and ginger contrast beautifully with creamy, mild scallops. This recipe is an homage to the magic of deglazing, which creates a rich, flavorful sauce to drizzle on top. This is a perfect dish to make when you want something that looks and tastes fancy, but requires minimal effort.

In a blender, combine orange zest and juice, tamari, honey, water, ginger, and garlic. Blend until completely smooth.

Place scallops on a baking sheet and pat dry with a paper or cloth towel. Prepare a serving plate for the scallops.

Heat a large sauté pan to high heat and add butter. When butter has melted and is bubbling, add scallops to the pan, leaving at least 1 inch of space between them. Sprinkle scallops with a pinch of sea salt, then sear scallops for approximately 2 minutes, until a golden-brown crust has formed around the edges. Use a turner spatula to flip the scallops and repeat on remaining side (including seasoning with salt). The second side takes a little less time, closer to 1 or 1½ minutes. Scallops are finished when they are completely opaque all the way through: no longer translucent. Do not overcook. Cooking time will vary with the thickness of the scallops.

Remove scallops from the pan onto your serving plate. Pour orange juice mixture into the pan. Use your turner spatula to scrape up any brown bits from the bottom of the pan, then use a whisk to mix everything together. Cook for 2 to 3 minutes, stirring, until the liquid has thickened so that it can coat the back of a spoon.

Pour sauce over scallops and enjoy immediately. I don't recommend reheating scallops; they almost invariably become rubbery.

1 teaspoon orange zest (approximately 1 medium navel orange)

⅓ cup freshly squeezed orange juice (approximately 2 medium navel oranges)

1 tablespoon low-sodium tamari

1 teaspoon honey

2 tablespoons water

1-inch piece ginger root* (sub ¼ teaspoon ground)

1 large clove garlic, peeled*

1 pound medium scallops, side muscles removed (you can ask someone to do this, but most frozen brands have removed them)

2 tablespoons butter (DF sub coconut oil or ghee)

2 pinches sea salt

*If you don't have a high-powered blender, grate ginger and mince garlic before adding to blender.

SUGGESTED SIDES

Tahini Ginger Mashed Sweet Potatoes (page 178)

Asian Marinated Cucumber Zucchini Salad (page 203)

Roasted Fennel, Orange & Wild Rice Salad (page 296)

note
You want a very hot pan here, but if it starts smoking, turn heat to medium-high or medium.

veggie

By now, the jig is up that I'm not vegan, or even vegetarian. I proudly enjoy quality meats in moderation: they give me energy and help keep my blood sugar balanced. However, sometimes I really enjoy a plant-based meal, or even a plant-based month. And I'm not talking about heaps of raw veggies and juicing; I crave hearty and flavorful food, no matter the protein.

Each recipe in this section is robust and satisfying, without feeling heavy. My goal with my plant-focused dishes is to ensure you don't think, "This is good . . . for a *vegan* meatloaf." Instead, I hope you'll utter aloud in a room full of people, "This is just GOOD!" These dishes are perfect for encouraging hard-core carnivores (a.k.a., my husband) to look forward to Meatless Monday, or to simply appreciate a variety of foods.

Whether you're a vegan, vegetarian, pescatarian, or a happy omnivore like me, you're sure to find something to delight your taste buds, as well as nourish your belly, in this chapter.

bbq chickpea & sweet potato veggie loaf

V Vg GF DF | **HANDS-ON TIME:** *35 to 45 min* | **TOTAL TIME:** *1 h, 40 to 50 min* | **YIELD:** *6 to 8 slices* ⊕

What is it about a "loaf" that is so appealing as the weather begins to cool? This particular loaf recipe is another happy-accident dish. One day I found myself with some leftover lonely BBQ sauce, a few sweet potatoes, and a hankering for chickpeas. When my slapdash creation came together, I was delighted that it exceeded all expectations. Packed with fiber and plant-based protein, this BBQ Chickpea & Sweet Potato Veggie Loaf is as filling at it is delicious, and it will keep your digestive system humming along. This is an ideal dish to bring to a holiday meal if you're vegan or vegetarian, as it can stand up to a bird or roast.

Preheat oven to 350° F and line a standard (8½ x 4½ x 2¾-inch) loaf pan with parchment paper or aluminum foil. Grease with 1 teaspoon olive oil.

In a small bowl, whisk together chia seeds and water and set aside.

In a food processor, combine oats, almond flour, chickpeas, and sunflower seeds. Pulse until the mixture forms a chunky paste, approximately 15 to 20 seconds. Empty mixture into a large bowl.

Heat a large sauté pan to medium heat and add remaining tablespoon olive oil. When oil is lightly shimmering, add sweet potato and onion. Cook, only stirring every 2 to 3 minutes, until vegetables have some golden-brown edges, approximately 8 to 10 minutes. Add splashes of water as necessary to prevent sticking. Turn heat to the lowest setting, and stir in garlic, tamari, nutritional yeast (if using), 2 tablespoons of BBQ sauce, and tomato paste. Cook, stirring, another minute.

Add sweet potato mixture to the chickpea mixture and stir to incorporate evenly. Stir in chia seed/water mixture, then mix in scallions and corn. Taste and add salt, if you like. Note that this is a fairly dry dough, and that is what you want.

Empty loaf mixture into loaf pan and press firmly into an even layer. Bake loaf for 25 minutes, then remove and coat with remaining ¼ cup BBQ sauce in an even layer. Bake another 20 minutes, then allow to cool 10 minutes before lifting out of the pan. Allow to cool another 15 minutes before slicing.

1 tablespoon plus 1 teaspoon olive oil

2 tablespoons chia seeds

6 tablespoons water

½ cup rolled oats

½ cup blanched almond flour

1 15-ounce can chickpeas, rinsed and drained

½ cup raw sunflower seeds

2 cups grated sweet potato (approximately 1 medium, and I leave the skin on)

1 cup grated white onion (approximately 1 small)

4 cloves garlic, minced

3 tablespoons low-sodium tamari

1 tablespoon nutritional yeast (optional)

¼ cup plus 2 tablespoons Remarkable BBQ Sauce (page 248) (sub other ketchup-based BBQ sauce), plus more for dipping (I serve an extra dollop on the side of each slice)

2 tablespoons tomato paste (sub more BBQ sauce)

⅓ cup thinly sliced scallions

1 cup frozen corn kernels

Sea salt to taste

SUGGESTED SIDES

Turmeric & Tahini Roasted Cauliflower
(page 189)

Pinewood Social Roasted Broccoli with
Almond Dipping Sauce (page 190)

Grilled Asparagus with Basil Walnut
Vinaigrette (page 193)

cold sesame noodles, the new generation

V GF DF | HANDS-ON TIME: *20 min* | TOTAL TIME: *1 h, 20 min* | YIELD: *4 to 8 servings* ❄ | OPTIONS: Vg P

Growing up, my absolute favorite meal was Mom's sesame noodles. As much as I love mayonnaise though, her recipe called for more than I like to use these days. I decided get creative and make a version sans-mayo. I'd never dream of choosing between the two, but I can say that my sesame noodles are can't-put-the-fork-down fabulous. A few years ago, I made my husband a batch when I was going out of town. He called me that night to say his dinner had been delicious. "Your dinner?" I asked. "There were at least 4 servings in that container!"

Cook spaghetti according to package directions. Drain and set aside in a large bowl. If pasta is going to sit out for longer than 20 minutes before you add sauce to it, toss noodles with 1 teaspoon olive, coconut, or toasted sesame oil to prevent them from sticking together.

In a medium-sized mixing bowl, combine all ingredients except noodles in the order listed and whisk to incorporate thoroughly. Stir half of the sauce into the bowl of noodles. Taste and add more sauce as you like. I add it all in, because I like really saucy noodles and I find they dry out in the fridge. You can also cover and refrigerate leftover sauce and add later.

Place in a tightly sealed container in the refrigerator for at least 1 hour before enjoying. Garnish with thinly sliced scallions, thinly sliced purple cabbage, or sesame seeds. Noodles will keep for 5 days.

1 8-ounce box spaghetti (P sub paleo spaghetti)

1 teaspoon olive, coconut, or toasted sesame oil (optional)

¼ cup tahini paste

¼ cup unsweetened, unsalted peanut butter (P sub tahini)

¼ cup toasted sesame oil

2 tablespoons plus 1 teaspoon low-sodium tamari

1 tablespoon honey (Vg sub maple syrup)

1 tablespoon sriracha

2 cloves garlic, finely minced

1 packed teaspoon freshly grated ginger (sub ¼ teaspoon ground)

½ teaspoon sea salt

6 tablespoons water

Scallions, purple cabbage, or sesame seeds (optional garnish)

SUGGESTED SIDES

Carrot Ginger Cabbage Slaw (page 182)

Asian Marinated Cucumber Zucchini Salad (page 203)

wild rice lentil burgers *with* when in doubt sauce

V GF DF | HANDS-ON TIME: *35 to 40 min* | TOTAL TIME: *1 h, 35 to 40 min* | YIELD: *7 burgers* | OPTIONS: Vg

Y'all. I am gaga over these veggie burgers. I crave this recipe more than almost any other in the cookbook. I've enjoyed many a veggie burger in my day, but I hadn't found one that 100% hit the spot. So I created it! These burgers look like traditional beef burgers, they hold together, and they have a chewy, hearty texture. As a result, they're enjoyed by plant-eaters and meat-eaters alike. They're full of savory umami goodness, and they can stand alone or with any toppings. I love to make a double batch and freeze leftovers, then add them to salads for a quick, nourishing lunch. My When in Doubt Sauce might be my favorite condiment in the entire book. It is ridiculously easy, and it makes almost everything taste better. I like to make extra, and I always find a use for leftovers. It is great as a dip for my Crispy Garlic Smashed Potatoes (page 177), Perfect Oven Fries (page 174), and Coconut-Crusted Baked Chicken Tenders (page 242) . . . to name a few.

Preheat oven to 350° F.

Begin making the burgers. To a small sauce pot, add wild rice, water, and 1 teaspoon sea salt. Bring to a boil, then reduce to a simmer on the lowest setting possible. Cover with a lid and cook for 45 to 50 minutes, or until the water looks completely evaporated. Remove pot from the heat and keep covered another 5 minutes before fluffing with a fork. If you see leftover water when you fluff, just add rice to a colander and drain extra water. Place rice in the refrigerator to cool (either in the pot or colander) for 20 minutes.

While rice is cooking, place pecans on a baking sheet and roast for 10 minutes at 350° F. Remove and set aside to cool.

Heat a small sauté pan to low heat and add 2 teaspoons olive oil. When oil moves easily around the pan, add garlic, dates, and onion powder and cook, stirring constantly, until garlic is softened and fragrant, approximately 1 to 1½ minutes. Do not allow garlic to start turning brown. Remove mixture from the heat and set aside to cool to lukewarm temperature.

(continued on next page)

BURGERS:

1 cup raw wild rice, rinsed and drained thoroughly

2⅓ cups water

1 plus ½ teaspoons sea salt, plus more to taste

1 cup raw pecans

2 plus 1 teaspoons olive oil

4 cloves garlic, minced

2 large medjool dates, pitted and chopped into ¼-inch pieces

1 teaspoon onion powder

½ cup rolled oats

¼ teaspoon black pepper

1 teaspoon dried basil

1 15-ounce can brown lentils, rinsed and well-drained

7 burger buns or English muffins

Mashed avocado, tomato, red onion, or lettuce (optional garnish)

WHEN IN DOUBT SAUCE (OPTIONAL):

¼ cup mayonnaise (Vg sub vegan mayonnaise)

¼ cup ketchup

¼ cup Dijon mustard

wild rice lentil burgers *with* when in doubt sauce (continued)

To a food processor, add rolled oats, remaining ½ teaspoon sea salt, pepper, and dried basil. Pulse until the oats turn into a grainy flour consistency, similar to cornmeal. Add garlic/date mixture, cooked wild rice, pecans, and lentils. Pulse until the mixture forms a chunky paste—you should still see some whole pieces of wild rice. Taste for more salt and add accordingly—I usually add an extra ½ teaspoon.

Use slightly dampened hands to form mixture into 7 patties, using ½ packed cup mixture per patty. Flatten them to approximately 1-inch thickness. Note that this is a dry dough, so you can use a little water to smooth the sides. Place patties on a baking sheet or large plate.

Heat a grill pan to high heat and brush with remaining 1 teaspoon olive oil. When grill pan is smoking, add burgers. Allow to cook without touching, until patties have achieved nice grill marks, approximately 3 minutes. Flip using a flat spatula and repeat. Turn heat to low and cover patties with a piece of aluminum foil or a large stainless steel lid. Allow burgers to steam for 3 minutes before serving.

If making sauce, whisk together mayonnaise, ketchup, and Dijon mustard until incorporated.

Burgers will keep tightly sealed in the refrigerator for 4 days; sauce keeps for 3 days.

SUGGESTED SIDES

Perfect Oven Fries Two Ways (page 174)

Perfect Harvest Salad with Cinnamon Date Vinaigrette (page 295)

SERVING SUGGESTIONS

Though we love these burgers with When In Doubt Sauce, you can top them with a variety of sauces and relishes. For example, the sauce shown in the photograph on page 279 is a sun-dried tomato pesto paired with mashed avocado.

refried black bean enchiladas
with sweet potato "cheese" sauce

V **Vg** **GF** **DF** | HANDS-ON TIME: *1 h* | TOTAL TIME: *1 h, 45 min* | YIELD: *8 to 10 servings*

This recipe was inspired by my sister-in-law, who adores anything black bean–related. The Sweet Potato "Cheese" Sauce is addicting on its own, but combined with my refried black beans, the result is a decadent Mexican dish that even the hardest-core carnivore will love. You won't believe it's completely dairy-free! Leftovers reheat well, so this is an ideal big-batch dish to feed your family for a few days.

To make the Sweet Potato "Cheese" Sauce, place cashews in a small sauce pot and cover with water by at least 1 inch. Bring to a boil and boil 5 minutes. Drain and rinse with cold water. Set aside.

Bring 2 quarts (8 cups) of water to a boil in a sauce pot. Add sweet potatoes and boil until easily pierced with a fork, 6 to 8 minutes. Drain and rinse with cold water for 1 minute to cool.

Place stock, tomatoes, cashews, sweet potatoes, nutritional yeast, garlic, sea salt, chili powder, and paprika in a blender. Puree until smooth. Taste for more nutritional yeast and sea salt and add accordingly. Set aside. This recipe makes approximately 4¼ cups.

(continued on next page)

SWEET POTATO "CHEESE" SAUCE:

1 cup raw cashews

2 cups sweet potatoes, peeled and chopped into 1-inch pieces (approximately 2 medium sweet potatoes)

½ cup vegetable stock

1 15-ounce can diced tomatoes

½ cup nutritional yeast, plus more to taste

1 clove garlic, roughly chopped

1 teaspoon sea salt, plus more to taste

1 teaspoon chili powder

½ teaspoon paprika

REFRIED BLACK BEANS:

¼ cup tahini paste

1 cup vegetable stock

1½ teaspoons sea salt, plus more to taste

¼ teaspoon black pepper

2 teaspoons dried oregano

¼ teaspoon cumin

3 tablespoons olive oil

1½ cups yellow onion, diced into ½-inch pieces (approximately 1 medium onion)

10 cloves garlic, minced

2 15-ounce cans black beans, drained and rinsed

2 cups frozen spinach

(continued on next page)

refried black bean enchiladas
with sweet potato "cheese" sauce (continued)

To make the refried black beans, combine tahini, stock, sea salt, pepper, dried oregano, and cumin in a mixing bowl and whisk to combine.

Preheat oven to 350° F and prepare a large casserole dish (at least 11 x 15 x 2 inches).

Heat a large sauté pan to medium heat and add olive oil. When oil is lightly shimmering, add onions. Cook, stirring, until onions are softened and translucent, approximately 3 to 4 minutes. Turn heat to low and add garlic. Cook another 30 seconds, stirring.

Add beans and tahini/stock mixture and stir to incorporate. Turn heat back to medium and cook, stirring every few minutes, until stock has mostly evaporated, approximately 3 to 4 minutes. Turn off heat. Use an immersion blender or potato masher to mash the black beans to form a chunky paste with some pieces intact. Stir in frozen spinach and turn heat back to low. Cook another minute or two, stirring, until spinach has thawed out. Taste for more salt and add accordingly.

To assemble, spread ½ of sweet potato sauce on the bottom of dish in an even layer. Wrap tortillas with ¼ cup black bean mixture (or ⅓ cup if using medium-sized tortillas). Carefully place tortillas in the dish, open sides down, and perpendicular to the dish. Pack them in. With small tortillas, you should be able to get two rows. With medium tortillas, you should get one row plus a few that you can place in crosswise. Cover enchiladas with remaining sauce.

Bake for 30 minutes, then allow to cool 10 minutes before topping with a drizzle of sriracha or dollops of salsa. Serve portions with shredded cabbage, lime wedges, cilantro, and avocado. Casserole will keep tightly sealed in the refrigerator for 5 days.

ASSEMBLY:

20 small or 12 medium soft corn tortillas

Sriracha or salsa

Thinly shredded cabbage

Lime

Cilantro

Avocado

SUGGESTED SIDES

Turmeric & Tahini Roasted Cauliflower (page 189)

Lightened-Up Green Pea Guacamole (page 197)

corn, kale & goat cheese chickpea cake

V **GF** | **HANDS-ON TIME:** *30 to 35 min* | **TOTAL TIME:** *1 h, 5 to 10 min* | **YIELD:** *8 servings* ⊕ **DF**

Whenever I'm brainstorming vegetarian dishes, one of my top priorities is satisfaction. Will eating a portion of this dish leave me and my husband kicking back the chair in happy contentment? If the answer is yes, it's a winner! This chickpea cake is a supreme example of that. Creamy chickpeas are full of fiber and protein, kale offers concentrated nutrition, and sweet corn + feta is a match made in heaven. I first served this chickpea cake to the founder of The Nashville Food Project, an organization that repurposes locally grown and leftover whole foods to feed the city's hungry constituency. When she gave me an enthusiastic seal of approval, I officially added it to the book and never looked back.

Preheat the oven to 350° F and grease a 9-inch quiche pan with 1 teaspoon olive oil. You could probably also use a cast-iron skillet, if you like.

Heat a small sauté pan to medium heat and add remaining 2 teaspoons olive oil. When oil is lightly shimmering, add garlic. Cook, stirring, until garlic is fragrant and starting to soften, approximately 1 minute. Add kale, turn heat to low, and cook, stirring, until kale is mostly wilted but retains some firmness, about another minute. Remove pan from heat and set aside to cool.

In a food processor, combine chickpeas, coconut milk, olive oil, eggs, onion powder, sea salt, black pepper, and baking soda. Puree until smooth. Add chickpea batter to a large mixing bowl. Stir in the garlic/kale mixture, frozen corn, and goat cheese. Pour batter into your prepared quiche pan. Bake for 45 minutes, until the top springs back when pressed gently and there are golden-brown edges.

If using, make Avocado Crema (page 265). Allow cake to cool 15 minutes before serving. Cake will keep tightly sealed in the refrigerator for 4 days.

1 plus 2 teaspoons extra-virgin olive oil

5 cloves garlic, minced

2 packed cups shredded kale leaves

1 15-ounce can chickpeas, drained and rinsed

½ cup canned full-fat coconut milk

2 tablespoons olive oil

4 large eggs

1 teaspoon onion powder

1½ teaspoons sea salt

¼ teaspoon black pepper

¼ teaspoon baking soda

½ cup frozen corn kernels

½ cup crumbled goat cheese

1 batch Avocado Crema (page 265) (optional)

SUGGESTED SIDES

Grilled Asparagus with Basil Walnut Vinaigrette (page 193)

Watermelon, Quinoa & Arugula Salad with Honey Lime Dressing (page 300)

Pinewood Social Roasted Broccoli with Almond Dipping Sauce (page 190)

mushroom & arugula walnut pesto pasta

V GF DF | HANDS-ON TIME: *35 min* | TOTAL TIME: *45 min* | YIELD: *6 to 8 servings* | OPTIONS: Vg P

This is my kind of comfort food. Pesto is one of my favorite condiments, and I love it with meaty, savory mushrooms. This pasta is a great vehicle for any protein. I top mine with sliced avocado and chickpeas, and I add rotisserie chicken to the rest for my guy. This pasta tastes equally good warm or cold, so it's an ideal lunch to bring to work, or when you need to satiate hunger fast!

Begin the pesto. Place walnuts on a baking sheet and heat oven to 350° F. Roast walnuts for 10 to 12 minutes, until fragrant and slightly darkened in color. Allow to cool 5 minutes. Set aside ¾ cup walnuts for the pesto. Chop the remaining ¼ cup for garnish and set aside.

Begin the pasta. Cook pasta slightly al dente (1 to 2 minutes less than package directions suggest; the noodles will still have a little "bite" to them when you chew). Drain in a colander and rinse with cold water for 1 minute. Toss with 1 teaspoon olive oil to prevent sticking. Set aside.

Make pesto by combining all pesto ingredients, except olive oil, in a food processor. Blend, stopping and scraping down the sides once, until ingredients are just combined (15 to 20 seconds total). Blend again and drizzle in olive oil. Continue blending until pesto reaches desired consistency—I like my pesto a little thinner, like a thick sauce. This recipe makes approximately 1¼ cups. You could also sub another pesto of choice and adjust seasonings accordingly.

To complete cooking of the pasta ingredients, heat a sauté pan to medium-low and add remaining 1 tablespoon olive oil and 2 tablespoons water. When water is bubbling, add mushrooms and onions. Cook for approximately 10 minutes, deglazing every 2 to 3 minutes by adding a splash of water and scraping up the brown bits with a spatula.

Add cooked pasta, ¾ cup pesto, sea salt, pepper, and nutritional yeast or parmesan. Stir to coat evenly. Taste for salt and add more accordingly. Add more pesto as desired as well. Serve over fresh arugula and top with remaining ¼ cup chopped walnuts. Pasta will keep tightly sealed in the refrigerator up to 4 days; leftover pesto will keep for 5 days.

note

Freeze pesto in silicone ice cube trays, then pop into a food storage bag to keep in the freezer. Whenever you need pesto, refrigerate what you want until softened, or leave on the counter at room temperature for 30 minutes.

ARUGULA WALNUT PESTO:

1 cup raw walnuts (sub another nut or seed of choice)

2 packed cups baby arugula

2 packed cups baby spinach

2 cloves garlic, roughly chopped

¾ teaspoon sea salt

Pinch black pepper

2 tablespoons fresh lemon juice

1 teaspoon honey (Vg omit— I don't like maple syrup in this)

2 tablespoons nutritional yeast (sub parmesan cheese)

⅓ cup olive oil

PASTA:

8 ounces pasta of choice (I like fusilli or spaghetti) (P sub paleo pasta)

1 tablespoon plus 1 teaspoon olive oil

8 ounces sliced white button or baby portabella mushrooms

½ cup white onion, chopped into ½-inch pieces (approximately ½ medium onion)

1 teaspoon sea salt, plus more to taste (I use 1½ teaspoons)

¼ teaspoon black pepper

2 tablespoons nutritional yeast (sub parmesan cheese)

Fresh arugula

SUGGESTED SIDES

Kale Caesar with Sweet Chili Pumpkin Seed Clusters (page 299)

Lemon Parmesan Cauliflower Steaks (page 186)

marinated tempeh sushi burritos

V **Vg** **GF** **DF** | HANDS-ON TIME: *25 to 30 min* | TOTAL TIME: *2 h, 30 min* | YIELD: *4 to 5 burritos* ❄

I almost didn't include this recipe in the book. I honestly forgot about it, until my cousin Rachel mentioned that they're a household favorite. I'm so glad she did, because as soon as I re-tested them, I had to agree! The marinated tempeh alone is worth sharing, as you can use it multiple ways: thrown on salads, sautéed with potatoes in a hash, or tossed in my Cold Sesame Noodles (page 277). However, these sushi burritos are definitely my favorite way to enjoy the tempeh, all wrapped up with creamy avocado and crunchy veggies. I love making these when I have a busy week ahead and need pre-made meals, as they hold up well in the fridge.

Combine all ingredients for tempeh (except tempeh) in a medium-sized mixing bowl. Whisk to incorporate and add salt to taste. Add tempeh slices to mixture and toss to coat. Cover and refrigerate 2 to 6 hours.

Preheat oven to 415° F and line a baking sheet with parchment paper. Grab marinating tempeh and take tempeh slices out, gently shaking off as much excess sauce as possible. Place tempeh slices in an even layer on the baking sheet (note that any sauce that gets on the parchment will burn in the cooking process. This will not affect the end result, but it will smoke). Reserve leftover marinade.

Bake tempeh for 15 minutes, turning halfway (minute 7 or 8). Allow to cool 10 minutes before assembling burritos.

To assemble: Spread a thin layer of mashed avocado on a tortilla. Top with a nori sheet, then spread a thin layer of leftover marinade on nori. Mentally divide the tortilla into three vertical sections. In the right-hand section, add approximately ¼ to ⅓ cup rice (if using). Line 4 to 6 tempeh slices vertically, leaving at least an inch of tortilla free. Top tempeh with a small amount of cabbage, carrots, and cucumber.

To roll, tuck in the bottom and top 1 inch of the tortilla. While tucking, roll tortilla closed, starting from the food-filled side and moving toward the empty side. Hold firmly for a few seconds to help it stick. Burrito components will keep separately in the refrigerator for 4 days, or assembled for 2 days. I like to make a few initially, then make the remainder 2 days later for lunches the rest of the week.

TEMPEH:

2 tablespoons plus 1 teaspoon toasted sesame oil

3 tablespoons low-sodium tamari

2 tablespoons apple cider vinegar

2 tablespoons maple syrup (sub honey)

2 tablespoons tahini paste (sub nut/seed butter of choice)

2 cloves garlic, minced

2 teaspoons freshly grated ginger root

¼ to ½ teaspoon sea salt

8 ounces organic tempeh, sliced into ½-inch-thick slices

ASSEMBLY:

Tortillas/wraps of choice

Avocado, mashed

Nori sheets

Cooked rice or other grain (optional but recommended)

Purple cabbage, thinly sliced

Carrots, thinly sliced

Cucumber, thinly sliced

SUGGESTED SIDES

Carrot Ginger Cabbage Slaw (page 182)

Sesame Maple Brussels Sprouts Bits (page 185)

Asian Marinated Cucumber Zucchini Salad (page 203)

note
Wrap one end of the burrito tightly with aluminum foil to make it easy to eat without falling apart.

maple balsamic–glazed tempeh & mushroom bake

Ⓥ Ⓥg Ⓖf Ⓓf | **HANDS-ON TIME:** *20 min* | **TOTAL TIME:** *5 h* | **YIELD:** *4 to 6 servings* | ❄

*G*ood golly. When I pulled this dish out of the oven and took one whiff of the caramelized, rich aroma, I knew I'd created something special. The flavors of this marinade infuse every crack and crevice of the tempeh, and roasting adds even more richness. This is another ideal holiday recipe for plant-eaters, and I guarantee everyone will be stealing bites! I always feel cozy and nourished after enjoying a bowl of this tempeh with rice and sautéed greens.

Gently whisk all ingredients together, except tempeh and mushrooms, in a 11 x 9 x 2-inch baking dish. Add tempeh and mushrooms and coat with marinade. Cover dish with aluminum foil and marinate for at least 4 hours and up to 24 hours, stirring occasionally.

Preheat oven to 350° F. Place baking dish in the oven, covered, and bake for 20 minutes. Uncover dish, flip the tempeh and mushrooms, and allow to bake another 20 minutes. Using a slotted spoon, remove tempeh and mushrooms from the dish, reserving extra marinade. Serve immediately. I like to enjoy this over cooked quinoa or wild rice, with a few slices of avocado. Feel free to drizzle on extra marinade, but I find it flavorful enough without.

Tempeh will keep tightly sealed in the refrigerator up to 4 days.

⅓ cup balsamic vinegar

1 tablespoon maple syrup

2 tablespoons low-sodium tamari

3 cloves garlic, minced

2 tablespoons olive oil

1 tablespoon minced fresh rosemary

1 teaspoon Dijon mustard

¼ teaspoon sea salt

1 8-ounce package organic tempeh, cut into 1-inch cubes

8 ounces sliced white mushrooms, wiped clean

SUGGESTED SIDES

Pan-Seared Beets with Pumpkin Crumble & Lemon Yogurt (page 181)

Creamy Green Bean Casserole (page 198)

recipes

SALADS & SOUPS

I am very particular about my salads and soups, and as a result, I have trouble finding dishes I really love when dining out. I'm not a "brothy" soup kinda girl, preferring thick textures, but those are often made with lots of heavy cream. Salads also seem to fall into one extreme or the other— they're either too light to satisfy, or too heavy to feel healthy.

Well, this chapter was my opportunity to create a middle ground between these extremes! With my soups, I use a handful of "trick" thickening ingredients that are completely dairy-free, such as hummus and quinoa. As a result, my soups are spoonably satisfying, but they won't leave you feeling sluggish. My salads are equally varied, with a little something for everyone and every season. I hope that you will also find some reliable dressing recipes that you can keep around for other DIY salads.

perfect harvest salad *with* cinnamon date vinaigrette

(V) (GF) | HANDS-ON TIME: *30 min* | TOTAL TIME: *1 h, 15 min* | YIELD: *4 to 6 servings* | OPTIONS: **(Vg) (DF) (P)**

This recipe was inspired by one my favorite salad experiences. I was with my brother and several friends, and we had just finished a glorious 4-mile hike in upstate New York in peak autumn. The trail finished in a quaint little town, and we stopped at the first cafe we saw for lunch. The salad I ordered was such a perfect combination of flavors and textures, in the dreamiest setting, that I'll never forget it. Although I can't recreate the experience for you, I hope that this offers you a small taste of that magical fall day.

Preheat oven to 350° F and line two baking sheets with parchment paper. Add hazelnuts to one sheet and roast for 12 to 14 minutes. Cool for 5 minutes, then place in a kitchen towel and twist at the top to close. Holding the towel with one hand, use the other hand to rub hazelnuts together to remove skin. Gently lay towel open on the counter and add hazelnuts to a small bowl, shaking off skin. It's okay if some of it doesn't come off. Chop hazelnuts. Set aside.

Turn oven heat to 400° F. In a mixing bowl, toss together sweet potatoes, olive oil, ¼ teaspoon sea salt, paprika, and cinnamon. Spread potatoes in an even layer on remaining baking sheet. Roast potatoes for 25 minutes, then remove and allow to cool at least 5 minutes before assembling salad.

While sweet potatoes are roasting, make Cinnamon Date Vinaigrette by combining all ingredients in a blender and pureeing until smooth. Vinaigrette will keep tightly sealed in the refrigerator up to 5 days. Recipe makes approximately ¾ cup.

Chop apple into ½-inch pieces, then toss apples with lemon juice.

To assemble, add mixed greens to a large salad bowl. Top salad with roasted chopped hazelnuts, roasted sweet potatoes, chopped apples, cranberries or cherries, and goat cheese (if using). Toss with dressing to taste. Add a sprinkle of sea salt, if desired. Serve immediately.

SALAD:

¾ cup raw hazelnuts (sub pecans but watch roasting time)

2 cups sweet potatoes, diced into 1-inch pieces

1 teaspoon olive oil

¼ teaspoon sea salt, plus more to taste

½ teaspoon paprika

¼ teaspoon cinnamon

1 medium apple (something sweet and red, like Honeycrisp or Pink Lady)

1 teaspoon fresh lemon juice

10 ounces mixed greens and/or baby spinach

⅓ cup dried cranberries or cherries (look for unsweetened or fruit-sweetened)

½ cup crumbled goat cheese (optional) (**(Vg) (DF) (P)** omit)

CINNAMON DATE VINAIGRETTE:

⅓ cup olive oil

¼ cup water

2 tablespoons apple cider vinegar

2 teaspoons Dijon mustard

1 large or 2 small medjool dates, pitted and chopped into ¼-inch pieces

¼ teaspoon cinnamon

¼ teaspoon sea salt, plus more to taste

2 tablespoons shallot, minced (sub 1 small clove garlic)

roasted fennel, orange & wild rice salad

V Vg GF DF | **HANDS-ON TIME:** *35 min* | **TOTAL TIME:** *2 h, 30 min* | **YIELD:** *6 to 8 servings* | ❄

*W*ild rice isn't actually a grain—it's the seed of an aquatic grass that is high in fiber, B vitamins, magnesium, and more. It can be a wonderful ingredient for anyone who has trouble with gluten or grains, and I adore its chewy texture and nutty flavor. Fresh, slightly acidic citrus is an ideal foil for this hearty little grass. Roasting fennel tones down its strong licorice flavor and brings out a mild, caramel sweetness. I urge you to give this unique salad a try; I think you'll be surprised by how much you love it.

Preheat oven to 350° F and roast pecans on a baking sheet for 10 to 12 minutes, until fragrant and slightly darkened. Cool, chop, and set aside.

Make the Citrus Vinaigrette by combining all ingredients in a blender and pureeing until smooth. You can also whisk it together, but blending emulsifies everything so it doesn't separate. Vinaigrette will keep tightly sealed in the refrigerator up to 5 days. Recipe makes approximately ¾ cup.

Continue preparing the salad ingredients. Rinse wild rice in a mesh strainer and drain completely. Add rice, stock, and ½ teaspoon sea salt to a sauce pot. Bring to a boil, reduce to simmer, and cover. Simmer for 45 minutes, then turn off heat and allow to sit another 10 minutes. If there is liquid left in the pot, drain rice.

While rice is cooking, roast fennel: Preheat oven to 400° F and line a baking sheet with parchment paper. In a mixing bowl, toss fennel slices with 1 teaspoon olive oil and ¼ teaspoon sea salt. Place in an even layer on sheet and roast for 25 minutes, or until fork-tender and golden brown around the edges. Set aside to cool at least 5 minutes.

Add rice to a large mixing bowl and toss with ¼ cup of Citrus Vinaigrette, as well as remaining ¼ teaspoon sea salt. Stir in roasted fennel slices, scallions, orange zest, and orange segments. Taste for more sea salt and add accordingly. Refrigerate for at least 1 hour or overnight. Right before serving, add more vinaigrette to taste and toss with pecans. Add mint if using. Salad will keep tightly sealed in the refrigerator up to 4 days.

note

To supreme any citrus, slice a thin layer off top and bottom. Sit fruit upright and slice off peel in downward motions. Hold citrus over a bowl and carefully slice white lines so segments fall into the bowl.

SALAD:

½ cup raw pecans

1 cup wild rice

2⅓ cups vegetable stock (sub low-sodium chicken stock)

½ plus ¼ plus ¼ teaspoon sea salt, plus more to taste

2 bulbs fennel, fronds and bases removed, sliced horizontally into ¼-inch-thick rounds and pulled apart into slices like onion rings

1 teaspoon olive oil

¼ cup thinly sliced scallions (approximately 2 scallions)

1 teaspoon orange zest (approximately 1 orange)

2 navel oranges, supremed into segments (see note)

2 tablespoons fresh mint, chopped (optional)

CITRUS VINAIGRETTE:

⅓ cup orange juice (approximately 1 navel orange)

2 tablespoons lemon juice (approximately 1 lemon)

1 clove garlic, roughly chopped (finely mince if whisking)

¼ plus ¼ teaspoon sea salt

¼ teaspoon black pepper

2 teaspoons maple syrup (sub honey)

⅓ cup olive oil

kale caesar *with* sweet chili pumpkin seed clusters

Ⓥ ⒼⒻ ⒹⒻ Ⓟ HANDS-ON TIME: *20 to 25 min* | TOTAL TIME: *1 h, 30 min** | YIELD: *2 to 4 servings* ❄ ⊕ OPTIONS: Ⓥg

Includes clusters.

I know, I know—everyone has their take on a kale Caesar. So, why did I feel the need to take up valuable cookbook real estate with this recipe? Because I wanted a kale Caesar that was a hybrid of classic and modern versions, and I had yet to find one. My take on Caesar salad uses shallots instead of garlic in the dressing, and hearty kale replaces romaine. I also swap croutons for my Sweet Chili Pumpkin Seed Clusters (page 80). The result is a dish reminiscent of the traditional favorite, with brighter, bolder, and more interesting flavors. I love to pair this salad with avocado and a soft-boiled egg.

Combine all ingredients for dressing in a high-powered blender and puree until smooth. Makes approximately ¾ cup.

To assemble: Place kale in a large mixing bowl and toss with dressing to taste. Use clean hands to massage dressing into the kale, until you feel the texture of the kale soften. Refrigerate for at least 30 minutes and up to 24 hours before serving. Top with Sweet Chili Pumpkin Seed Clusters.

If you have extra dressing, I like to keep it around to "rehydrate" any leftovers. Salad and dressing will keep tightly sealed in the refrigerator up to 3 days.

CAESAR DRESSING:

1 tablespoon fresh lemon juice

2 teaspoons Dijon mustard

½ teaspoon maple syrup

1 teaspoon low-sodium tamari

2 tablespoons minced shallots

2 tablespoons water

2 tablespoons mayonnaise (Ⓥg sub vegan mayonnaise)

¼ cup olive oil

¼ teaspoon sea salt

1 teaspoon onion powder

¼ teaspoon garlic powder

Pinch black pepper

SALAD:

2 bunches kale, stemmed and chopped into 2-inch pieces

1 batch Sweet Chili Pumpkin Seed Clusters (page 80)

watermelon, quinoa & arugula salad
with honey lime dressing

V **GF** | HANDS-ON TIME: *25 to 30 min* | TOTAL TIME: *2 h* | YIELD: *4 to 6 servings* ❄ ⊕ | OPTIONS: **Vg** **DF**

*T*his is another reliable flavor combination that I've updated with some LL Balanced tweaks, and it absolutely radiates summer in the South. Perfectly cooked quinoa, full of protein and fiber, is an ideal vessel for the other vibrant ingredients. Each and every forkful offers a salty bite of feta, a bright pop of mint, a juicy burst of watermelon, and a rich crunch from walnuts. The combination is unbeatable! This salad can absolutely stand alone as an entree, but feel free to pump it up with grilled shrimp or chickpeas.

Preheat oven to 350° F and roast walnuts on a baking sheet for 10 to 12 minutes, until fragrant and slightly darkened in color. Allow to cool, then chop. Set aside.

After making a batch of Easiest Fluffy Quinoa (page 207), place it in a large salad bowl, cover, and refrigerate until chilled, at least 1 hour.

While quinoa is chilling, make dressing. Whisk ingredients for Honey Lime Dressing together in a bowl or puree in a blender until smooth. Dressing will keep tightly sealed in the refrigerator up to 5 days. Recipe makes approximately ½ cup.

Remove salad bowl from the fridge and add remaining ingredients. Add ½ of the dressing and toss to coat; taste and add dressing accordingly. Serve immediately. Salad will keep tightly sealed in the refrigerator for 4 days.

SALAD:

½ cup raw walnuts

1 batch Easiest Fluffy Quinoa (page 207)

2 cups seedless watermelon, diced into ½-inch pieces

¼ packed cup fresh mint, sliced into thin ribbons

½ cup feta cheese crumbles, plus more to taste (**Vg** **DF** omit, but might need extra salt)

1 8-ounce bag baby arugula

HONEY LIME DRESSING:

2 tablespoons lime juice

1 tablespoon honey (**Vg** sub maple syrup, but note this will change the flavor slightly)

⅓ cup olive oil

½ teaspoon sea salt

note

If you want to keep the arugula crisp because you plan to have leftovers, leave it out of the toss process. Add a handful of arugula to the base of each serving bowl and top with quinoa mixture.

husband-favorite salad *with* cucumber mint dressing

V **GF** | HANDS-ON TIME: *20 min* | TOTAL TIME: *20 min* | YIELD: *4 to 6 servings* | 🕐 | OPTIONS: **Vg** **DF** **P**

*W*help, the name says it all. *Bon appétit!*

J.K. I created this salad because my hubby loves a big ole' classic romaine salad—and I can't blame him. The health world is so focused on the "dark leafies" that lighter, crunchier greens get left in the dust. Romaine lettuce is hydrating and nutritious, contains vitamins C and B, fiber, folic acid, and potassium. Not too shabby! The best part of this salad, however, is my Cucumber Mint Dressing. It is refreshing, light, and just a touch sweet. If you have a picky eater or just want to reward a loved one who always dutifully eats the veggies you make, this will seem like an indulgent treat.

Combine all ingredients for Cucumber Mint Dressing in a blender and puree until smooth. Recipe makes approximately 1½ cups.

Combine romaine, tomatoes, cucumber, avocado, and optional garnishes of choice in a large mixing bowl. Add dressing to taste. Toss to coat and serve immediately. Salad will keep for 24 hours in the fridge tossed with dressing. If you don't want to eat the whole salad at once, keep dressing and avocado separate until serving.

note

To keep salad fresh in the fridge, cover it with damp paper towels, pressed in around the edges of the greens.

CUCUMBER MINT DRESSING:

1 cup cucumber, peeled and sliced into ¼-inch-thick rounds (approximately ½ medium cucumber)

¼ cup plain yogurt (**Vg** **DF** **P** sub coconut milk or non-dairy yogurt)

¼ cup packed fresh mint, plus more for garnish

1 to 2 cloves garlic, peeled and roughly chopped

2 teaspoons Dijon mustard

1½ teaspoons honey (**Vg** sub maple syrup)

2 tablespoons apple cider vinegar

¼ teaspoon sea salt

Pinch black pepper

3 tablespoons olive oil

SALAD:

12 ounces romaine lettuce, sliced into 1-inch ribbons

1½ cups cherry tomatoes, sliced in half

1½ to 2 cups cucumber, peeled and sliced into ½-inch-thick half-moons (approximately 1 medium cucumber)

1 large ripe avocado, diced into 1-inch pieces

Sweet Chili Pumpkin Seed Clusters (page 80), freshly chopped mint or basil, or feta or goat cheese (optional garnish) (**DF** **P** omit cheese)

famous bryant family chili

GF | **HANDS-ON TIME:** *40 min* | **TOTAL TIME:** *1 h, 20 min* | **YIELD:** *10 servings* | **OPTIONS:** DF

Chili was the first home-cooked meal my mom ever made for my dad when they were married in 1977, and it was her go-to entertaining dish for years. My brothers and I were lucky enough to enjoy her chili throughout our childhood as well, and I began making it when I moved to New York City. My roommates dubbed it the Famous Bryant Family Chili, and the name stuck. As much as I love the original recipe, it's a little heavier than I'd prefer. My version uses half beef/half chicken, and I sauté my vegetables in a little butter instead of using bacon grease. Despite my changes, Mom gave this her seal of approval, so I know you will as well!

Heat a large pot to medium-high and add beef and chicken. Cook, using a wooden spoon or spatula to break up the meat, for 8 to 10 minutes or until no pink remains and the meat has some golden-brown edges. At first the meat will seem like it's sticking, but as it cooks it will render natural fat to help unstick. Scoop meat out into a heatproof bowl and set aside.

Turn heat to medium-low and add butter. When butter has melted, add onion and bell pepper. Cook, stirring, until veggies are softened, approximately 6 minutes. Turn heat to lowest setting and add garlic. Cook, stirring, until garlic is softened and fragrant, approximately 1 minute. Add meat back to pot, along with chili powder, cumin, paprika, and sea salt. Cook, stirring, another minute, then add remaining ingredients. Stir to combine ingredients evenly.

Bring to a simmer if not already simmering and cover pot with a lid. Allow to simmer 45 minutes to an hour before serving. Leftover chili will keep tightly sealed in the refrigerator for up to 4 days or in the freezer for 2 months.

1 pound ground beef (I use 85/15)

1 pound ground chicken or turkey (I use a mixture of dark and white meat)

1 tablespoon butter (DF sub olive oil)

2 cups white onion, diced into ¼-inch pieces (approximately 1 large or 2 small onions)

2½ to 3 cups mixed bell peppers, diced into ½-inch pieces (I use 1 yellow and 1 green pepper)

5 cloves garlic, minced

3 tablespoons chili powder

1 tablespoon cumin

2 tablespoons paprika

1½ teaspoons sea salt

1 28-ounce can unsalted crushed tomatoes (can sub diced)

1 15-ounce can unsalted diced tomatoes

2 tablespoons sriracha (depending on spice preference)

2 tablespoons molasses

¼ cup coconut sugar (sub light brown sugar, or 3 tablespoons honey or maple syrup)

¼ cup tomato paste

¼ cup low-sodium tamari

1 15-ounce can unsalted black beans, drained and rinsed

1 15-ounce can unsalted kidney beans, drained and rinsed

30-minute sweet potato & lentil curry

GF   HANDS-ON TIME: *10 min*   TOTAL TIME: *30 min*   YIELD: *6 to 8 servings*   OPTIONS: V Vg DF

I make this dish all throughout the winter. It is so simple, quick, and nourishing, and it's the perfect amount of food to enjoy for a week of lunches. Red lentils are a fantastic source of fiber, iron, and plant protein, and they can help stabilize blood sugar, which keeps sugar cravings at bay. Adding sweet potatoes to curry adds a lovely sweetness, as well as beta-carotene and vitamin C. This anti-inflammatory dish is a great choice if you're feeling under the weather, as it will soothe and heal you from the inside out.

Combine spices (curry powder through black pepper) in a small bowl and set aside.

Heat a large sauce pot to medium heat and add butter. When butter has melted, add onions and sauté for 2 to 3 minutes or until translucent and fragrant.

Add garlic and spices. Sauté another 30 seconds, stirring. Add tomato paste, stock, sweet potatoes, and red lentils. Stir everything together and bring to a simmer.

Once simmering, turn heat to lowest setting. Simmer stew for 20 minutes, stirring occasionally, or until sweet potatoes are fork-tender. Taste for salt and add accordingly. You can blend stew with an immersion blender or in a mixer for a creamier texture.

Serve over rice, pasta, or eat straight-up. Leftovers will keep tightly sealed in the refrigerator for 4 days or frozen for 1 month.

1 teaspoon curry powder

1 teaspoon turmeric

½ teaspoon cumin

1 teaspoon sea salt, plus more to taste

½ teaspoon black pepper

2 tablespoons butter
(DF sub coconut oil)

1 cup sweet yellow onion, chopped into ½-inch pieces (approximately ½ medium onion)

3 cloves garlic, minced

2 tablespoons tomato paste

3½ cups chicken stock
(V Vg sub vegetable stock)

2 rounded cups sweet potatoes, peeled and chopped into 1-inch pieces (approximately 1 large sweet potato)

1 cup canned red lentils, rinsed thoroughly and drained

SERVING SUGGESTIONS

Sometimes I split this into two containers and mix pulled rotisserie chicken or sausage into one container for my husband.

spicy black bean quinoa soup

GF | HANDS-ON TIME: *30 to 35 min* | TOTAL TIME: *55 min to 1 h* | YIELD: *4 to 6 servings* | ⊕ ⏱ | OPTIONS: V Vg DF

*A*dding whole grains to soup is another way to thicken them up without dairy. This Spicy Black Bean Quinoa Soup is like a festive hug in a bowl; it is so warming and satisfying. I prefer to enjoy mine topped with avocado, salsa, and plain yogurt, but I often add cooked sausage for my husband. If you are a lover of all things in the Mexican flavor profile, I'd wager this soup will make you extremely happy!

Combine spices (chili powder through sea salt) in a small bowl and set aside.

Heat a large sauce pot (around 4 quarts) to medium heat and add olive oil. Swirl to coat the bottom with olive oil and add onion and jalapeño. Cook, stirring, until onion is softened and translucent, approximately 3 to 4 minutes. Turn heat to low and add garlic and spices. Cook, stirring constantly, another minute.

Add remaining ingredients, except quinoa and optional items, to the pot. Stir to incorporate ingredients evenly. Bring soup to a simmer, then cover and simmer 25 minutes. If you don't have quinoa made in advance, I suggest cooking quinoa while the soup is simmering.

After 25 minutes, use an immersion blender to puree soup—it's okay if there are small pieces of beans left. Alternatively, add soup to a blender in batches, then add back to pot. Stir in quinoa and chicken, if using, and heat soup completely through before serving. Soup will keep tightly sealed in the refrigerator for 5 days, or frozen up to 2 months.

note

The soup will seem thin at first, but it will thicken significantly as the quinoa absorbs liquid. Taste for more salt or sriracha and add accordingly. I personally use 2½ teaspoons sea salt total and 1½ tablespoons sriracha, total.

2 teaspoons chili powder

1 teaspoon cumin

1 teaspoon dried oregano

1½ teaspoons sea salt, plus more to taste

1 tablespoon olive oil

1 cup white onion, diced into ¼-inch pieces

2 tablespoons to ¼ cup jalapeño, diced into ¼-inch pieces (approximately ½ to 1 medium jalapeño)*

5 cloves garlic, minced

6 cups low-sodium chicken stock (V Vg sub vegetable stock)

2 15-ounce cans unsalted black beans, drained and rinsed

1 tablespoon lime juice

2 tablespoons low-sodium tamari

1 to 1½ tablespoons sriracha (start with 1 tablespoon and add to taste)

1 tablespoon maple syrup

1 batch Easy Fluffy Quinoa (page 207) (approximately 3 cups cooked)

2 cups cooked and shredded chicken (optional) (V Vg omit)

Scallions, avocado, fresh lime juice, cilantro, salsa, diced green pepper, or plain yogurt (optional garnish) (DF omit yogurt)

*Use according to your spice preference. Some jalapeños are significantly hotter than others. Take a teeny bite of yours to help determine how much you should use.

mushroom, rosemary & hummus soup

GF DF | HANDS-ON TIME: *30 min* | TOTAL TIME: *50 min* | YIELD: *4 to 6 servings* | OPTIONS: V Vg

*W*ait! Don't turn the page! I know this combination sounds bizarre, but I promise it works. Hummus is another fantastic way to add body and staying power to a soup, and it also adds a creamy texture. Meaty mushrooms and earthy, pungent rosemary are a powerful duo, and they sing when allowed to cook down together. Slightly lighter than the other soups in this chapter, this Mushroom, Rosemary & Hummus Soup hits the spot equally well. I actually prefer to sip this soup out of a mug, and it is one of our favorite cold-weather dishes.

Heat a large stock pot to medium heat and add olive oil. When oil moves easily around the pan, add shallots and mushrooms. Cook for approximately 10 minutes, stirring every minute or so, until most of the water released from the mushrooms has evaporated. Add garlic, sea salt, and pepper, and cook, stirring, another minute. Add stock, tamari, vinegar, rosemary, and honey. Stir to combine and bring to a simmer. When soup begins to simmer, turn heat to low, cover, and simmer for 20 minutes.

Turn off heat and remove rosemary sprigs. Some rosemary leaves will have fallen off, which is what you want. Stir in hummus—it's okay if it doesn't mix in completely—then use an immersion blender to puree soup. Alternatively, if you want a creamier texture, carefully add soup in batches to a blender and puree until smooth. I blend half the soup, pour that into a large mixing bowl, puree the second half, and then pour it all back in the stock pot.

Bring soup to a simmer and simmer another 10 minutes. Taste for more salt and add to taste. Serve immediately.

2 tablespoons olive oil

½ cup shallots, minced (approximately 1 large or 2 small shallots)

16 ounces sliced baby portabella mushrooms, rinsed thoroughly and patted dry

4 cloves garlic, minced

½ teaspoon sea salt, plus more to taste (I use 1 teaspoon)

¼ teaspoon black pepper

6 cups low-sodium chicken stock (V Vg sub vegetable stock)

1½ tablespoons low-sodium tamari

2 tablespoons balsamic vinegar

2 sprigs fresh rosemary

1 tablespoon honey (Vg sub molasses)

¾ cup plain hummus

peanut, ginger & chickpea slow cooker stew

GF **DF**   HANDS-ON TIME: *20 min*   TOTAL TIME: *5 h, 20 min*   YIELD: *6 servings*   🍲   OPTIONS: **V** **Vg**

*T*his is as easy as recipes get. You throw all the kiddos into the pool, let them splash around all day, and the result is . . . well, an absolutely killer stew. This is such a great dish when you're planning for a lazy night on the couch, but you don't want to spend money on overly salty take-out. Pairing this Peanut, Ginger & Chickpea Slow Cooker Stew with white rice feels indulgent and exotic, but it is healthy enough to enjoy every week. Plus, anything with peanut butter is just better, amiright? If you're on the fence about purchasing a slow cooker, I think this stew alone is worth it!

To a slow cooker, add all ingredients except carrots, chickpeas, and starch (if using). Stir to combine. Turn slow cooker to high and cook for 4 hours. Add carrots and chickpeas and cook another hour. Taste for more salt and coconut sugar and add accordingly. If using starch, add 1 tablespoon soup liquid to a small bowl with starch and stir together. Add mixture to slow cooker and stir to incorporate. Soup will thicken slightly in a minute or so.

I love to serve this soup over white rice or quinoa. Soup will keep tightly sealed in the refrigerator for 5 days and frozen up to 1 month.

½ medium yellow onion, sliced into ¼-inch-thick half-moons (or as thin as you can get them)

1 medium green bell pepper, sliced into ½-inch-thick strips

1 medium red bell pepper, sliced into ½-inch-thick strips

1 15-ounce can diced tomatoes

1 15-ounce can full-fat coconut milk

1 cup low-sodium chicken (**V** **Vg** sub vegetable stock)

¼ cup low-sodium tamari

½ cup unsalted, unsweetened peanut butter

1 to 2 tablespoons coconut sugar (start with 1; I use 2 tablespoons; sub light or dark brown sugar or maple syrup)

2 tablespoons freshly grated ginger root

1 teaspoon sea salt, plus more to taste (start with 1; I use 1½ teaspoons total)

¼ teaspoon black pepper

1 teaspoon garlic powder

1 medium or 2 small carrots, peeled into thin strips with a vegetable grater (you can also slice into ¼-inch-thick rounds if that's easier)

1 15-ounce can chickpeas, drained and rinsed

1 tablespoon arrowroot starch for thickening (sub non-GMO cornstarch) (optional)

recipes

9

DESSERT

··

I have a bona fide, grade-A sweet tooth. As a child, I had a meticulous system with which I organized my Halloween candy, making it last throughout the year. As an adult, I've swapped my candy bars for high-quality dark chocolate, but I have a little something sweet almost every day.

Thankfully, it comes easily to me to set dessert boundaries, but I know that many people struggle with portion control. Whole-foods–based desserts using natural sweeteners can be much easier to enjoy in moderation. I primarily stick to almond and coconut flour when baking, as the protein and fiber help you stop at one treat. I also love using fresh and dried fruit, nuts, and even legumes (!) as dessert ingredients to amp up the nutrition and satiation factor. It's important to remember that natural sugars are still sugar, and only you can determine how much is okay for you. Whatever you decide, there's a little something for everyone in this chapter.

Don't forget to take note of the ideas for quick, healthy snacks and treats that are scattered throughout.

··

chocolate-covered, almond butter–stuffed dates

Ⓥ ⒼⒻ   HANDS-ON TIME: *25 min*   TOTAL TIME: *55 min*   YIELD: *10 servings*   🕐 ❄   OPTIONS: **Ⓥg ⒹⒻ Ⓟ**

I make these nuggets of chocolatey goodness at least twice per month. I love how they can serve as both dessert and a sweet-tooth satisfying snack. They're a great option when you finish a light meal and want a little something more, or as a pre-workout energy boost. These stuffed dates are an incredible textural experience—you bite through crackling chocolate, then gooey, caramel-y dates, then into the cookie-dough like center.

Line a baking sheet with parchment paper. Pit dates by creating a slit lengthwise that exposes the pit but doesn't split the date in half. Remove pits. Spread dates on baking sheet with the slits facing upward, slightly opened.

In a small bowl, whisk together almond butter, coconut flour, vanilla, and sea salt. This will turn into a semi-thick paste. Dampen teaspoon and fingers with water to help prevent sticking, and fill each date with 1 rounded teaspoon almond butter mixture.

In a prepared double boiler, add chopped chocolate and coconut oil and bring to medium-low heat. If you don't have one, make a double boiler by adding several inches of water to a small pot and bringing to a simmer. Once simmering, place a stainless steel or glass bowl on top that is big enough that it won't sink in. Heat chocolate and coconut oil, stirring constantly, until it is almost completely melted but there are tiny chocolate lumps left (approximately 2 minutes). Remove from heat and continue to stir until smooth.

Place each date gently into the melted chocolate and use a fork to roll it around, coating completely with chocolate. Lift dates, using fork, back onto baking sheet. Sprinkle with garnish of choice.

Place dates in the freezer for 30 minutes until chocolate has hardened. Gently loosen dates from parchment and enjoy. Place leftover dates in a tightly sealed container and keep refrigerated; will last for 1 week.

10 large medjool dates, pit-in

¼ cup unsalted, unsweetened almond butter (or nut/seed butter of choice)

2 tablespoons coconut flour

½ teaspoon vanilla extract

¼ teaspoon sea salt, plus more for garnish

½ cup chopped dark chocolate or chocolate chips (I recommend around 72%) (**Ⓥg ⒹⒻ Ⓟ** sub dairy-free dark chocolate)

1 tablespoon coconut oil

Sea salt, cacao nibs, coconut flakes, or sesame seeds (optional garnish)

ideas for
QUICK SNACKS

Easy dipped dried fruit: Medjool dates, dried unsulphured apricots, dried strawberries or dried mango, dipped in a tablespoon or two of almond butter, peanut butter, or sunbutter. Sprinkle on cinnamon or coconut flakes.

5-ingredient no-bake truffles

(V) (Vg) (GF) (DF) (P) | HANDS-ON TIME: *20 min* | TOTAL TIME: *50 min* | YIELD: *15 truffles* ❄ 🕐

*Y*ou won't believe that these decadent, luscious truffles are made from nuts, fruit, and a little cocoa powder. This is one of the first healthy recipes I ever made, and I almost sold them at a juice bar in New York City. I love these truffles so much that I actually requested them at my wedding! Not only are they nutrient-dense sources of fiber, potassium, vitamin E, and anti-inflammatory polyphenols, they're ridiculously easy to make. I like them straight out of the fridge, but you can also microwave for 5 to 8 seconds to make them soft and gooey.

1½ cups raw walnuts

1 tightly packed cup pitted medjool dates

1 teaspoon vanilla extract

3 tablespoons and 1 teaspoon unsweetened cocoa powder, plus 2 tablespoons for optional coating

¼ teaspoon sea salt, plus more for optional garnish

Line a baking sheet with parchment paper. Place all ingredients in a food processor and pulse until the ingredients start to come together, approximately 30 seconds. You want to be able to pinch the mixture with your fingers and have it stick together. Avoid over-mixing, as it will make the truffles chewy.

Empty mixture onto your baking sheet and prepare a bowl of room temperature water and a dampened dish towel. Wet your fingertips to prevent sticking, scoop out approximately 2 loosely packed tablespoons of mixture, and roll into a ball. Place truffle on baking sheet. Repeat with remaining mixture, wiping off hands as necessary with your dish towel to make rolling easier. Refrigerate for at least 30 minutes before enjoying. Place leftover truffles in an airtight sealable container and keep refrigerated for up to 5 days.

Optional: After making truffles, sprinkle on extra sea salt for a garnish as desired, or add 2 tablespoons cocoa powder to a plate and roll truffles in cocoa powder. Shake off excess powder. Refrigerate.

ideas for
QUICK SNACKS

Frozen fruit and coconut milk cup: Mix frozen fruit with a few tablespoons coconut milk and allow to thaw 10 minutes before enjoying. Can sprinkle on cinnamon, chopped nuts, or drizzle with a little honey or maple syrup, depending on how sweet the fruit is. I like cherries, blueberries, and peaches best.

grapefruit & basil granita

Ⓥ Ⓥⓖ Ⓖⓕ Ⓓⓕ Ⓟ   **HANDS-ON TIME:** *25 min*   **TOTAL TIME:** *24 h, 25 min*   **YIELD:** *6 to 8 servings*   ❄

This recipe is another one that makes me feel like Ina Garten: sophisticated, effortlessly elegant, dressed in linen, and ready to entertain at a moment's notice. In reality, there's a 95% chance I'm wearing yoga pants and serving out of a plastic container, but it's lovely to have recipes that inspire me otherwise! Granitas sound fancy, but they're actually incredibly simple. I particularly adore the combination of tangy grapefruit with earthy basil; it is so refreshing and a perfect palate cleanser after a heavy meal. I usually serve this granita in the spring and summer, but feel free to play with different flavors as the seasons change: maybe cherry and pomegranate in winter, pear and thyme in fall, or pineapple and mint in summer.

Grab an 8 x 8-inch baking dish.

Add grapefruit juice to a large heatproof mixing bowl. To a small sauce pot, add basil, maple syrup, and water. Bring to a boil and boil 5 minutes. Strain basil mixture into the grapefruit juice bowl and whisk to combine evenly.

Pour grapefruit-basil mixture into your baking dish, cover with aluminum foil, and freeze for 24 hours. Be sure to place on a flat surface in the freezer, so it doesn't freeze in an uneven layer.

When granita has been frozen for 24 hours, remove and use a fork to scrape mixture into fluffy ice shavings. Serve immediately, ideally in martini glasses or shot glasses. This granita has a strong flavor, and it shouldn't be eaten like a bowl of ice cream or smoothie!

2 cups freshly squeezed grapefruit juice, strained (approximately 4 large grapefruits or 6 small)

½ packed cup fresh basil leaves

⅓ cup maple syrup

½ cup water

---
ideas for
QUICK SNACKS

Homemade cinnamon toast: Toast 1 slice healthy bread of choice and spread with 1 teaspoon butter or coconut oil, ½ teaspoon dried sweetener, and a pinch of cinnamon (be sure to add toppings while bread is hot).

summer peach & blueberry crumble
with coconut cashew cream

V **VG** **GF** **DF** | HANDS-ON TIME: *20 min* | TOTAL TIME: *1 h* | YIELD: *6 to 8 servings* 🕐

*T*here is one herald of summer that I anticipate every year—The Peach Truck. The Peach Truck come from Pearson Farm in Georgia, and they're here in Nashville from May to September. These peaches are juicy and sweet; the perfect representative of peak seasonal summer fruit. After we've gotten our fill of enjoying them whole, I like to throw together this gorgeous and foolproof crumble. Slightly tart blueberries are a foil to the peaches, and my crumble topping melts into the fruit as it cooks.

To make the Coconut Cashew Cream (optional): If you have a high-powered blender, combine ingredients and puree until smooth. If you do not have a high-powered blender, you have two options: a long soak or a quick boil. For the long soak, soak the cashews in room temperature water in a small bowl for 4 to 6 hours, then drain before blending. For the quick boil, add the cashews to boiling water for 10 minutes, then drain and rinse with cold water until they are room temperature. Regardless of method, refrigerate at least 1 hour before serving. Recipe makes ¾ cup.

Preheat oven to 375° F.

Prepare the fruit. In a large mixing bowl, combine peaches, blueberries, dates, lemon juice, and arrowroot. Toss to coat evenly. Empty mixture into a cast-iron skillet.

Now, mix the crumble. In a separate mixing bowl, combine oats, almond flour, sugar, cinnamon, and sea salt. Stir to combine. Add coconut oil and use fingertips to mix oil into the ingredients until a crumble consistency forms.

Scatter crumble topping evenly over fruit mixture. Bake for 35 minutes, or until fruit is bubbling and tender. Wait 10 minutes to cool and top with Coconut Cashew Cream. Crumble will keep tightly sealed in the refrigerator for 4 days. I suggest keeping the Coconut Cashew Cream separate if you plan to have leftovers.

FROZEN FRUIT VERSION:

Winter crumble hankerings? Feel free to use frozen fruit and bake another few minutes, or substitute for another seasonal fruit of your choosing in the same ratio.

COCONUT CASHEW CREAM (OPTIONAL):

½ cup canned full-fat coconut milk

½ cup raw whole cashews

2 tablespoons maple syrup

FRUIT:

4 ripe peaches, skin on, cored and chopped into 1-inch pieces

2 cups fresh blueberries

½ cup medjool dates, pitted and chopped into ½-inch pieces (sub raisins)

2 tablespoons lemon juice

2 tablespoons arrowroot starch

CRUMBLE:

½ cup rolled oats

½ cup blanched almond flour (sub almond meal, wheat, oat, spelt, or gluten-free all-purpose flour)

6 tablespoons coconut sugar (sub light brown sugar)

1 teaspoon cinnamon

1 teaspoon sea salt

¼ cup melted coconut oil

note

To chop your peach, just poke your knife into the flesh around the stem until you feel the pit, then gently slice down, curving the knife around the edge of the pit. Repeat this with a cut going crosswise to the first, and you should have four slabs of peach flesh for chopping.

pineapple mojito popsicles

(V) (GF) (DF) (P) | **HANDS-ON TIME:** *15 min* | **TOTAL TIME:** *6 h, 15 min* | **YIELD:** *10 popsicles* | ❄ | **OPTIONS:** (Vg)

When it comes to popsicles, people tend to either go creamy/ chocolatey, or they're loyal to the fruity/tangy category. For the latter folks, these Pineapple Mojito Popsicles are an absolute dream. Their sweetness is balanced by the "zip" and acidity of lime and mint, and pineapple can aid in digestion. These popsicles are a refreshing summery treat that please kiddos and adults alike, and they couldn't be easier to make. P.S. For the adults, you could easily sub tequila or rum for some of the water. Just sayin'!

Combine all ingredients in a blender and puree until smooth. Taste for more honey and add accordingly. Pour evenly into popsicle molds and add sticks according to your specific mold's directions. Freeze at least 6 hours. To serve, run hot water over molds, being careful not to get water on the popsicles, just until loose enough to remove. To store, stack popsicles between pieces of parchment paper and wrap in plastic wrap. Will keep in the freezer up to 1 week.

2 rounded cups fresh pineapple, cut into 1-inch chunks

1 cup water

¼ cup packed fresh mint leaves

½ teaspoon lime zest (approximately 2 limes)

¼ cup lime juice

1 tablespoons honey, plus more to taste ((Vg) sub maple syrup)

---
ideas for
QUICK SNACKS

Elvis banana: 1 ripe banana, drizzled with peanut butter and honey. Can also add cinnamon, coconut flakes, chopped nuts, or chocolate chips.

---
note

My popsicle molds hold 3 ounces each.

Yes, say many in
Louvre, Jean-Luc Martinez, who
described free ports as the greatest museums no one can see.
Some see even higher stakes for
contemporary works, as they can
be whisked off, their paint hardly
dry, before ever entering the
public's consciousness. Storage
Kaplan International
with Mr. Daleyot and

coconut avocado popsicles

(V) (Vg) (GF) (DF) (P)   HANDS-ON TIME: *10 to 15 min*   TOTAL TIME: *6 h, 10 to 15 min*   YIELD: *10 popsicles*   ❄ ⊕

When I was deciding if I should move home to Nashville, a few foodie gems helped sway me back to the motherland. One was Las Paletas, a gourmet popsicle shop that uses creative ingredients like hibiscus, chili, and avocado. When I finally enjoyed their famed avocado paleta, it didn't disappoint, and I knew I wanted an LL Balanced version for the cookbook. These Coconut Avocado Popsicles are downright dreamy—rich and velvety with just enough sweetness. Plus, they're full of nourishing healthy fats. Even my 3-year-old niece Vivian loves these unique popsicles!

Add coconut milk, water, avocado, vanilla, and maple syrup in a blender and puree until smooth. Pour evenly into popsicle molds and add sticks according to your specific mold's directions. Note that this is a thick liquid, so I sometimes find it easier to spoon the mixture into each mold instead of pouring. Before placing in the freezer, gently tap the molds on the counter to fill in any air bubbles.

Freeze at least 6 hours. To serve, run hot water over molds, being careful not to get water on the popsicles, just until loose enough to remove.

If using garnishes, place popsicles on a parchment-lined baking sheet. Apply Chocolate Drizzle (page 334) over popsicles, then sprinkle on toasted coconut. Place back in the freezer another 5 minutes. Use a turner spatula to flip popsicles and repeat on opposite side.

To store, stack popsicles between pieces of parchment paper and wrap in plastic wrap. Will keep in the freezer up to 1 week.

1 15-ounce can full-fat coconut milk

½ cup water

½ cup mashed ripe avocado

1 teaspoon vanilla extract

⅓ cup maple syrup

Chocolate Drizzle (page 334; optional garnish)

⅓ cup toasted coconut flakes (see page 105; optional garnish)

note

Chop up any leftover popsicles and blend them up in a smoothie for extra-healthy fat, creaminess, and flavor.

note

My popsicle molds hold 3 ounces each.

strawberry bourbon ice cream

V Vg GF DF | HANDS-ON TIME: *30 min* | TOTAL TIME: *11 h* | YIELD: *8 servings* | 🌢 ❄ | OPTIONS: P

*H*eavens to Betsy, this ice cream. This is not-so-wicked, wickedly delicious, creamier-than-ice-cream ice cream. My trick of using pureed cashews with coconut milk results in a luscious, silky texture that stands up to its dairy-based counterpart. Although I've made countless ice cream flavors, this strawberry bourbon is easily a favorite. The flavor profile is both sophisticated and classic, and it's quintessentially Southern. If you're not feeling the strawberry, feel free to substitute the same amount of other berries, stone fruits, or even pears.

Make sure you freeze the base of your ice cream maker at least 24 hours before making ice cream.

In a small saucepan, combine 2 tablespoons of the maple syrup, strawberries, and water. Heat to medium and cook, stirring and mashing strawberries as they soften, until mixture has reduced to a jam consistency. This can take anywhere from 10 to 15 minutes, depending on whether you use fresh or frozen strawberries. Empty mixture into a heatproof bowl and refrigerate.

Prepare ice cream maker by placing on counter and plugging in. Leave bowl in the freezer until the last minute.

To a high-powered blender, add remaining 6 tablespoons maple syrup, cashews, coconut milk, lemon juice, bourbon, olive oil, and sea salt. Blend until completely smooth. Quickly remove ice cream maker bowl from the freezer and place on base. Pour cashew mixture into the bowl. Complete and churn according to manufacturer directions. Mine takes approximately 18 minutes.

(continued on next page)

2 plus 6 tablespoons maple syrup

2 rounded cups frozen or fresh strawberries, hulls removed

¼ cup water

1 cup raw cashews, soaked in warm water 4 to 8 hours, drained and rinsed

1 15-ounce can full-fat coconut milk

1 tablespoon fresh lemon juice

2 tablespoons bourbon (sub whiskey or rum) (P omit)

2 tablespoons olive oil

Pinch sea salt

note

If you remove the bourbon and strawberries in this recipe, or the bananas, vanilla, and peanut butter in the second, you have an amazing simple base for whatever ice cream flavors you like. Get creative adding fruit, chocolate chips, nuts, spices, or crumbled baked goods like The Best Soft-Baked Chocolate Chip Cookies (page 345) or Holy Fudge Black Bean Brownies (page 341).

For a chocolate ice cream, add ⅓ cup cocoa powder, 2 more tablespoons maple syrup, and 1 teaspoon vanilla extract.

strawberry bourbon ice cream *(continued)*

While ice cream is churning, line a standard (8 ½ x 4 ½ x 2 ¾-inch) loaf pan or shallow dish with parchment paper. When ice cream is finished churning, turn mixture out into prepared dish. Remove strawberry mixture from the refrigerator and carefully stir into ice cream.

Cover ice cream tightly with aluminum foil or plastic wrap and freeze at least 6 hours before enjoying. Allow ice cream to sit out at room temperature for 15 to 30 minutes before scooping (time depends on the temp of the room). Ice cream will keep tightly covered for 1 week.

note

You could leave out the alcohol if you want to serve this to kids or just prefer it without. It might slightly change the texture, but it will still taste wonderful. Also, I love to serve this topped with the oat crumble from my Ambrosia Salad recipe (page 204).

ideas for

QUICK SNACKS

My favorite trail mix: Mix together equal parts dark chocolate chips, dried cherries, and roasted cashews. Enjoy in moderation.

banana peanut butter elvis ice cream

V GF | HANDS-ON TIME: *20 min* | TOTAL TIME: *11 h* | YIELD: *8 servings* | ▲ ❄ | OPTIONS: **Vg DF P**

I think the name says it all here. Using the same base as my Strawberry Bourbon Ice Cream, I indulged my inner kiddo with this variation. As a Tennessee gal, I immediately thought of The King when I had my first scoop. Elvis's favorite sandwich was peanut butter, banana, grape jelly, and bacon, and while I don't use the latter two in my recipe, I still think he would approve! There's absolutely no way to be sad when you eat this ice cream, so I suggest planning to make it when you just need a little mood booster.

Make sure you freeze the base of your ice cream maker at least 24 hours before making ice cream.

Prepare ice cream maker by placing on counter and plugging in. Leave bowl in the freezer until the last minute.

Combine all ingredients except bananas and peanut butter in a blender and puree until smooth. Quickly remove ice cream maker bowl from the freezer and place on base. Pour cashew mixture into the bowl. Complete and churn according to manufacturer directions. Mine takes approximately 18 minutes.

While ice cream is churning, line a standard (8½ x 4½ x 2¾-inch) loaf pan or shallow dish with parchment paper. Slice bananas in half lengthwise, then chop into ½-inch pieces. When ice cream is finished churning, quickly turn mixture out into a medium mixing bowl and stir in bananas and peanut butter. Leave some whole streaks of peanut butter unmixed. Immediately add ice cream to lined loaf tin or dish and spread in an even layer.

Cover ice cream tightly with aluminum foil or plastic wrap and freeze at least 6 hours before enjoying. Allow ice cream to sit at room temperature for 15 to 30 mins before scooping (time depends on the temp of the room). Ice cream will keep tightly covered for 1 week.

1 cup raw cashews, soaked in room temperature water for 4 to 8 hours, drained and rinsed

½ cup maple syrup

1 15-ounce can full-fat coconut milk

2 teaspoons vanilla extract

1 tablespoon fresh lemon juice

2 tablespoons olive oil

Pinch sea salt

2 ripe bananas

⅓ to ½ cup peanut butter (use more if you want a very pronounced peanut butter flavor) (**P** sub almond butter)

⅓ to ½ cup semi-sweet chocolate chips or toasted coconut flakes (optional garnish) (**Vg DF P** sub dairy-free dark chocolate)

ideas for
QUICK SNACKS

The simplest smoothie: Blend ¾ cup milk of choice, 1 frozen banana, 1 teaspoon sweetener of choice, 1 tablespoon nut butter, splash vanilla extract, and a handful of ice. Add more liquid as necessary to achieve desired consistency.

maple peanut butter freezer fudge
with chocolate drizzle

Ⓥ Ⓥg Ⓖf Ⓓf | HANDS-ON TIME: *10 min* | TOTAL TIME: *1 h, 10 min* | YIELD: *12 pieces* | ❄ | OPTIONS: Ⓟ

This recipe clocks in at 10 minutes hands-on time from start to finish, but that doesn't mean it's any less delicious than other desserts! Coconut oil, tahini, and peanut butter create a melt-in-your mouth texture that rivals any traditional fudge. However, unlike the fudge of your childhood, mine is relatively low in sugar and full of healthy fats. As a result, I also use this freezer fudge as pre-workout snack! Feel free to play around with add-ins or toppings: dried cranberries, goji berries, chia seeds, coconut flakes, finely chopped nuts, or even a puffed rice cereal.

If making Chocolate Drizzle, whisk all ingredients together until smooth. Use as you would Magic Shell chocolate sauce—this will be liquid or semi-solid at room temperature, but will harden when added to something cold.

Whisk all ingredients for fudge together in a mixing bowl. If using mini cupcake molds, fill each almost completely. I do a mixture of mini cups and hearts. Freeze for 1 hour. Pop cups out of the molds. If garnishing, top with Chocolate Drizzle and sprinkle with sea salt. Freeze another 10 minutes. Enjoy straight out of the freezer. Fudge will keep tightly sealed for 2 weeks in freezer.

CHOCOLATE DRIZZLE (OPTIONAL):

2 tablespoons melted coconut oil

2 tablespoons unsweetened cocoa powder

2 tablespoons maple syrup

FUDGE:

½ cup peanut butter, tahini paste, almond butter, or a mix—I prefer half peanut butter and half tahini (Ⓟ sub non–peanut butter)

⅓ cup melted coconut oil

¾ teaspoon maple extract

2 tablespoons maple syrup

Sea salt flakes (optional garnish)

note

You will need a silicone mini cupcake tray or other small silicone molds.

ideas for
QUICK SNACKS

2-ingredient berry nice cream: In a food processor, blend 3 to 4 frozen bananas with 1 cup frozen berries of choice. Stop to scrape down with a spatula as necessary. If you're having trouble blending, add tablespoons of water or milk until mixture moves.

nashville gooey butter cake

V GF P | **HANDS-ON TIME:** *20 min* | **TOTAL TIME:** *1 h, 10 min* | **YIELD:** *16 squares* DF

*M*y newest sister-in-law is a St. Louis native, and she included a square of St. Louis gooey butter cake in her wedding welcome bag. I tried one bite and was completely smitten . . . I mean, it basically tastes like underbaked sugar cookie dough. For an LL Balanced version, I use cashews to create the "gooey" layer, and I replace refined sugar and flour with coconut sugar and almond flour. I adore my Nashville Gooey Butter Cake squares best with a dollop of my 20-Minute Chia Berry Jam (page 118) and whipped cream, but my husband prefers them plain. You could also sprinkle on some chocolate chips when they're hot out of the oven!

Preheat oven to 350° F.

Line an 8 x 8-inch baking pan with parchment paper, allowing a few inches of paper to hang over the sides. Add all base layer ingredients to a standing mixer or mixing bowl, if you have a hand mixer. Blend on medium speed until ingredients are incorporated. You could also whisk, if you don't have either mixer. Turn mixture out into baking pan and spread into an even layer.

Combine top layer ingredients in high-powered blender and blend until incorporated and smooth. This will be a liquid. Pour over base layer. Place dish on the middle rack and bake for 22 minutes, or until the edges are firm to touch but the center is sticky and can be easily punctured. The top layer will still jiggle a little when you move the pan. Allow to cool 15 minutes before lifting out of the pan using parchment paper, then cool another 5 minutes before slicing into squares.

Dust with arrowroot starch, if using, and serve with 20-Minute Chia Berry Jam (page 118) or other topping of choice. Cake will keep tightly sealed in the refrigerator up to 4 days.

BASE LAYER:

1½ cups blanched almond flour

2 large eggs

¼ cup coconut sugar

6 tablespoons softened butter (room temperature)

¼ teaspoon sea salt

1½ teaspoons vanilla extract

TOP LAYER:

2 large eggs

1 cup cashews, soaked in hot water 10 minutes, then drained

6 tablespoons maple syrup

1 teaspoon apple cider vinegar

Arrowroot starch (optional garnish)

note

This cake is true to its name, and some of the center pieces will be completely gooey. These are my favorites. But feel free to play with cooking longer if you'd like.

ideas for
QUICK SNACKS

Pumpkin pudding: Whisk together ⅓ cup pumpkin puree, 1 tablespoon liquid sweetener, ⅓ cup canned full-fat coconut milk, 1 tablespoon nut butter, and a pinch of cinnamon.

snickerdoodle cupcakes
with vanilla buttercream frosting

Ⓥ ⒢ Ⓟ | HANDS-ON TIME: *25 min* | TOTAL TIME: *50 min* | YIELD: *12 cupcakes* | 🕐 🄳🄵

I am slightly embarrassed by how many trials it took to get these cupcakes just right. I take my cupcakes seriously! The effort was well worth the result though, because these cupcakes have a light, tender crumb and are reminiscent of the classic snickerdoodle. My Vanilla Buttercream Frosting certainly isn't a health food, but it doesn't contain the gobs of powdered sugar found in traditional recipes. This recipe is everything you want for a celebratory sweet treat, and it won't send your energy crashing. The best of both worlds!

Preheat oven to 350° F and line a 12-cup cupcake tin with cupcake liners.

To make the cupcakes, in a large mixing bowl, whisk together flours, salt, baking powder, baking soda, cinnamon, and cream of tartar.

In a smaller bowl, whisk together coconut milk, olive oil, maple syrup, and eggs. Add wet mix to dry ingredients and mix to incorporate evenly.

Fill each cupcake liner approximately ⅔ full with batter, approximately ¼ cup per cupcake. This is a thick batter, so I suggest keeping a bowl of lukewarm water by to dampen your scooping utensil, which helps prevent sticking. Use damp fingertips to pat the batter into a flat layer in each tin.

Bake for 17 minutes, or until a toothpick comes out clean. Cool 5 minutes before removing from cupcake tin and placing on a slotted baking sheet or cooling rack. I use a fork to help lift them out of the tins.

When the cupcakes are cool or almost cool, make the Vanilla Buttercream Frosting. This is so you can add frosting right away; otherwise, it should be refrigerated, which hardens it, and then you'll have to wait for it to soften again.

In the bowl of a standing mixer or mixing bowl (if you have a hand mixer), whisk together all of the frosting ingredients except coconut oil. Turn mixer or hand-mixer to high speed and begin whipping mixture. Slowly drizzle in coconut oil and whip until light and fluffy with medium peaks, approximately 2 minutes. You can frost immediately, as long as cupcakes are completely cool.

CUPCAKES:

1¼ cups almond flour

½ cup coconut flour

¼ teaspoon sea salt

1½ teaspoons baking powder

¼ teaspoon baking soda

1 tablespoon plus 1 teaspoon cinnamon

1 teaspoon cream of tartar
(optional, but helps create an authentic snickerdoodle flavor)

¾ cup canned full-fat coconut milk

¼ cup olive oil

¼ cup maple syrup

3 large eggs

VANILLA BUTTERCREAM FROSTING:

¾ cup butter, room temperature

¼ cup arrowroot starch
(sub non-GMO cornstarch)

¼ cup maple syrup

1½ teaspoons vanilla extract

Pinch sea salt

¼ cup melted coconut oil

VANILLA/CHOCOLATE VERSION:

I have also made these cupcakes a classic vanilla/chocolate combination by subbing the cinnamon for 1½ teaspoons vanilla extract, and using my 1-Minute Ganache (page 341) as a frosting.

holy fudge black bean brownies
with 1-minute ganache

V **GF** | HANDS-ON TIME: *15 min* | TOTAL TIME: *1 h, 50 min* | YIELD: *12 to 15 brownies* | ❄ | OPTIONS: **Vg** **DF**

*H*ands down, no question, game over—this is the most popular recipe on my website. The idea of beans in dessert can seem off-putting at best and torturous at worst, but I promise it works! These brownies are the best I've ever had, healthy or no, and there isn't a hint of bean flavor. Instead, they're decadent, moist, and gratuitously chocolatey–everything you want in a brownie. Although these brownies can stand alone, adding my 1-Minute Ganache takes them to another stratosphere of dessert goodness. Oh and p.s., they're one of the easiest recipes in this book.

Preheat oven to 375° F and line a standard (8½ x 4½ x 2¾-inch) loaf pan with parchment paper, making sure there are at least 5 inches of parchment overflowing on each side.

For brownies, combine all ingredients except chopped chocolate in a food processor or high-powered blender. Puree until completely smooth, scraping down the side as needed.

Empty mixture into a mixing bowl and stir in chopped chocolate/ chocolate chips. Turn dough into loaf tin and shake gently to create an even layer. At this point, you can trim back some of the parchment, but leave an inch or two overhanging.

Bake for 50 minutes or until a toothpick comes out with only a tiny bit of batter. Remove from the oven and refrigerate brownies for 30 minutes.

If making 1-Minute Ganache, combine all ingredients in a small sauce pot and turn heat to medium-low. Cook, whisking, until ingredients are evenly incorporated and there are small bubbles forming around the edge. This should only take 1 minute. Remove ganache from the stove and allow to cool 20 minutes before using. The recipe makes approximately ¾ cup.

Add the ganache and optional toppings to the brownies. Refrigerate another 15 minutes before slicing. If you want the ganache to solidify even further, refrigerate for 1 hour before slicing. If you're not using ganache, allow brownies to cool 45 minutes to 1 hour after baking before slicing (no refrigeration required).

Brownies will keep tightly sealed in the refrigerator up to 5 days.

BROWNIES:

1 15-ounce can unsalted black beans, drained and rinsed thoroughly

6 tablespoons cocoa powder

¾ cup maple syrup

2 teaspoons vanilla extract

¼ cup unsalted almond butter (sub nut/seed butter of choice, but note that it will have a different flavor)

¼ teaspoon baking soda

¼ teaspoon salt

3½ ounces dark chocolate, roughly chopped into ¼-inch pieces (recommend 72%) (**Vg** **DF** sub dairy-free dark chocolate)

Coconut flakes, cacao nibs, or fresh fruit (optional garnish)

1-MINUTE GANACHE (OPTIONAL):

⅓ cup maple syrup

2 tablespoons butter (**Vg** **DF** sub coconut oil)

2 tablespoons canned full-fat coconut milk

¼ cup cocoa powder

1 teaspoon vanilla extract

Pinch sea salt

chewy ginger cookies *with* molasses date caramel

V GF P | HANDS-ON TIME: *25 min* | TOTAL TIME: *55 min* | YIELD: *15 cookies* | ⏱ ❄

I don't like cookies that don't contain chocolate. That is, I didn't, until I made these Chewy Ginger Cookies. I created them for my best friend, Kate, who loves anything with ginger. Except, as soon as I tasted one, I couldn't bear to give them all away (don't judge). These cookies have a lovely balance of spice and sweet, with a hint of earthiness from molasses. The texture is both tender and chewy, pleasing multiple cookie palates.

If making Molasses Date Caramel, add coconut milk and dates to a blender and puree until as smooth as possible—you will still see tiny pieces of date. Add mixture to a small sauce pot and turn to medium heat. As soon as the mixture starts simmering, turn heat to low. Cook, stirring every 30 seconds, until mixture has reduced by ½ and is a light brown color, approximately 10 minutes.

Remove from heat and stir in molasses and sea salt. Refrigerate mixture in a heatproof container until completely cooled.

For cookies, preheat oven to 325° F and line two baking sheets with parchment paper. Mix ¼ cup coconut sugar and ¼ teaspoon ground ginger and spread on a plate.

In a large mixing bowl, combine remaining ginger, flours, cinnamon, salt, and baking powder. Whisk to incorporate.

In a standing mixer or hand mixer, combine remaining 1 cup coconut sugar, eggs, and butter. Mix on high speed for 1 minute, until mixture has formed small soft peaks and lightened in color. Add molasses. Mix another 30 seconds until molasses is incorporated and mixture has slightly firmer peaks—when you turn your spatula upside down, the peaks will hold for just a second before collapsing.

Fold wet mixture into dry until incorporated. Cover dough and refrigerate for 30 minutes. Remove from fridge. Fill a small bowl with room temperature water and place next to baking sheets and coconut sugar plate. Scoop and roll 2-inch balls of dough. Roll them in coconut sugar mixture to coat and place balls on baking sheet. I do 7 to 8 balls per baking sheet, leaving plenty of room for them to expand.

(continued at right)

MOLASSES DATE CARAMEL (OPTIONAL):

1 cup canned full-fat coconut milk

½ cup packed pitted medjool dates

1 teaspoon molasses

¼ teaspoon sea salt

COOKIES:

1 plus ¼ cups coconut sugar

1 plus ¼ teaspoon ground ginger

1¼ cups blanched almond flour

6 tablespoons coconut flour

1½ teaspoons ground cinnamon

½ teaspoon sea salt

½ teaspoon baking powder

1 egg plus 1 egg white

¼ cup room temperature grass-fed butter

2 tablespoons molasses

(recipe instructions continued)

Use damp fingers to flatten balls to approximately ½-inch thickness. Bake for 20 minutes, then allow to cool 10 minutes before topping with caramel (if using) and enjoying.

Cookies will keep tightly sealed on the countertop for 2 days or in the refrigerator for 5 days. Reheat in the oven at 300° F for 5 minutes.

the best soft-baked chocolate chip cookies

V GF   HANDS-ON TIME: *15 to 20 min*   TOTAL TIME: *35 to 40 min*   YIELD: *12 cookies*   OPTIONS: DF P

*E*veryone needs a reliable chocolate chip cookie recipe, and there are a million available for you to choose from. But who wants to sort through a million cookie recipes (okay, me, but that's beside the point)? The point is, why take the time, when you have one that's consistently easy, scrumptious, and about as healthy as a chocolate chip cookie gets? These cookies have become a staple in many readers' homes, and they're fun to make as a family. Despite tasting decadent, there's actually very little sugar per cookie. Note that these are soft-baked in texture, which is my personal favorite. If you're a crispy cookie kinda person, my CCC's might not be for you. Then again, they've converted many to join the soft-baked camp!

Preheat oven to 350° F. Line a baking sheet with parchment paper.

Combine almond flour, baking soda, coconut sugar, and sea salt in a large mixing bowl. Whisk to incorporate.

In a separate smaller bowl, whisk together egg, olive oil, coconut milk, and vanilla extract until combined.

Add wet ingredients to dry and stir to incorporate evenly. Stir in chopped chocolate.

Place a small bowl of room temperature water between your batter and baking sheet. Dampen fingers and dollop 2 level tablespoons of dough per cookie onto the baking sheet. Leave at least 1 inch of room between cookies. This is a sticky batter, so be patient with it. With damp fingers, pat your dollops of dough into a round shape and flatten to approximately ½-inch thickness.

Bake for 11 minutes, or until cookies are just barely set on top, with a light golden brown around the bottom edges. They will seem under-baked, but they will continue to firm up.

Allow to cool 10 minutes before using a spatula to loosen from the baking sheet—enjoy! Cookies will keep sealed on the counter for 48 hours or refrigerated for up to 5 days. To reheat, microwave at 10 second intervals until chocolate is starting to melt.

1½ cups blanched almond flour

½ teaspoon baking soda

6 tablespoons coconut sugar (sub light brown sugar)

¼ teaspoon sea salt

1 large egg

2 tablespoons olive oil (sounds strange in a cookie, but it adds a wonderful hint of umami)

2 tablespoons canned full-fat coconut milk

1 teaspoon vanilla extract

½ cup dark chocolate, chopped to ¼-inch pieces (I recommend 72%, but semi-sweet works too and is a good option for kids, as it is a little sweeter) (DF P sub dairy-free dark chocolate)

OTHER VERSIONS:

Some readers have reported adding nuts and/or dried fruit to these bars. Play around with pecans, walnuts, cranberries, cherries, coconut flakes— the sky's the limit!

APPENDIX

weekly menus

SPRING

	MONDAY	TUESDAY	WEDNESDAY	THURSDAY	FRIDAY
BREAKFAST	Aloha Smoothie Bowl	Blueberry Coconut Morning Porridge	Blueberry Coconut Morning Porridge	Aloha Smoothie Bowl	Aloha Smoothie Bowl
LUNCH	Wild Rice Lentil Burgers; raw veggies with hummus	BBQ Chicken Quinoa Casserole; Husband-Favorite Salad	BBQ Chicken Quinoa Casserole; Husband-Favorite Salad; and/or veggies with hummus	Mushroom & Arugula Walnut Pesto Pasta*	Mushroom & Arugula Walnut Pesto Pasta*
DINNER	BBQ Chicken Quinoa Casserole; Husband-Favorite Salad	Wild Rice Lentil Burgers; raw veggies with hummus	Wild Rice Lentil Burgers; Sesame Maple Brussels Sprouts Bits	Orange & Ginger Seared Scallops; Carrot Ginger Cabbage Slaw; Sesame Maple Brussels Sprouts Bits	Orange & Ginger Seared Scallops; Carrot Ginger Cabbage Slaw; Sesame Maple Brussels Sprouts Bits

*Toss Mushroom & Arugula Walnut Pesto Pasta with fresh arugula when serving.

RECIPES USED

Aloha Smoothie Bowl x 3 (page 105)
Blueberry Coconut Morning Porridge x 2 (page 113)
Wild Rice Lentil Burgers (page 278)
BBQ Chicken Quinoa Casserole (page 248)
Husband-Favorite Salad (page 303)
Mushroom & Arugula Walnut Pesto Pasta (page 286)
Sesame Maple Brussels Sprouts Bits (page 185)
Orange & Ginger Seared Scallops x 2 (page 270)
Carrot Ginger Cabbage Slaw (page 182)

ADDITIONAL ITEMS:

Raw veggies
Hummus
Extra arugula

COOKING SCHEDULE

Saturday: Grocery shop. Freeze smoothie bowl fruit. Make Remarkable BBQ Sauce, if you did not buy packaged. Make Cucumber Mint Dressing for Husband-Favorite Salad.

Sunday: Make BBQ Chicken Quinoa Casserole. Make Wild Rice Lentil Burgers. Slice raw veggies.

Monday night: Make a double batch of Blueberry Coconut Morning Porridge.

Wednesday night: Make Mushroom & Arugula Walnut Pesto Pasta. Make Carrot Ginger Cabbage Slaw.

Thursday and Friday night: Make Orange & Ginger Seared Scallops fresh each night.

SUMMER

	MONDAY	TUESDAY	WEDNESDAY	THURSDAY	FRIDAY
BREAKFAST	LL's Daily Green Smoothie	Blueberry Ginger Breakfast Smoothie	LL's Daily Green Smoothie	Blueberry Ginger Breakfast Smoothie	LL's Daily Green Smoothie
LUNCH	Watermelon, Quinoa & Arugula Salad*	Tarragon Almond Chicken Salad; Lemon Parmesan Cauliflower Steaks	Watermelon, Quinoa & Arugula Salad*; Lamb Burgers	Cold Sesame Noodles*; Asian Marinated Cucumber Zucchini Salad	Cold Sesame Noodles*; Asian Marinated Cucumber Zucchini Salad
DINNER	Tarragon Almond Chicken Salad; Lemon Parmesan Cauliflower Steaks	Watermelon, Quinoa & Arugula Salad*; Lamb Burgers	Tarragon Almond Chicken Salad; Lemon Parmesan Cauliflower Steaks; and/or greens of choice with dressing	Lamb Burgers; greens of choice with dressing	Leftovers/ Time to get creative!

*If heartier meals are desired, add chickpeas and avocado to the Watermelon, Quinoa & Arugula Salad or Cold Sesame Noodles.

RECIPES USED

LL's Daily Green Smoothie x 3 (page 90)
Blueberry Ginger Breakfast Smoothie x 2 (page 93)
Watermelon, Quinoa & Arugula Salad (page 300)
Tarragon Almond Chicken Salad (page 234)
Lemon Parmesan Cauliflower Steaks (page 186)
Lamb Burgers (page 230)
Cold Sesame Noodles (page 277)
Asian Marinated Cucumber Zucchini Salad (page 203)

ADDITIONAL ITEMS:

Greens of choice
Dressing of choice
Chickpeas (optional)
Avocados (optional)

COOKING SCHEDULE

Saturday: Grocery shop and make sure all smoothie fruit is frozen.

Sunday: Make Watermelon, Quinoa & Arugula Salad with a double batch of vinaigrette; toss quinoa with ½ vinaigrette and refrigerate. Make Tarragon Almond Chicken Salad.

Wednesday night: Make Cold Sesame Noodles and Asian Marinated Cucumber Zucchini Salad.

note

The goal of these menu plans is to help you be efficient with grocery dollars and time, so there is a purposeful reliance on leftovers. Most recipes will be made ahead of time and reheated on serving days. Exceptions: smoothies and some other breakfast and seafood dishes are to be made and enjoyed immediately, without leftovers. Some other in-between recipes are to be made and eaten immediately, but will provide leftovers as well. Note that cooking instructions will only indicate any steps to be taken ahead of the serving time shown in the chart.

weekly menus *(continued)*

AUTUMN

	MONDAY	TUESDAY	WEDNESDAY	THURSDAY	FRIDAY
BREAKFAST	Sunflower SuperSeed Flatbread with mashed avocado, salt and pepper, and an optional fried egg	10-Minute Whipped Banana Almond Porridge	Sunflower SuperSeed Flatbread with mashed avocado, salt and pepper, and an optional fried egg	10-Minute Whipped Banana Almond Porridge	Sunflower SuperSeed Flatbread with mashed avocado, salt and pepper, and an optional fried egg
LUNCH	Perfect Harvest Salad*	Slow Cooker Indian Butter Chicken; Baked Coconut Rice	Leftovers/Time to get creative!	Maple Balsamic–Glazed Tempeh & Mushroom Bake; Simple Spicy Garlicky Greens	Maple Balsamic–Glazed Tempeh & Mushroom Bake; Simple Spicy Garlicky Greens
DINNER	Slow Cooker Indian Butter Chicken; Baked Coconut Rice	Perfect Harvest Salad*	Maple Balsamic–Glazed Tempeh & Mushroom Bake; Simple Spicy Garlicky Greens	Shockingly Delicious Asian Salmon Cakes; Turmeric & Tahini Roasted Cauliflower	Shockingly Delicious Asian Salmon Cakes; Turmeric & Tahini Roasted Cauliflower

*Add chickpeas or protein of choice.

RECIPES USED

Sunflower SuperSeed Flatbread (page 169)
10-Minute Whipped Banana Almond Porridge x 2 (page 127)
Perfect Harvest Salad (page 295)
Slow Cooker Indian Butter Chicken (page 238)
Baked Coconut Rice (page 208)
Maple Balsamic–Glazed Tempeh & Mushroom Bake (page 290)
Simple Spicy Garlicky Greens (page 194)
Shockingly Delicious Asian Salmon Cakes (page 266)
Turmeric & Tahini Roasted Cauliflower (page 189)

ADDITIONAL ITEMS:

Avocados
Eggs (optional)
Chickpeas (optional)
Protein of choice (optional)

COOKING SCHEDULE

Saturday: Grocery shop. Make Sunflower SuperSeed Flatbread.

Sunday: Roast sweet potatoes and pecans for Harvest Salad; make Cinnamon Date Dressing. Make Coconut Baked Rice.

Monday morning: Start slow cooking the Slow Cooker Indian Butter Chicken.

Tuesday night: Marinate the tempeh and mushrooms for the Maple Balsamic–Glazed Tempeh & Mushroom Bake.

WINTER

	MONDAY	TUESDAY	WEDNESDAY	THURSDAY	FRIDAY
BREAKFAST	Crispy Fried Egg Power Breakfast; Green Immuni-Tea	Power C Sunshine Smoothie; protein of choice	Crispy Fried Egg Power Breakfast; Green Immuni-Tea	Power C Sunshine Smoothie; protein of choice	Crispy Fried Egg Power Breakfast; Green Immuni-Tea
LUNCH	Taco salad made with The Best 15-Minute Taco Meat	Quinoa Lentil Pizza Crust, Pepperoni Version; Lemon Parmesan Cauliflower Steaks	Leftovers/Time to get creative!	Famous Bryant Family Chili; Creamy Green Bean Casserole	Curried Honey Mustard Salmon Sautéed Greens & Rice Bowl
DINNER	Quinoa Lentil Pizza Crust, Pepperoni Version; Lemon Parmesan Cauliflower Steaks	Taco salad made with The Best 15-Minute Taco Meat	Famous Bryant Family Chili; Creamy Green Bean Casserole	Curried Honey Mustard Salmon Sautéed Greens & Rice Bowl	Famous Bryant Family Chili; Creamy Green Bean Casserole

RECIPES USED

Crispy Fried Egg Power Breakfast x 3 (page 133)

Green Immuni-Tea x 3 (page 106)

Power C Sunshine Smoothie (page 98)

The Best 15-Minute Taco Meat (page 215)

Quinoa Lentil Pizza Crust, Pepperoni Version (page 219)

Lemon Parmesan Cauliflower Steaks (page 186)

Famous Bryant Family Chili (page 304)

Creamy Green Bean Casserole (page 198)

Curried Honey Mustard Salmon Sautéed
    Greens & Rice Bowl (page 258)

ADDITIONAL ITEMS:

Breakfast protein of choice

Salad ingredients for taco salad

COOKING SCHEDULE

Saturday: Grocery shop. Freeze smoothie fruit. Mix LL's Special Spice Mixture for eggs.

Sunday: Soak lentils and par-bake Quinoa Lentil Pizza Crust. Make a double batch of 10-Minute New York Chunky Pizza Sauce.

Monday morning: Make a triple batch of Green Immuni-Tea.

Tuesday night: Prepare Creamy Green Bean Casserole but don't bake until Wednesday night.

weekly menus *(continued)*

PALEO

	MONDAY	TUESDAY	WEDNESDAY	THURSDAY	FRIDAY
BREAKFAST	Pesto Chicken & Spinach Frittata	Pesto Chicken & Spinach Frittata	Pesto Chicken & Spinach Frittata	Chocolate Chia Avocado Pudding; fresh berries	Chocolate Chia Avocado Pudding; fresh berries
LUNCH	Kale Caesar with Sweet Chili Pumpkin Seed Clusters*	Kale Caesar with Sweet Chili Pumpkin Seed Clusters*	Leftovers/Time to get creative!	Spicy Asian Chicken Collard Cups; Perfect Oven Fries	Spicy Asian Chicken Collard Cups; Perfect Oven Fries
DINNER	Beef & Veggie Stir Fry; Tahini Ginger Mashed Sweet Potatoes	Beef & Veggie Stir Fry; Tahini Ginger Mashed Sweet Potatoes	Spicy Asian Chicken Collard Cups; Perfect Oven Fries	Curried Honey Mustard Salmon Strawberry, Pecan & Goat Cheese Salad	Curried Honey Mustard Salmon Strawberry, Pecan & Goat Cheese Salad

*Add canned wild tuna or sardines for protein, if desired.

RECIPES USED

Pesto Chicken & Spinach Frittata (page 137)

Chocolate Chia Avocado Pudding (page 124)

Kale Caesar with Sweet Chili Pumpkin Seed Clusters (page 299)

Spicy Asian Chicken Collard Cups (page 245)

Perfect Oven Fries (page 174)

Beef & Veggie Stir Fry (page 225)

Tahini Ginger Mashed Sweet Potatoes (page 178)

Curried Honey Mustard Salmon Strawberry, Pecan & Goat Cheese Salad (page 258) (Note: Omit goat cheese.)

ADDITIONAL ITEMS:

Fresh berries

Canned wild tuna or sardines (optional)

COOKING SCHEDULE

Saturday: Grocery shop. Make Arugula Walnut Pesto for Pesto Chicken & Spinach Frittata.

Sunday: Roast Sweet Chili Pumpkin Seeds. Make Kale Caesar but leave off toppings. Prepare Pesto Chicken & Spinach Frittata for baking but don't bake until Monday morning. Marinate beef for Beef & Veggie Stir Fry. Par-boil sweet potatoes for Tahini Ginger Mashed Sweet Potatoes.

Wednesday night: Make Chocolate Chia Avocado Pudding to set overnight.

VEGAN

	MONDAY	TUESDAY	WEDNESDAY	THURSDAY	FRIDAY
BREAKFAST	Strawberry Shortcake Smoothie Bowl	Strawberry Shortcake Smoothie Bowl	10-Minute Whipped Banana Almond Porridge	10-Minute Whipped Banana Almond Porridge	Strawberry Shortcake Smoothie Bowl or Green Overnight Oat Pudding
LUNCH	Green Overnight Oat Pudding	Green Overnight Oat Pudding	Leftovers/ Time to get creative!	Refried Black Bean Enchiladas; Lightened-Up Green Pea Guacamole	Maple Balsamic–Glazed Tempeh & Mushroom Bake; Simple Spicy Garlicky Greens
DINNER	BBQ Chickpea & Sweet Potato Veggie Loaf; Pinewood Social Roasted Broccoli	BBQ Chickpea & Sweet Potato Veggie Loaf; Pinewood Social Roasted Broccoli	Refried Black Bean Enchiladas; Lightened-Up Green Pea Guacamole	Maple Balsamic–Glazed Tempeh & Mushroom Bake; Simple Spicy Garlicky Greens	Refried Black Bean Enchiladas; Lightened-Up Green Pea Guacamole; and/ or Simple Spicy Garlicky Greens

RECIPES USED

Strawberry Shortcake Smoothie Bowl x 2 or 3 (page 97)

10-Minute Whipped Banana Almond Porridge x 2 (page 127)

Green Overnight Oat Pudding x 2 or 3 (page 114)

Refried Black Bean Enchiladas (page 281)

Lightened-Up Green Pea Guacamole (page 197)

Maple Balsamic–Glazed Tempeh & Mushroom Bake (page 290)

Simple Spicy Garlicky Greens (page 194)

BBQ Chickpea & Sweet Potato Veggie Loaf (page 274)

Pinewood Social Roasted Broccoli (page 190)

COOKING SCHEDULE

Saturday: Grocery shop. Freeze fruit for smoothie bowl.

Sunday: Prepare Green Overnight Oat Pudding to set overnight. Make BBQ Chickpea & Sweet Potato Veggie Loaf. Make Almond Dipping Sauce for Pinewood Social Roasted Broccoli.

Wednesday night: Marinate tempeh and mushrooms for Maple Balsamic–Glazed Tempeh & Mushroom Bake.

SUGGESTED QUICK MEALS WHEN YOU DON'T HAVE LEFTOVERS

Canned wild seafood mixed with mayo, salt, and pepper over greens, with balsamic and olive oil

Thaw a wrap or 2 slices of bread and make an avocado toast/wrap with hummus, any sliced veggies or greens, any nuts or seeds, and thin layers of Dijon mustard and sriracha

2 hard-boiled eggs mashed with avocado or mayo, salt, and pepper, eaten with raw cucumber slices and crackers or non-vegetable oil potato chips

Grilled chicken sausages with ketchup and store-bought kimchi

Any smoothie you have the ingredients for!

My 10-Minute Whipped Banana Almond Porridge

Cook plain oats and season with salt, pepper, and a drizzle of olive oil. Top with roasted salted nuts, poached fried eggs, avocado, and any cooked veggies you have.

special occasions

VEGAN PICNIC

Anti-Inflammatory Root Veggie Hummus (page 76)

Sunflower SuperSeed Flatbread (page 169)

Roasted Fennel, Orange & Wild Rice Salad (page 296)

Ambrosia Fruit Salad with Oat Crumble (page 204)

PALEO PICNIC

Spicy Golden Deviled Eggs (page 71)

Tarragon Almond Chicken Salad (page 234)

Kale Caesar with Sweet Chili Pumpkin Seed Clusters (page 299)

The Best Soft-Baked Chocolate Chip Cookies (page 345)

VEGAN BBQ

Green Goddess Avocado Dip (page 75)

Grilled Asparagus with Basil Walnut Vinaigrette (page 193)

Wild Rice Lentil Burgers (page 278)

Pineapple Mojito Popsicles (page 324)

BBQ Chickpea & Sweet Potato Veggie Loaf (page 274)

PALEO BBQ

Lamb Burgers (page 230) (omit bun or use paleo buns)

Crispy Garlic Smashed Potatoes (page 177)

Asian Marinated Cucumber Zucchini Salad (page 203)

Marinated Skirt Steak (page 222)

Coconut Avocado Popsicles (page 327)

KID'S BIRTHDAY PARTY

PB&J No-Bake Energy Squares (page 62)

Workout Water (page 89)

Tacos made with The Best 15-Minute Taco Meat (page 215)

Coconut-Crusted Baked Chicken Tenders (page 242)

Pinewood Social Roasted Broccoli with Almond Dipping Sauce (page 190)

Snickerdoodle Cupcakes with Vanilla Buttercream Frosting (page 338)

ADULT'S CASUAL BIRTHDAY PARTY

Sriracha Garlic Roasted Edamame (page 83)

Lightened-Up Green Pea Guacamole (page 197)

Lamb Burgers (page 230)

Turmeric & Tahini Roasted Cauliflower (page 189)

Nashville Gooey Butter Cake (page 337)

Strawberry Bourbon Ice Cream (page 328)

BRIDAL/ENGAGEMENT/BABY SHOWER

Rosemary Roasted Pecans (page 61)

Cleansing Raspberry Ginger Water (page 86)

Sweet Potato & Kale Eggy Muffin Cups (page 140)

Bananas Foster Walnut Muffins (page 158)

Watermelon, Quinoa & Arugula Salad (page 300)

5-Ingredient No-Bake Truffles (page 319)

HOLIDAY MEAL

Tahini Ginger Mashed Sweet Potatoes (page 178)

Turmeric & Tahini Roasted Cauliflower (page 189)

Apricot & Rosemary Glazed Pork Tenderloin (page 229)

Maple Balsamic–Glazed Tempeh & Mushroom Bake (page 290)

Kale Caesar with Sweet Chili Pumpkin Seed Clusters (page 299)

Holy Fudge Black Bean Brownies (page 341)

FANCY DINNER PARTY

Fig & Olive Tapenade with Whipped Goat Cheese Crostini (page 68)

Lemon Parmesan Cauliflower Steaks (page 186)

Simple Spicy Garlicky Greens (page 194)

Marinated Skirt Steak with Sesame Horseradish Mayonnaise (page 222)

Orange & Ginger Seared Scallops (page 270)

Grapefruit & Basil Granita (page 320)

FALL/WINTER BRUNCH

Pumpkin Spice Protein Pancakes (page 131)

Crispy Potato, Rosemary & Goat Cheese Frittata (page 143)

Tempeh Pecan Breakfast "Sausage" (page 144)

Apple Cinnamon Coffee Cake (page 162)

Perfect Harvest Salad (page 295)

SPRING/SUMMER BRUNCH

Spicy Golden Deviled Eggs (page 71)

Blender Green Juice (page 102)

Customizable Oat Johnnycakes (page 118)

Grilled Sweet Potato Avocado Toast (page 121)

Sylvia's Blueberry Bran Muffins (page 165)

Ambrosia Fruit Salad with Oat Crumble (page 204)

GAME DAY

Kale & Artichoke Dip (page 65)

Teriyaki Slow Cooker Meatball Skewers (page 66)

Perfect Oven Fries (page 174)

Lightened-Up Green Pea Guacamole (page 197)

Quinoa Lentil Pizza Crust, Pepperoni Version (page 219)

Chocolate-Covered, Almond Butter–Stuffed Dates (page 316)

Metric Conversion

In this book, temperatures are listed in Fahrenheit; volumes are given in teaspoons, tablespoons, cups, and occasionally fluid ounces; and weights are given as ounces and pounds. Anything less than one is shown as a fraction. If you wish to convert these to metric, please use the following formulas:

FRACTIONS TO DECIMALS

$\frac{1}{8}$ = .125

$\frac{1}{4}$ = .25

$\frac{1}{2}$ = .5

$\frac{3}{4}$ = .75

TEMPERATURE

To convert from Fahrenheit to Celsius, subtract 32, multiply by 5, then divide by 9.

For example, if you wanted to change 350° F to C:

- 350 – 32 = 318
- 318 x 5 = 1590
- 1590 / 9 = 176.66

VOLUME

Multiply US teaspoons by 4.93 to get milliliters

Multiply US tablespoons by 14.79 to get milliliters

Multiply US cups by 236.59 to get milliliters

Multiply fluid ounces by 29.57 to get milliliters

For example, if you wanted to convert 3 ½ tablespoons to milliliters:

- 3.5 T x 14.79 ml = 51.76 ml

WEIGHT

Multiply ounces by 28.35 to get grams

Multiply pounds by .45 to get kilograms

For example, if you wanted to convert 5 ounces to grams:

- 5 oz. x 28.35 g = 141.75 g

And to convert 2 pounds to kilograms:

- 2 lb. x .45 kg = .9 kg

index

Note: Page numbers in *italics* indicate photos of recipes.

index of recipes by category

(Dairy-Free; Paleo; Vegan; Vegetarian)

ABOUT THE AUTHOR

Laura Lea Goldberg is a Certified Holistic Chef with a holistic wellness business in Nashville, Tennessee. Laura Lea graduated from the University of Virginia in 2008 and moved to New York City, where she worked in legal and finance jobs for four years. Laura Lea found herself disillusioned by New York corporate culture, which seemed to reward output at the expense of personal health, as well as the social cycle of over-indulging and under-sleeping. Laura Lea began studying holistic health and cooking fresh, produce-focused meals. She marveled at the profound improvement on her physical and emotional state; particularly, her ability to cope with stress and anxiety. She became determined to make a career out of sharing this simple but forgotten connection. In 2012 she discovered the Natural Gourmet Institute in Chelsea, New York. The program focuses on cooking with whole, mostly plant-based foods, and includes nutrition and healing courses. In September 2012, Laura Lea quit her job at a hedge fund and enrolled in the program.

PHOTO COURTESY OF KATE DAVIS PHOTO.

After graduating in August 2013, Laura Lea returned to her hometown of Nashville and created her website, LLBalanced.com. The goal of LL Balanced is to increase awareness about the relationship between food and mental, emotional, *and* physical health, so that people can live their most vibrant, productive, and happy lives. Through LL Balanced, Laura Lea provides her clients and readers with easy, family-friendly, and, of course, healthy recipes. Her dishes are often remakes of Southern-influenced comfort food, with the intention of having the best of both worlds. Laura Lea also contributes articles and recipes for *Nashville Lifestyles, Greatist,* and *Shape Magazine,* among others. She has also appeared in *Southern Living* and *Food Republic.* Laura Lea has a regular cooking segment on WSMV Channel 4, where she demonstrates how to make some of her most popular dishes.

MORE GREAT BOOKS *from*
SPRING HOUSE PRESS

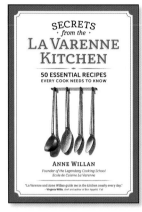

**Secrets from
the La Varenne Kitchen**
978-1-940611-15-0
$17.95 | 136 Pages

**A Colander, Cake Stand, and
My Grandfather's Iron Skillet**
978-1-940611-36-5
$24.95 | 184 Pages

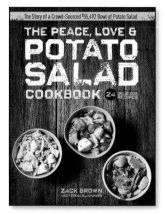

**The Peace, Love &
Potato Salad Cookbook**
978-1-940611-38-9
$16.95 | 80 Pages

The Cocktail Chronicles
978-1-940611-17-4
$24.95 | 200 Pages

The Hot Chicken Cookbook
978-1-940611-19-8
$19.95 | 128 Pages

The Natural Beauty Solution
978-1-940611-18-1
$19.95 | 128 Pages

SPRING HOUSE PRESS

Look for these Spring House Press titles at your favorite bookstore, specialty retailer, or visit *www.springhousepress.com*.
For more information about Spring House Press, call 717-208-3739 or email us at *info@springhousepress.com*.